Cornell Studies in English

Edited by Joseph Quincy Adams, Lane Cooper,
Clark Sutherland Northup, and
Martin Wright Sampson

Plays & Masques at Court
During the Reigns of
Elizabeth, James
and Charles

By Mary Susan Steele, Ph.D.
Professor of English in Judson College

New Haven: Yale University Press
London, Humphrey Milford
Oxford University Press
1926

PLAYS AND MASQUES AT COURT
1558-1642

PREFACE

ALTHOUGH many lists, more or less formal, have been made of dramatic performances at the English Court, there has been since the time of Fleay[1] no attempt to compile a list of court plays and masques for the period 1558–1642. It is well known that Fleay's work, while still valuable for reference, contains many errors and omissions. Murray, in 1910, as a part of a larger undertaking, gathered up the published records of plays acted at Court during the period.[2] But his tables, although fuller and more accurate than those of Fleay, must now be supplemented by the result of later research. The list of plays and masques prepared by Wallace,[3] and the more recent "Court Calendar" by Chambers,[4] both of which are based on a collation of original documents, are at once more accurate and more comprehensive than any which preceded them; but Wallace ends with the year 1585, and Chambers with the death of Shakespeare. The student, therefore, for a large part of the great English dramatic period, must still depend on scattered sources. For this reason it has seemed worth while to attempt to bring together in one volume as complete a list of court plays and masques for the years 1558–1642 as may at present be assembled.

In this study, the term "court performance" has been extended to include all dramatic representations before the sovereigns and other members of the royal family, on progress as well as in their usual residences. Certain university plays, with masques and plays given in private houses in honor of royal guests, have therefore found a place in the list. On the other hand, mere shows, pageants, and the like, which seem to form a distinct type of entertainment, have not been included.

[1] F. G. Fleay, *A Chronicle History of the English Stage*, 1890.
[2] J. T. Murray, *English Dramatic Companies*, 2 vols., 1910.
[3] C. W. Wallace, *Evolution of the English Drama*, 1912, pp. 199–209.
[4] E. K. Chambers, *Elizabethan Stage*, iv, Appendix A, supplemented by Appendix B.

The compilation is in the main a record of plays. I have tried to present all the significant details of each performance, and to indicate where further information may be found. In the case of masques, I have not attempted to make use of all the illustrative material frequently so abundant and voluminous in the Jacobean and Caroline periods; rather I have chosen to list chronologically those masques known to have been performed before members of the royal family at Court or elsewhere, with, when possible, the exact dates and places of performance, and to leave other matters to the historian.

The materials upon which such a study must be based are, it is scarcely necessary to say, of two kinds: the official records of court performances found in the office-books of the Revels and in payments to actors; and contemporary allusions found in correspondence, memoirs, diaries, and the like. A little material may also be gathered from title-pages, prologues, and epilogues. It is probable that our knowledge of the first source is nearly complete, although further search may add a little fresh information, especially for the years following the death of Shakespeare. As for the second, it is only to be expected that many more small "finds" will be made from time to time.

For the Elizabethan period, the records of the Office of the Revels have been edited by Albert Feuillerat.[1] Besides the very valuable Inventory of 1560, these records include the Accounts of the Office, which extend, with certain gaps, from 1558 to 1602. After 1589, however, the Accounts furnish no details of performances.

Payments to actors for plays presented at Court are available through two sources, the Registers of the Privy Council, and the Accounts of the Treasurer of the Chamber. George Chalmers published in his *Apology for the Believers in the Shakespeare Papers* (1797) extracts from the Council Registers of payments from

[1] *Documents Relating to the Office of the Revels in the Time of Queen Elizabeth*, Louvain, 1908.

January 10, 1562-3, to June 24, 1601.[1] These payments may now be found in more accurate form in the *Acts of the Privy Council of England*, New Series, 1890, edited by J. R. Dasent.

The Chamber Accounts furnish more detailed and more reliable information about plays than the poorly-kept Registers of the Council. Peter Cunningham, in 1842, published a series of payments extending from January 21, 1560-1, to April 22, 1603, which were, as he says, "derived from the original Office Books of the Treasurers of the Chamber during a part of the reign of Queen Elizabeth."[2] A more nearly complete series is to be found in the Declared Accounts, which are abstracts of the Original Accounts, and which, says Chambers, are equally full so far as payments to actors are concerned. In 1906 Chambers published a brief summary of the new information contained in them.[3] Mrs. C. C. Stopes, in 1910, printed from the Declared Accounts "contracted notices" of court plays from 1558 to 1597.[4] In 1912, Wallace, after a fresh examination of the records, published the series of payments from 1558-1585.[5] Lastly, Chambers, in 1923, printed from these Accounts a digest of the information contained in them about plays from 1558 to 1616.[6] The work of these last-mentioned scholars constitutes, of course, the best published source of information about payments for the period which it covers. Chambers' digest appeared in time to enable me to check my list of plays by it, and to add the small amount of new information which it contained. I have recorded all the divergencies among these published materials which are of any consequence.

[1] Later reprinted in the Boswell-Malone *Variorum Shakespeare*, 1821, vol. iii.

[2] *Extracts from the Accounts of the Revels at the Court in the Reigns of Queen Elizabeth and King James I*, pp. xxvii-xxxiv.

[3] "Court Performances before Queen Elizabeth," *Modern Language Review*, ii, 1-13.

[4] *William Hunnis and the Revels of the Chapel Royal*, Note to Chapters xviii and xx. Similar notices of various payments, mostly to the Earl of Leicester's Company, also appear in her *Burbage and Shakespeare's Stage*, 1913.

[5] *Evolution of the English Drama*, pp. 210-225. He announced his intention of completing the series to 1642, but he has not yet done so.

[6] *Elizabethan Stage*, iv, Appendix B.

Sources for the reigns of James I and Charles I may conveniently be considered together. Only two Original Accounts of the Office of the Revels survive, one for the year 1604–5 and one for 1611–12. Cunningham, the discoverer of these documents, was long under unjust suspicion of forgery, and the information they contain was either disregarded by scholars or used with reservations. Thanks to the research of Ernest Law,[1] however, their authenticity is no longer seriously questioned, although the puzzling discrepancies between them and the Chamber Accounts still engage attention.[2] The records of the Office during the long administration of Sir Henry Herbert, who supervised court dramatic entertainment from 1623 to 1642, exist in a very incomplete state. Those which survive have been brought together and edited by Professor Adams.[3]

Payments for court performances during this period must be collected from several sources. With one exception, noted below, no payments are to be found in the Registers of the Privy Council. The Jacobean Registers begin with May 1, 1613, the earlier volumes having been destroyed by fire. And in 1615 the signing of warrants was taken over by the Lord Chamberlain. One exception occurs in the warrant issued July 11, 1617, for payment to "certaine players" [Lady Elizabeth's] for three plays acted before the King on his journey to Scotland.[4]

Chalmers, in 1797, published from "a MS. book in the Lord Chamberlain's office" a series of payments from April 27, 1634, to March 20, 1640–1.[5] Cunningham published extracts from the Accounts of the Treasurer of the Chamber for the period 1603 to 1619.[6] He also printed, a few years later, payments from Novem-

---

[1] *Some Supposed Shakespeare Forgeries,*1911; *More about Shakespeare "Forgeries,"* 1913.
[2] See Chambers, *Eliz. Stage,* iv, 136–141.
[3] J. Q. Adams, *Dramatic Records of Sir Henry Herbert,* 1917.
[4] See E. K. Chambers and W. W. Greg, "Dramatic Records from the Privy Council Registers, 1603–1642," Malone Society's *Collections,* Parts IV and V, 1911.
[5] *Apology,* pp. 507–12.
[6] *Revels,* pp. xxxiv–xlv.

ber 1, 1612, to June 28, 1613, derived originally from the Accounts of Lord Harrington, which give the titles of a number of plays, as well as the sums paid[1]. In 1909 Chambers gleaned some new information from the Declared Accounts, consisting of plays acted from February 20, 1603-4, to Christmas, 1615-6.[2] Mrs. Stopes, in 1910, printed payments from April 10, 1628, to March 10, 1640-1.[3] In the same year Murray printed from the Inner Temple Library MS. 515, No. 7, described as "A Booke conteyneing severall particulars with Relation to the Kings servants petitions Warrants Bills &c and may be supposed to be a Copy of some part of the Lord Chamberlaine of the Households Booke in and about the yeare 1622."[4] This document gives the titles of, as well as the payments for, nine plays acted from November 5, 1621, to March 5, 1621-2. Mrs. Stopes, again, gives abstracts of payments to the King's Company from December 3, 1603, to March 20, 1640-1.[5] For payments later than 1616, with which year the authoritative digest by Chambers previously referred to closes, one must reconcile discrepancies in the material as best he may. Here again I have recorded all which seem important.

Concerning contemporary allusions to plays performed at Court, little need be said except that those which have been discovered form an interesting supplement to the official records. Allusions to masques, naturally, are more frequent, for masques attracted more attention than plays, which were merely an accepted part of the routine of amusement. After 1589, when the Revels Accounts no longer furnish information about perform-

---

[1] "Plays at Court, Anno 1613," *The Shakespeare Society's Papers*, 1845, ii, 123-126. Extracts of these titles, printed from the original source, the Rawlinson MS. in the Bodleian, are also to be found in Halliwell-Phillipps, *Outlines*, ii, 87; in *Transactions of the New Shakespeare Society*, 1875-6, pp. 419-20; and in Chambers, *Eliz. Stage*, iv, Appendix B.
[2] "Court Performances under James I," *Modern Language Review*, iv, 153-166.
[3] "Shakespeare's Fellows and Followers," *Jahrbuch*, xlvi, 95ff.
[4] *English Dramatic Companies*, ii, 192-194.
[5] *Burbage*, pp. 253-262.

ances, contemporary mention affords the principal source of knowledge regarding masques shown before Elizabeth.

For masques of the reigns of James I and Charles I, one finds the careful study by Paul Reyher[1] of great value. In a few instances I have been able to supplement Reyher's list, especially with material from the Venetian State Papers, the Calendars of which had reached about the year 1617 when his work appeared.

My aim in making this list has been to produce a trustworthy handbook of court dramatic performances. The task was undertaken as a doctoral dissertation, under the direction of Professor Joseph Q. Adams. It is a pleasure to record my obligation to Professor Adams for the suggestion of the subject, and for generous advice and assistance upon many points. In work which has involved so much detail I have probably not been able, in spite of care, to escape errors, and for such defects I am entirely responsible.

[1] *Les Masques Anglais,* 1909.

TABLE OF CONTENTS

THE REIGN OF ELIZABETH
1558-1603

THE REIGN OF ELIZABETH

THE SEASON 1558-1559

WHEN Elizabeth came to the throne on November 17, 1558, she found the Office of the Revels ready to supply her with the plays, masques, and other diversions which were an established part of the holiday amusement of the English Court. No doubt she indicated her desires; but the first weeks and months of her reign were crowded with problems more serious than those of the selection of pastimes, and the opening entry in the Revels Accounts reflects something of the uncertainty under which the officers labored in their preparations for the festivities of the first Christmas:

Translatinge newe makinge garnysshinge furnysshinge and fynnysshinge of dyuers and sundrye garmentes Apparell vestures and propertyes aswell of Maskes as for playes and other pastymes sett forthe and shewen in her Maiesties presence with the chaunge and Alteracion of the same to serve her Highnes pleasure and determynacion as occasion required from tyme to tyme upon comaundement to be in Areddines when it was called ffor. videlicet agaynst Christmas Neweyeres tyde & Twelf tyde that yeare. and ageanste the Coronacion foloinge after Twelftyde.

According to Nichols, the Queen spent Christmas at Westminster. The Court seems to have remained there until after Shrovetide. (See Feuillerat, *Doc.*, pp. 89, 93, 95.)

1558-9. MASQUES OF UNCERTAIN DATE.

Under this heading are grouped five masques to which exact dates probably can not be assigned. All that can be said with assurance is that they were performed before April or May, 1560, when an inventory of the Revels stuff was taken, and that they are not among the known masques of Mary's reign. They appear, however, to belong to the years 1558-1559, since no one of them is mentioned in the record of the employment of materials

I

delivered from the Wardrobe to Sir Thomas Benger, who became Master of the Revels on January 18, 1559–60.

The entries which follow show the vacant dates of January 16, 22, February 2 (?) and 5 (the second set of mummers in the double masque described by Il Schifanoya is unidentified). Any attempt to distribute the masques among these dates would be a matter of guesswork.

The Inventory of 1560, in which the record of these masques is preserved, is edited by Feuillerat in his *Documents Relating to the Office of the Revels in the Time of Queen Elizabeth* (pp. 18–46). It consists of a "rear-account"—which includes a survey of the Revels stuff in 1555, an account of the different masques in which the material was used, and a list of the stuffs received from the Royal Wardrobe with an account of their employment—and a description of the condition of the masquing garments in April or May, 1560, when the Inventory was taken. In order to separate the Elizabethan masques from those performed earlier, it has been necessary to compare the Inventory with other Revels documents, also published by Feuillerat, in his *Edward VI and Mary*.

My analysis of the document was completed before that of Chambers (*Elizabethan Stage*, i, 155 ff.) appeared, and shows substantially the same results.

[*A Masque of*] *Hungarians.*

"All the blewe and purple clothe of gold" of the *Masque of Mariners* [performed in 1554] was "translated into vi hungarians garmentes with longe sleves." The only clue to the date lies in the fact that two of these garments were utilized for "winges and collors of the patriarkes maske," which was given on January 6, 1559–60, and four for "wemens kirtels of Dianas Nymphes," in a masque which was probably shown on February 27 of the same year. (See Feuillerat, *Doc.*, p. 19.)

"*A Maske of Marryners.*"

This masque is distinct from the masque of the same title which had been performed during Queen Mary's reign. It is later in date

2

than the *Masque of Fishermen* (February 7, 1558–9), for some of the "greene clothe of Silver" used in that masque was "agayne translated into *A Maske of Marryners.*" On the other hand, it precedes *"a maske of Turkes"* of unknown date. (Feuillerat, *Doc.*, p. 19.)

"A Maske of Turkes."

All that is known of the date of this masque is to be found in the record of the "imploymente" of certain pieces of green cloth of silver which had been used for the "Maryners viij" of the preceding reign, and which were later "translated into lyninge of the Almaynes sloppes and agayne cut in peces to payne ffissher mens sloppes & bodies and agayne translated in to *A Maske of Marryners* and againe translated into Torchebearers for *a maske of Turkes.*" (Feuillerat, *Doc.*, p. 19.) The "ffissher men" appeared on Shrove Tuesday.

"A Maske of Conquerers."

Some of the garments which had been worn by the Greek Worthies of Mary's reign were "translated into *A Maske of Conquerers* and againe the beste of that taken oute and translated in to *A Maske of Moores.*" (Feuillerat, *Doc.*, p. 20.)

"A Maske of Moores vj."

The torch-bearers were "viij white ffriers." (*Ibid.*, p. 25.) This masque preceded the *Masque of Clowns*. It also preceded the *Masque of Patriarchs* shown on January 6, 1559–60, for the "vj Scaplers for Moores . . . were translated to turne vp the handes of the patriarke." (Feuillerat, *Doc.*, pp. 26, 41.)

1558–9. JANUARY 6 (FRIDAY). WESTMINSTER.

A farce and a masque at Court.

On January 23 Il Schifanoya wrote to the Castellan of Mantua:

As I suppose your Lordship will have heard of the farce performed [*farsa fatta*] in the presence of her Majesty on the day of the Epiphany, and I not having sufficient intellect to interpret it, nor yet the mummery performed after supper on the same day, of

3

crows in the habits of Cardinals, of asses habited as Bishops, and of wolves representing Abbots, I will consign it to silence. (*Cal. State Papers, Venetian*, 1558–1580, p. 11.)

Various ecclesiastical garments, some of which probably belong to this masque, are mentioned in the Inventory of 1560. And in the Revels Accounts there is a record of payment to William Cleye "for him and his companye to wayte with a barge of viij ores to carry and recarry the Revells stuffe and attendauntes thereon betweene the blacke fryers and the corte when soe ever he was called betwene christmas day and twelfe daye." (Feuillerat, *Doc.*, p. 83.)

1558–9. JANUARY 16 (MONDAY). WESTMINSTER.

A "Maske shewen the morowe after the Coronacion." (Feuillerat, *Doc.*, p. 88.)

1558–9. JANUARY 22 (SUNDAY). WESTMINSTER.

A "Maske shewen on the sondaye seven nighte after the Coronacion." (Feuillerat, *Doc.*, p. 88.)

1558–9. FEBRUARY 2 (THURSDAY).

No performance is recorded. But the Revels charges against "the Coronacion and Candellmas" suggest that there may have been a masque. (See Feuillerat, *Doc.*, p. 84.)

1558–9. FEBRUARY 5 (SHROVE SUNDAY). WESTMINSTER.

"*A Maske of swartrutters* shewen on shrovesonday at nighte." (Feuillerat, *Doc.*, p. 94.)

On February 6 Il Schifanoya wrote to the Mantuan Ambassador at Brussels:

Last evening at the Court a double mummery was played: one set of mummers rifled the Queen's ladies, and the other set, with wooden swords and bucklers, recovered the spoil. (*Cal. State Papers, Venetian*, 1558–1580, p. 27.)

Chambers (*Eliz. Stage*, i, 156) suggests the Hungarians as appropriate antagonists to the Swartrutters.

1558–9. FEBRUARY 6 (SHROVE MONDAY).

No performance is recorded. Wallace (*Evol. E. D.*, p. 199) assumes from the payments to William Cleye on Sunday, Monday, and Tuesday "to carry and recarry the Revells Stuff and attend-auntes thereon betweene the blacke fryers and the courte" that a masque was performed. The two recorded performances, however, would probably account for the journey on Monday.

1558–9. FEBRUARY 7 (SHROVE TUESDAY). WESTMINSTER.

Fishermen, Fishwives, and Marketwives appeared in one or more masques on Shrove Tuesday night. (Feuillerat, *Doc.*, pp. 19, 21, 25, 28, 45, and 94.) The Fisherman had a drum and fife, and the Fishwives and Marketwives had six minstrels.

Chambers (*Eliz. Stage*, i, 157) suggests that the Fishermen may have been torchbearers to a double masque of Fishwives and Marketwives. There is in the Inventory, however, a distinct reference to a "Maske of ffisshermen" (Feuillerat, p. 21), seemingly identical with the Fishermen of Shrove Tuesday.

1559. MAY 24 (WEDNESDAY). WESTMINSTER.

"*A Maske of Astronoers.*" (Feuillerat, *Doc.*, p. 97.)

"A banckett howse at westminster" was "then made." It is probable that the masque was performed in this Banqueting House, as part of the entertainment of the French Embassy.

From the Revels Accounts it is evident that the date of performance was before May 25. The correct date is probably May 24, for on that date, according to Machyn (*Diary*, p. 198), the French were received by the Queen.

SUMMER, 1559

1559. JULY 11 (TUESDAY). GREENWICH. BANQUETING HOUSE.

A masque before the Queen.

Nichols gives the following account of the occasion:

5

The 10th of the same month, the Queen, being still at Greenwich, well knew how pomps and shews, especially military, with her own presence thereat, delighted her subjects, and perhaps herself too; now therefore was set up in Greenwich Park a goodly banqueting-house for her Grace, made with fir poles, and decked with birch branches, and all manner of flowers, both of the field and garden, as roses, julyflowers, lavender, marygolds, and all manner of strewing herbs and rushes; there were also set up tents for the kitchen, and for the officers, against tomorrow, with provisions laid in of wine, ale, and beer. There was also made up a place for the Queen's pensioners, who were to run with spears. The challengers were three, the earl of Ormond, Sir John Perrot, and Mr. North; and there were likewise defendants of equal valour, with launces and swords.

About five in the afternoon came the Queen, with the ambassadors and divers lords and ladies, and stood over the Park Gate to see the exercise; and after, the combatants ran chasing one the other. After this, the Queen came down into the Park, and took her horse, and rode up to the banqueting-house, and the three ambassadors, and so to supper. After was a mask; and then a great banquet; and then followed a great casting of fire, and shooting of guns, till twelve at night. (*Progresses Elizabeth*, i.)

It is impossible to say, on the basis of this account, whether the masque was performed on July 10 or later. I have followed Machyn, who, in the *Diary* (pp. 203–4), dates the performance July 11.

1559. AUGUST 6 (SUNDAY). NONSUCH.

A masque before the Queen, given by the Earl of Arundel. Nichols supplies the following account:

August the 5th, the Queen being now at Eltham, in Kent, one of the antient houses of the kings, removed thence unto Nonsuch, another of her houses, of which the noble earl of Arundel seems to be now house-keeper; there the Queen had great entertainment with banquets, especially on Sunday night, made by the said earl; together with a mask. (*Progresses Elizabeth*, i.)

See also Machyn's *Diary*, ed. by Nichols, p. 206.

1559. AUGUST 7 (MONDAY). NONSUCH.

A play before the Queen by the Children of Paul's.

The entertainment of the Queen by the Earl of Arundel was continued on the following evening with a play. Nichols concludes the account thus:

On Monday was a great supper made for her; but before night she stood at her standing in the further Park and there she saw a course. At night was a play of the children of Paul's, and their [musick-]master Sebastian. (*Progresses Elizabeth*, i.)

Machyn (*Diary*, p. 206) refers to it as "a play of the chylderyn of Powlles and ther master Se[bastian], master Phelypes, and master Haywod."

Fleay conjectures that the play performed by the boys was *Nice Wanton*. (*Stage*, p. 57.)

1559. BEFORE AUGUST 24. HORSLEY.

"*A Maske of Shypmenn and maydes of the cuntrye* then made and shewen at horseleye." (Feuillerat, *Doc.*, p. 105.)

The masque was given before August 24, on which date the Court removed to Hampton. A Banqueting House was erected for the occasion. (See *ibid.*, pp. 106, 107.)

West Horsley was the seat of Lord Admiral Clinton.

THE SEASON 1559–1560

1559–60. MASQUES OF UNCERTAIN DATE.

The following masques are mentioned in the Inventory of 1560 as having been furnished, at least in part, from stuff delivered to Sir Thomas Benger.

"*Colownes viij*. Hindes Torcheberes to the Cloyens. viij." (Feuillerat, *Doc.*, pp. 40, 41.)

This masque followed the *Masque of Moors* of uncertain date, for the black velvet employed in the latter which was not stolen by the lords was "cut into high shoes for *the cloynes maske*." (*Ibid.*, p. 24.) It also followed a masque in which were "twoo Cardinalls and two bishoppes" (probably that of January 6, 1558–9), and one in which two "grasiers," also called "Ientlemen of the contrey," appeared. (*Ibid.*, pp. 25, 28.) Possibly the last was the masque at Horsley.

A more definite indication of the date is given by the "translation" of materials which had been used in the *Masque of Astronomers*, performed in May, 1559, into garments for the Clowns. (*Ibid.*, pp. 26, 28.)

"*Acteons vj*. Hunters. torcheberers to the Actions. viij." (Feuillerat, *Doc.*, pp. 38–39.)

Some of the garments used in this masque had been "translated" from those of a masque in which "ffryers," "monkes," and "Sumpners" had appeared. (*Ibid.*, pp. 24, 25.) It preceded the *Masque of Diana*, for seven girdles used in the latter were made from the lining of Actaeon's jerkin and slops. (*Ibid.*, p. 36.) Chambers (*Eliz. Stage*, i, 157) must therefore be wrong in assigning it to Shrove Tuesday.

"*Nusquams vj*. Turkes Commoners torcheberers to the Musquams. vj." (Feuillerat, *Doc.*, p. 39.)

White velvet which had been "imployed into two white ffriers . . . which were againe translated into Morisshe fryers" was "againe translated and imployed to the performance of the Nusquams and so restethe." (*Ibid.*, p. 24.) Again, "Satten Incarnate" which had been "imployed in to depe hoodes and scaplers of iiij ffryers" was again used to decorate the undersleeves of torchbearers to the Nusquams. (*Ibid.*, p. 26.)

1559/1559–60. DATE UNCERTAIN.

"A play by the children of the chapple." (Feuillerat, *Doc.*, p. 34.)

1559. DECEMBER 31 (SUNDAY). WHITEHALL.

A play before the Queen which displeased her.

Henry Machyn writes in his *Diary*:

The sam day at nyght at the quen court ther was a play a-for her grace, the wyche the plaers plad shuche matter that they wher commondyd to leyff off, and contenent the maske cam in dansyng. (*Diary*, p. 221. See also *Progresses Elizabeth*, i.)

Fleay (*Stage*, pp. 58, 60), followed by Murray (*English Dramatic Companies*, i, 335, *n.*), conjectures that the play was *Misogonus*, that it was written by Richard Edwards, and that it was performed by the Children of the Chapel.

1559. DECEMBER 31 (SUNDAY). WHITEHALL.

A masque before the Queen "on neweyeres even." (Feuillerat, *Doc.*, p. 110.)

See the note to the preceding entry.

This is the first of the "ffower Maskes with there torche berers sett forthe and shewen before ye queenes maiestie at whyte Hawle on neweyeres even Neweyeres daye and Twelf daye att nighte." See the following entries.

1559–60. JANUARY 1 (MONDAY). WHITEHALL.

"A *Maske of Barbarians* . . . Shewen on Newyeares daye at Nighte. 1559." (Feuillerat, *Doc.*, p. 20.)

The Barbarians were six in number, and their torch bearers were six "venecyans." (*Ibid.*, pp. 39–40.)

1559–60. JANUARY 6 (SATURDAY). WHITEHALL.

"*A Maske of Patriarkes* shewen on Twelff nighte." (Feuillerat, *Doc.*, p. 30. Cf. p. 110.)

1559–60. JANUARY 6 (SATURDAY). WHITEHALL.

A "*Maske of Italyen wemen* on twelf nighte." (Feuillerat, *Doc.*, p. 32. Cf. p. 110.)

1559–60. FEBRUARY 25, 26 (SHROVE SUNDAY, MONDAY). WHITEHALL.

Two masques of men.

"Toe Maskes of men & one maske of wemen with there torche berers & A Rocke of founteyne and other furnyture thereto apertenente" were "prepared to be sett forth & shewen in ye quenes presence at whighte Hall during ye tyme of Shroftyde." (Feuillerat, *Doc.*, p. 110.)

1559–60. FEBRUARY 27 (SHROVE TUESDAY). WHITEHALL.

"*Dyana and vj Nymphes* Huntresses withe her. Maydens Torcheberers to the Nymphes viij." (Feuillerat, *Doc.*, pp. 43, 44.)

"One maske of wemen" was shown at Whitehall during Shrovetide. (*Ibid.*, p. 110.) Twelve yards of red sarcenet were used "in two paire of Sloppes & Scarfes for the womens Drom and ffife on Shroftuidaye at nighte." (*Ibid.*, p. 34.) Undoubtedly this was the *Masque of Diana*, for the latter is the only undated masque of women mentioned in the Inventory of 1560 as having been furnished from stuff delivered to Sir Thomas Benger. (See *ibid.*, pp. 30–35.)

THE SEASON 1560–1561

Chambers (*Eliz. Stage*, iv, 79) points out the fact that one of the Christmas plays may have been Thomas Preston's *Cambyses*. He quotes from Christopher Playter to Mr. Kytson, February 21:

at the corte new plays, which lasted almost all night—the name of the play was *huff-suff-and ruff*, with other masks, both of the ladies and gents.

No masques are officially recorded. But on December 10, 1560, a warrant was issued for the delivery to Sir Thomas Benger of silks "for the making of certeyne masking garmentes." (See Feuillerat, *Doc.*, p. 112.)

1558–1560. DATE UNCERTAIN.

A play by the Queen's interlude players?

£6. 13*s*. 4*d*. was paid to the Queen's interlude players "for her hyghnes accustomed Rewarde dewe vnto them at Newe yeres tyde." (Wallace, *Evol. E. D.*, p. 210.)

The amount suggests a play rather than the annual pension paid to these players.

1558–1560. DATE UNCERTAIN.

Two plays at Court?

£13. 6s. 8d. was paid "to players of enterludes." (Chambers, *Eliz. Stage.* iv, 142.)

1560/1560–1. CHRISTMAS.

A play before the Queen "at Christmas" by Lord Robert Dudley's Company. Payment £6. 13s. 4d. on warrant dated January 21, 1560–1. (Wallace, *Evol. E. D.*, pp. 210–11. See also Cunningham, *Revels*, p. xxvii; Stopes, *Burbage*, p. 246.)

1560/1560–1. CHRISTMAS.

A play before the Queen "at Christmas" by the Children of Paul's (Sebastiane Wescott). Payment £6. 13s. 4d., on the same warrant as that for the preceding play. (Wallace, *Evol. E. D.*, pp. 210–11. See also Cunningham, *Revels*, p. xxvii; Stopes, *Burbage*, p. 246.)

THE SEASON 1561–1562

1561/1561–2. DATE UNCERTAIN.

A play before the Queen by the Children of Paul's (Sebastian westcote). Payment £6. 13s. 4d., on warrant dated at Westminster, March 9, 1561–2. (Wallace, *Evol. E. D.*, p. 211. See also Cunningham, *Revels*, p. xxvii.)

1561. OCTOBER 25–28. WHITEHALL.

A masque of the wise and foolish virgins, in honor of the French escort of Mary, Queen of Scots.

A notice of this masque occurs in a reminiscence of Queen Elizabeth by Pierre de Bourdeilles, Abbé et Seigneur de Brantôme, who was a member of the party which, in August, 1561, accompanied Mary Stuart from France to Scotland. On their return in October the French were entertained at the English Court. On that occasion the Queen expressed her great admiration for King Henry II of France. Brantôme writes:

J'ay ouy conter à la reyne d'Angleterre qui est aujourd'huy, que c'estoit le roy et le prince du monde qu'elle avoit plus desiré de voir, pour le beau rapport qu'on luy en avoit faict, et pour sa grande renommée qui en volloit partout. M. le connestable, qui vit aujourd'huy [Henri, duc de Montmorency] s'en pourra bien ressouvenir. Ce fut lorsque, tournans d'Escosse M. le grande prieur de France, de la maison de Lorraine, et luy, la reyne leur donna un soir à soupper, où aprés se fit un ballet de ses filles, qu'elle avoit ordonné et dressé, representans les vierges de l'Evangile, desquelles les unes avoient leurs lampes allumées, et les autres n'avoient ny huille ny feu, et en demandoient. Ces lampes estoient d'argent fort gentiment faictes et elabourées; et les dames estoient tres belles, bien honnestes et bien apprises, qui prindrent nous autres François pour dancer; mesmes la reyne dança, et de fort bonne grace et belle majesté royalle. ("Le Roy Henry II," in Brantôme, *Œuvres*, ed. Mérimée and Lacour, iv, 126–7. The passage is pointed out by Reyher, in *Masques Anglais*, p. 125.)

The precise date of performance has not been ascertained. On October 25, according to Machyn (p. 270), "the in-bassadurs of France that cam owtt of Scotland" were brought to Court, and three days later they were entertained at Whitehall with bull- and bear-baiting.

1561/1561–2. CHRISTMAS.

A play before the Queen "at Christmas" by Lord Robert Dudley's Company. Payment £6. 13*s*. 4*d*., on warrant dated January 6, 1561–2. (Wallace, *Evol. E. D.*, p. 211. See also Stopes, *Hunnis*, p. 318; *Burbage*, p. 246; Chambers, *M. L. R.*, ii, 3.)

1561/1561–2. CHRISTMAS.

A play before the Queen "at Christmas" by the Children of Paul's (Sebestiano westcote). Payment £6. 13*s*. 4*d*., on the same warrant as that for the preceding play. (Wallace, *Evol. E. D.*, p. 211. See also Stopes, *Hunnis*, p. 318; *Burbage*, p. 246; Chambers, *M. L. R.*, ii, 3.)

1561–2. JANUARY 15 (THURSDAY). BAYNARD'S CASTLE.

A masque in honor of the Queen, given by the Earl of Pembroke.

Machyn supplies the following account:

The xv day of January the Quen['s] grace cam to Beynard Castyll to the yerle of Penbroke to dener, and many of here consell, and tared soper, and at nyght there was grett chere and a grett bankett, and after a maske, and here grace tared all nyght. (*Diary*, p. 275.)

1561–2. JANUARY 18 (SUNDAY). WHITEHALL.

Gorboduc, or Ferrex and Porrex, acted before the Queen by the students of the Inner Temple.

Machyn's account is as follows:

The xviij day of January was a play in the quen hall at West-mynster by the gentyll-men of the Tempull, and after a grett maske, for ther was a grett skaffold in the hall, with grett try-humpe as has bene sene; and the morow after the skaffold was taken done. (*Diary*, p. 275.)

The title-page of the edition of 1565 reads:

The Tragedie of Gorboduc, whereof three Actes were wrytten by Thomas Nortone, and the two laste by Thomas Sackuyle. Sett forthe as the same was shewed before the Quenes most excellent Maiestie, in her highnes Court of Whitehall, the . xviij. day of January, Anno Domini. 1561. By the Gentlemen of Thynner Temple in London.

1561–2. JANUARY 18 (SUNDAY). WHITEHALL.

A masque at Court, after the performance of *Gorboduc*.
See the note to the preceding entry.

1561–2. FEBRUARY 1 (SUNDAY).

A "masket" at Court.
Machyn writes in his *Diary*:

The furst day of Feybruary at nyght was the goodlyest masket cam owt of London that ever was seen, of a C. and d'ᵍ gorgyously be-sene, and a C. cheynes of gold, and as for trumpettes and drumes, and as for torchelyght a ij hundred, and so to the cowrt, and dyvers goodly men of armes in gylt harnes, and Julyus Sesar played. (*Diary*, p. 276.)

The word "played," says Nichols, has been added in another hand. It is therefore by no means certain that a play of *Julyus Sesar* was performed. Nichols suggests that Julius Caesar may have been personated among the men of arms. (*Ibid.*, p. 389.)

1561–2. FEBRUARY 8–10 (SHROVETIDE).

No performances are recorded. But it is probable that there were masques. In "A breefe Certifficathe of mony owinge," which was endorsed January 20, 1561–2, the officers of the Revels add a "memorandum" to the effect that "the Charges for Shroftyde nowe nexte ensuinge . . . by estimacion will amounte to the some of one hundred pounds or thereabowtes." (See Feuillerat, *Doc.*, p. 113.)

SUMMER, 1562

1562. MAY–JULY.

Three "devices to be shewed before the quenes Matie by waye of maskinge, at Nottingham castell, after the meteinge of the quene of Scottes" [endorsed "Maij 1562"] were planned for a projected meeting between Elizabeth and Mary; but the meeting never took place. Negotiations for it were dropped in July. The plot of the "devices" is printed by E. K. Chambers and W. W. Greg, in "Dramatic Records from the Landsdowne MSS.," Malone Soc. *Collections*, I, 2, 144–48. It may also be found in Collier, *History of English Dramatic Poetry*, 1879, i, 178–81.

On May 10, 1562, a warrant was issued for the delivery of silks to Sir Thomas Benger "for the better furnyshinge and settinge forthe of suche maskes and Revelles as shalbe shewed by hym." (See Feuillerat, *Doc.*, p. 114.)

THE SEASON 1562–1563

1562/1562–3. CHRISTMAS.

A play before the Queen "in Christmas" by Lord Robert Dudley's Company. Payment £6. 13*s*. 4*d*., on warrant dated at Westminster, January 10, 1562–3. (Wallace, *Evol. E. D.*, p. 211.

See also Cunningham, *Revels*, p. xxviii; Stopes, *Burbage*, p. 246; Dasent, *Acts*, vii, 134; Chalmers, *Apology*, p. 394.)

1562/1562–3. CHRISTMAS.

A play before the Queen "in Christmas" by the Children of Paul's. Payment £6. 13*s*. 4*d*., on the same warrant as that for the preceding play. (Wallace, *Evol. E. D.*, p. 211. See also Cunningham, *Revels*, p. xxviii; Stopes, *Burbage*, p. 246; Dasent, *Acts*, vii, 134, in which the payee, "Sebastian Wescotte," is given; Chalmers, *Apology*, p. 360, in which the play is undated.)

THE SEASON 1563–1564

1563/1563–4. CHRISTMAS; FEBRUARY 2 (WEDNESDAY). WINDSOR.

"Cristmas and Candellmas . . . iij Plays at wyndsor." (Feuillerat, *Doc.*, p. 116.)

No warrants for payment have been discovered.

SUMMER, 1564

1564. JUNE. RICHMOND.

"The ixth of Iune Repayringe and new makinge of thre maskes with thare hole furniture and diuers devisses and a Castle ffor ladies and a harboure ffor Lords and thre harrolds and iiij Trompetours too bringe in the devise with the men of Armes and showen at the Courtte of Richmond before the Quenes Maiestie and the ffrench Embassitours &c." (Feuillerat, *Doc.*, p. 116.)

The Ambassador was Artus de Cossé, Seigneur de Gonnor, who came to confirm the treaty of Troyes.

1564. JULY 5 (WEDNESDAY). SACKVILLE HOUSE.

A comedy before the Queen at the house of Sir Richard Sackville.

On July 10 Guzman de Silva wrote to the King of Spain:

After supper . . . I was about to take my leave when she told me not to go yet, as she wished me to see a comedy that was to be acted . . . The Queen came out to the hall, which was lit with many torches, where the comedy was represented. I should not have understood much of it if the Queen had not interpreted, as she told me she would do. They generally deal with marriage in the comedies . . . . (*Cal. State Papers, Spanish*, 1558–1567, p. 367.)

For the date and place of performance, see Chambers, *Eliz. Stage*, iv, 81.

1564. JULY 5 (WEDNESDAY). SACKVILLE HOUSE.

A masque in honor of the Queen, given by Sir Richard Sackville. De Silva, in the letter previously quoted from, wrote:

The comedy ended, and then there was a masque of certain gentlemen who entered dressed in black and white, which the Queen told me were her colours, and after dancing awhile one of them approached and handed the Queen a sonnet in English praising her. . . . This ended the feast, and the Queen entered a gallery where there was a very long table with every sort and kind of preserves and candied fruits that can be imagined, according to the English custom. It must have been two in the morning and the Queen had to return to Westminister by water, although it was very windy.

CAMBRIDGE, AUGUST, 1564

For a general account of the Queen's visit to Cambridge and of the plays presented before her, see F. S. Boas, *University Drama in the Tudor Age*, pp. 89–98.

1564. AUGUST 6 (SUNDAY). KING'S COLLEGE CHAPEL.

The *Aulularia* of Plautus, acted before the Queen by students chosen from several colleges.

On July 12, 1564, Sir William Cecil, Chancellor of Cambridge, notified the Vice-Chancellor, Edward Hawford, Master of Christ's College, of the Queen's intention to "repayre thither in her progresse, and to remayne in that Universitye three days." On July 15 Edmund Grindal, Bishop of London, also wrote to the

Vice-Chancellor, urging that the Queen be entertained with all manner of scholastical exercises, and "playing of Comedies & Tragedies."

The Queen arrived on August 5. On the evening of the following day the first play was presented before her. A detailed account of this performance, and of the preparations which had been made for it and for the performances which were to follow, is taken from the Latin of Nicholas Robinson:

For they appointed several of their number to attempt the presentation of tragedies, comedies, and other plays, in order that she might drink in as it were with a certain pleasure the sweetness of all these things, if she should be willing, amid the weightier affairs of the commonwealth, to adapt herself to these light jests. And in order that the plays might be more agreeably presented to the eyes and ears of all, and that everyone might watch undisturbed, there was made in the chapel of King's College, a place very beautiful on account of its workmanship, and spacious enough besides, a sort of structure of rather thick boards, five feet high, whose length and breadth was adequate for any scene. To this, from the upper chancel, was built a way elevated a little above the floor, by which the Queen, safe from the exuberance of the onlookers, might ascend aloft to this structure, on which was made ready for her by means of certain steps, a place of greater honor, covered with tapestry interwoven with gold, which was the seat of her royal Majesty, so that she might easily be seen by all the spectators. For there were built in the space which divides the chapel in the middle other seats for the nobles and most renowned ladies, and for others next to this space in convenient places, because the Queen determined that she would sit alone in the other. On account of the darkness the royal attendants bore lighted torches in their hands to the sides of the stage. In truth, nothing was more ample than the lights. In this royal theatre, constructed and adorned at great outlay, was presented on a stormy Sunday night, that very charming comedy of Plautus, the *Aulularia*, which they eargerly devoured, by the wit of which life is somewhat stirred, as by a rustic dance. And although some, either sleepy, or ignorant of the Latin dialogue, with difficulty endured the waste of so many hours, the Queen remained with a very placid countenance, to the last *plaudite*, and showed no sign of weariness. How much charm, in truth, was added to the wit of Plautus by the industry and efforts of Dr. Kelke, it will not be necessary to tell many. For it was decided by common opinion that here was to be revered a master of all grace, gesture, staging, the Roscius of his age, as it were, skilled in the presentation of theatrical performances. There were given to him as companions and assistants four younger tutors selected from the four larger colleges, who had excelled the rest in instructing youth. They had charge of one comedy and tragedy, as if they had been the servants of the whole University. The students of King's College wished the other plays to be theirs.

But the time came when bodies wearied by these strenuous exercises would be refreshed. And so when the Queen had been honorably conducted to her lodging, all betook themselves to their various places. (Nichols, *Progresses Elizabeth*, iii.)

The principal account in English is, according to Boas (*University Drama*, p. 90), from the pen of Matthew Stokys, University Registrary:

Which ended [evening prayer], she departed back, by the same way, to the play *Aulularia Plauti*. For the hearing and playing whereof, was made, by her Highness surveyor and at her own cost, in the body of the King's College Church, a great stage containing the breadth of the church from the one side to the other, that the chappels might serve for houses. In the length it ran two of the lower chappels full, with the pillars on a side.

Upon the south-wall was hanged a cloth of state, with the appurtances and half-path, for her Majesty.

In the rood-loft, another stage for ladies and gentlewomen to stand on. And the two lower tables, under the said rood-loft, were greatly enlarged and rayled for the choyce officers of the Court.

There was, before her Majesty's coming, made in the King's College Hall, a great stage. But, because it was judged by divers to be too little, and too close for her Highness and her company, and also far from her lodging, it was taken down.

When all things were ready for the plays, the Lord Chamberlayn and Mr. Secretary came in, bringing a multitude of the guard with them, having every man in his hand a torch-staff, for the lights of the play (for no other lights were occupied); and would not suffer any to stand upon the stage, save a very few upon the north side. And the guard stood upon the ground, by the stage side, holding their lights. From the quire door unto the stage was made as 'twere a bridge, rayled on both sides; for the Queen's Grace to go to the stage: which was straightly kept.

At last her Highness came, with certain Lords, Ladies, and Gentlewomen: all the Pensioners going on both sides, with torch staves. But the sword was not carried, neither the maces. And so took her seat, and heard the play fully. Which was played by certain selected persons, chosen out of all Colleges of the town, at the discretion of Mr. Roger Kelke, D. D. who was, by the Vicechancellor and Heads of Colleges, specially appointed to set forth and to teach such plays as should be exhibited before her Grace. To whom were joined four others thought mete for that charge, chosen out of the four principall colleges.

When the play was ended, her Majesty departed to her lodging about twelve of the clock, in such order as she came. (*Ibid.*, i.)

A brief anonymous account, also in English, adds the details that the play began "at ix^{ne} of the clock after supper," and that the actors "were chosen through the whole university, King's-colledge being only excepted." (*Ibid.*, iii.)

1564. AUGUST 7 (MONDAY). KING'S COLLEGE CHAPEL.

Dido and Aeneas, acted before the Queen by the students of King's College.

Robinson continues:

On this night was presented the tragedy of *Dido and Aeneas*, composed for the most part in Virgilian verses. A certain former associate of King's College undertook the labor of composition, who in his zeal for learning imitated the song of Vergil, but with a thinner pipe; not infelicitously, however, he worked out the course of the narrative into the form of a tragedy. A new work, yet charming and polished, and approved by the votes of the learned, it somewhat offended, perhaps by its length, the fastidious and critical. King's College furnished all the actors. The stage, which had been built in the chapel, was arranged as we have indicated on the previous day. The Queen, having been occupied for several hours with the sad calamity of Dido, at length betook herself to rest, pleasing to mortals. And this was the end of the third day. (Nichols, *Progresses Elizabeth*, iii.)

The account given by Stokys is very brief:

And, about nine of the clock [the Queen] came, as the night before, to a play, called Dido; which was exhibited and played by and at the charges of the company of the King's College. (*Ibid.*, i.)

The author of the anonymous account in English describes the play as written "in hexametre verse, without anie chorus," and continues:

While this was a handling, the Lo. Robert, steward to the universitie, and Mr. secretarie Cecil, chancellor, to signifye their good wille, and that things might be orderlye done, vouchsafed to hold both books on the scaffold themselves, and to provide also that sylence might be kept with quietness. (*Ibid.*, iii.)

The play was written by Edward Haliwell, a former fellow of the College. A brief summary of the plot, in Latin verse, may be found in Abraham Hartwell's *Regina Literata*, printed by Nichols.

Thomas Preston "acted so admirably well in the tragedy of *Dido*, before Queen Elizabeth, when she was entertained at Cambridge in 1564, and did so genteelly and gracefully dispute before her, that she gave him 20^{li} per ann. for so doing." (Cunningham, *Revels*, pp. xix–xx, from Oldys' MS. Notes on Langbaine.)

1564. AUGUST 8 (TUESDAY). KING'S COLLEGE CHAPEL.

Ezechias, by Nicholas Udall, acted before the Queen by the students of King's College.

Robinson describes the occasion as follows:

On that night was presented that heroic deed of Hezekiah, who inflamed by jealousy for the divine honor, crushed the brazen image of the serpent. From this sacred fount Nicholas Udall drew as much as he deemed sufficient for the proper magnitude of a comedy, put the whole into English verse, and called it *Ezechias*. How much wit and charm in so grave and sacred a matter, and yet how much truth in a fixed, uninterrupted course! The Queen deigned to be present. Again only the students of King's College acted. But after it had been contemplated long enough, it was time for rest. These things were done on the fourth day. (Nichols, *Progresses Elizabeth*, iii.)

Stokys writes:

At night, about the accustomed houre, and in the same manner, her Highness came to the play, called *Ezechias*, in English; which was played by the King's College, and the charges thereof by them born. (*Ibid.*, i.)

The anonymous account is even briefer, and adds no new details.

The play is not extant. A summary of the plot may be found in Hartwell's *Regina Literata*.

1564. AUGUST 9 (WEDNESDAY).

Ajax Flagellifer was prepared for presentation before the Queen but was not acted.

Stokys writes:

Great preparations and charges, as before in the other plays, were employed and spent about the tragedy of Sophocles, called *Ajax Flagellifer* in Latin, to be this night played before her. But her Highness, as it were tyred with going about the colleges, and hearing of disputations, and over-watched with former plays (for it was very late nightly before she came to them, as also departed from them) and furthermore minding early in the morning to depart from Cambridge, and ride to a dinner unto a house of the Bishop of Ely at Stanton; and from thence to her bed at Hinchinbrook (a house of Sir Henry Cromwell; in Huntingdonshire, about twelve miles from Cambridge) could not, as otherwise, no doubt, she would (with like patience and chearfulness as she was present at the other) hear the said tragedy, to the great sorrow, not only of the players, but of all the whole University. (Nichols, i.)

Of the preparation Robinson says:

They brought warlike arms, garments remarkable for splendor, and all the rest of the equipment from London and other very remote places, selected persons from the whole University, and found a place both suitable and large enough. (*Ibid.*, iii.)

The author of the anonymous English account says that the play was to have been performed by the students of King's College only; but this is evidently an error.

1564. AUGUST 10 (THURSDAY). HINCHINBROOK.

A masque or show acted before the Queen at Hinchinbrook, the seat of Sir Henry Cromwell, by Cambridge students.

On August 19, 1564, Guzman de Silva, Spanish Ambassador in England, wrote to the Duchess of Parma:

When the Queen was at Cambridge they represented comedies and held scientific disputations, and an argument on religion in which the man who defended Catholicism was attacked by those who presided in order to avoid having to give him the prize. The Queen made a speech praising the acts and exercises, and they wished to give her another representation, which she refused in order to be no longer delayed. Those who were so anxious for her to hear it followed her to her first stopping-place, and so importuned her that at last she consented.

The actors came in dressed as some of the imprisoned Bishops. First came the Bishop of London carrying a lamb in his hands as if he were eating it as he walked along, and then the others with different devices, one being in the figure of a dog with the Host in his mouth. They write that the Queen was so angry that she at once entered her chamber using strong language, and the men who held the torches, it being night, left them in the dark, and so ended the thoughtless and scandalous representation. (*Cal. of State Papers, Spanish*, i, 375.)

As Boas points out, the Cambridge authorities would scarcely have sanctioned such a production as a part of the Queen's entertainment. It is more probable, he thinks, that De Silva, who wrote from London, confused it with the countermanded *Ajax Flagellifer*, and that the burlesque was an "unauthorized addition by some of the younger scholars, who followed Elizabeth to Hinchinbrook in order to perform it." (See *Univ. Drama in the Tudor Age*, pp. 382–85.)

THE SEASON 1564–1565

1564/1564-5. CHRISTMAS. WHITEHALL.

A masque. (Feuillerat, *Doc.*, p. 116.)
See the note to the following entry.

1564/1564–5. Christmas. Whitehall.

"Edwardes tragedy" by the Children of the Chapel.

"Diuers townes and howsses and other devisses and Clowds" were provided "ffor a maske and a showe and a play by the childerne of the chaple." In the margin is written, "Edwardes tragedy." (Feuillerat, *Doc.*, p. 116.)

It is generally agreed among scholars that the play was Richard Edwards's *Damon and Pythias*, printed in 1571 "as the same was shewed before the Queenes Maiestie, by the Children of her Graces Chappell." W. Y. Durand ("Notes on Richard Edwards," *Journal of English and Germanic Philology*, iv, 348 ff.) shows that the Queen spent Christmas in London, and that the play, therefore, was doubtless given at Whitehall.

1564/1564–5. Christmas. Whitehall.

Two plays before the Queen "at Christmas" by the Earl of Warwick's Company. Payment £6. 13s. 4d. each, on warrant dated at Westminster, January 18, 1564–5. (Wallace, *Evol. E. D.*, p. 211. See also Cunningham, *Revels*, p. xxviii; Dasent, *Acts*, vii, 187; Chalmers, *Apology*, p. 394.)

1564/1564–5. Christmas. Whitehall.

A play before the Queen "this Christmas" by the Children of Paul's (Sebastian westcote). Payment £6. 13s. 4d., on warrant dated at [Westminster], January 18, 1564–5. (Wallace, *Evol. E. D.*, p. 211. See also Cunningham, *Revels*, p. xxviii; Dasent, *Acts*, vii, 187, in which the amount is given as £7. 13s. 8d.; Chalmers, *Apology*, p. 360.)

Possibly this is the play for which the "Eyrringe" was done in January. See the note to the following entry.

1564–5. January.

"*Heautontimoroumenos* Terentii and *Miles gloriosus* Plauti plaied by the children of the grammer schoole in the colledge of Westminster and before the Quenes maiestie anno 1564." (Scott, "Westminster Play Accounts," *Athenaeum*, i [1903], 220.)

Among the expenses for the plays, as published by Dr. Scott, are sixpence for pins and sugar candy "at ye rehersing before Sir Thomas Benger," and eleven shillings for "one Plautus geuen to ye Queenes maiestie and fowre other unto the nobilitie."

In the Revels Accounts there is a record of charges for "Eyrringe in Ienevery ffor cayrtene playes by the gramar skolle of west-mynster and the childerne of powles." (Feuillerat, *Doc.*, p. 117.)

1564–5. FEBRUARY 2 (FRIDAY).

A play before the Queen "on Candlemas daye last past" by the Children of Paul's (Sebastian westcote). Payment £6. 13s. 4d., on warrant dated at Westminster, March 9, 1564–5. (Wallace, *Evol. E. D.*, p. 211. See also Cunningham, *Revels*, p. xxviii; Dasent, *Acts*, vii, 204.)

1564–5. FEBRUARY 18 (SUNDAY).

"A play maid by Sir percivall hartts Sones." (Feuillerat, *Doc.*, p. 117.)

"Diuers Cities and Townes and the Emperours pallace & other devisses" were furnished by the Revels Office, and charged under the date of February 18. (*Ibid.*, p. 117.)

Sir Percival Hart, notes Feuillerat, "had been one of the Sewers of the Chamber to Henry VIII. In May, 1531, £3. 6s. 8d. was given by the King for 'the Cristenyng of percyvall hartes Childe'."

1564–5. FEBRUARY 18 (SUNDAY).

"*A maske of huntars* and diuers devisses and a Rocke, or hill ffor the ix musses to Singe vppone with a vayne of Sarsnett Dravven vpp and downe before them." (Feuillerat, *Doc.*, p. 117.)

The expenses of the masque are entered under the date February 18.

1564–5. MARCH 4–6 (SHROVETIDE).

"Diuers showes made by the gentillmen of greys Ine." In the margin, "*Diana. pallas.*" (Feuillerat, *Doc.*, p. 117.)

Apparently it is of a Gray's Inn "show" that De Silva wrote, on March 12 [O. S.]:

When this supper was ended we went to the Queen's rooms and descended to where all was prepared for the representation of a comedy in English, of which I understood just so much as the Queen told me. The plot was founded on the question of marriage, discussed between Juno and Diana, Juno advocating marriage and Diana chastity. Jupiter gave a verdict in favour of matrimony after many things had passed on both sides in defence of the respective arguments. The Queen turned to me and said, "This is all against me." (*Cal. State Papers, Spanish*, 1558–1567, p. 404.)

1564–5. MARCH 4–6 (SHROVETIDE).

"Foure masks too of them nott occupied nor sene with thare hole furniture which be verie fayr and Riche of old stuff butt new garnished . . . to seme new." (Feuillerat, *Doc.*, p. 117.)

On March 12 Guzman de Silva wrote, in the letter already quoted from, of an entertainment given at Shrovetide to the Queen by the Earl of Leicester:

After the comedy there was a masquerade of satyrs, or wild gods, who danced with the ladies, and when this was finished there entered 10 parties of 12 gentlemen each, the same who had fought in the foot tourney, and these, all armed as they were, danced with the ladies—a very novel ball, surely.

SUMMER, 1565

1565. JULY 16 (MONDAY). DURHAM PLACE.

Two masques at the marriage of Henry, son of Sir Francis Knollys, to Margaret, daughter of Sir Ambrose Cave.

On July 23 De Silva wrote:

The Queen stayed through the entertainment. . . . After supper there was a ball, a tourney, and two masques, the feast ending at half-past one. (*Cal. State Papers, Spanish*, i, 452.)

THE SEASON 1565–1566

1565/1565–6. DATE UNCERTAIN.

Sapientia Solomonis [Sixt Birck] acted before the Queen and the "inclita princeps Cecilia" by "puellorum cohors Nutrita magnificis . . . sumptibus." (See the prologue and epilogue, printed by Churchill and Keller, in the *Jahrbuch*, xxxiv, 226, 228. Cf. Boas, *University Drama*, p. 21, *n*.)

Chambers (*Eliz. Stage*, ii, 72–3) ascribes the play to the Children of Westminster. Cecilia, sister of the King of Sweden, and wife of the Margrave of Baden, was in England from September, 1565, to the summer of 1566.

1565/1565–6. CHRISTMAS.

Two plays before the Queen "at the Courte this Christmas" by the Children of Paul's (Sebestyan Westcote). Payment £6. 13*s*. 4*d*. each, on warrant dated at Westminster, January 3, 1565–6. (Wallace, *Evol. E. D.*, p. 211. See also Chambers, *M. L. R.*, ii, 3.)

1565/1565–6. CHRISTMAS. THE SAVOY.

A play before the Queen "at the Ladye Cicilias lodging at the Savoye" by the Children of Paul's. £6. 13*s*. 4*d*., on the same warrant as that for the preceding play. (Wallace, *Evol. E. D.*, p. 211. See also Chambers, *M. L. R.*, ii. 3.)

1565–6. FEBRUARY 24–26 (SHROVETIDE).

A masque at the marriage of Henry Earl of Southampton to Mary Browne, daughter of Anthony Lord Montague. The Queen was present. (Chambers, *Eliz. Stage*, i, 162.)

SUMMER, 1566

1566. JULY 1 (MONDAY).

A masque at the marriage of Thomas Mildmay to Frances, sister of Thomas Earl of Sussex. The Queen was present.

On July 6 De Silva wrote:

On the 1st of this month a sister of Sussex was married, and the French Ambassador was asked to dinner, I being asked to supper, as the Queen was invited. There was a masquerade, and a long ball, . . . (*Cal. State Papers, Spanish*, 1558–1567, p. 565.)

OXFORD, SEPTEMBER, 1566

For a general account of the Queen's visit, and of the plays performed before her, see F. S. Boas, *University Drama in the Tudor Age*, pp. 98–108. The English account of the ceremonies written by Thomas Neale and preserved in the Twyne MS. has been available only through the accounts based on it by Wood in his *History and Antiquities of the University of Oxford*, and by Stephens in his *Brief Rehearsall*.

1566. SEPTEMBER 1 (SUNDAY). CHRIST CHURCH HALL.

Marcus Geminus, a Latin play, acted before the Court and the Spanish Ambassador. The Queen was not present.

The Queen in her progress, accompanied by many members of the Court, and by the Spanish Ambassador, Guzman de Silva, arrived in Oxford on Saturday, August 31. As Stow notes, the exercises provided by the University for her entertainment "agreed much with those which the Universitie of Cambridge had used two yeares before." On Sunday evening, wearied no doubt by the journey and by the orations which had greeted her at every turn, the Queen kept her lodging, to the keen disappointment of those who had expected her to be present at the play. The verbose description of the occasion given by John Bereblock in his *Commentaries* must be quoted, however, on account of the important details which it furnishes about the stage:

At nightfall a most splendid play was presented, which to those who had looked forward to it all day at leisure was a crowning recompense in its brilliance. Nothing, now, more costly or magnificent could be imagined than its staging and arrangement. In the first place there was a remarkable proscenium there, with an approach thrown open from the great solid wall; and from it a hanging wooden bridge, supported also by props, is stretched across to the great hall of the college by means of a small, highly burnished cable running through the cross pieces, the whole being adorned with festal garlands and with an embossed and painted canopy. Through this bridge, without commotion and without contact from the pressing crowd, the Queen might hasten by an easy ascent to the play, when it was ready. The hall was panelled with gilt, and the roof inside was arched and frescoed; in its size and loftiness you would say that it copied after the grandeur of an old Roman palace, and in its magnificence that it imitated some model of antiquity.

In the upper part of the hall, where it looks to the west, a stage is built, large and lofty, and many steps high. Along all the walls balconies and scaffoldings were constructed; these had many tiers of better seats, from which noble men and women might look on, and the people could get a view of the plays from round about. Cressets, lamps, and burning candles made a brilliant light there. With so many lights arranged in branches and circles, and with so many torches, here and there, giving forth a flickering gleam of varying power, the place was resplendent; so that the lights seem to shine like the day and to aid the splendor of the plays by their very great brightness. On each side of the stage magnificent palaces and well equipped houses are built up for the actors in the comedies and for the masked persons. On high a seat had been fixed, adorned with cushions and tapestries and covered with a golden canopy; this was the place made ready for the Queen. But she, indeed, was certainly not present on this night.

When, now, everything had been prepared in this fashion, and the house was filled comfortably full, straightway we could see on the stage Geminus Campanus, whom Duillius and Cotta (on account of their hatred and unscrupulous rivalry) accuse before Alexander Severus. Slaves, farmers, and peasants, corrupted by bribes, are introduced as witnesses. Nothing could be more laughable than to observe them, exulting vulgarly in their certain success, now quarreling about the punishment of Geminus, now wrangling over the sharing of his property: and then to see them deploring their bad luck with lamentings and tears like women. When this scene had been sufficiently acted out, freedmen of a more honorable stamp are finally brought forward,—men who could not be induced by threats or rewards to make a wrongful accusation. So by *their* writings, *their* testimony, witness and examination, the conspiracy was made clear. The slaves, therefore, formerly accusers, now at the Emperor's command are fixed on the cross. Druillius and Cotta are deservedly punished, the freedmen are rewarded, Geminus is acquitted; and great applause is won from all. When the play is finished, we disperse for the night. (Translation by W. Y. Durand, *Pub. M. L. Assoc.*, xx [1905],

504–506. For the Latin, see Nichols, *Progresses Elizabeth*, i, and Plummer, *Elizabethan Oxford*, pp. 123–25.)

Nicholas Robinson, who wrote perhaps the most detailed account of the plays at Cambridge, has left a briefer description of this occasion, which supplements that of Bereblock. Again I quote from Durand's translation:

This day was closed by a sort of History of a certain Geminus, which History some learned men of Christ's College had turned into the form of a comedy, but in prose; and they acted it on the stage, in the hall of the same college, where all was splendid enough in the way of magnificence and decoration, with regal costliness; and this was done with the aid of Master Edwards, who remained almost two months at the University for completing a certain English work which he gave on the following night. (*Ibid.*, p. 507. For the Latin see Nichols, *op. cit.*, and Plummer, pp. 178–9.)

According to the brief account communicated by Gutch from Wood's MSS., the Spanish Ambassador so highly commended the performance to the Queen that she exclaimed, "In truth, I will lose no more sport hereafter, for the good report that I hear of these your good doings." (Nichols, *op. cit.*, iii.)

Other accounts of the occasion are those by Stephens, in *A Brief Rehearsall* (Nichols, i, and Plummer, p. 199); and Wood, in his *History and Antiquities of the University of Oxford*.

1566. SEPTEMBER 2 (MONDAY). CHRIST CHURCH HALL.

The first part of *Palamon and Arcyte*, by Richard Edwards, acted before the Queen.

Richard Edwards, Master of Arts of Christ Church, and since 1561 Master of the Children of the Chapel Royal, was well fitted to write a successful play for the occasion. It seems at rehearsal to have aroused enthusiasm. Thomas Neale relates that at a preliminary performance "before certayne courtiers" in the lodging of Roger Marbeck, Canon of Christ Church, it "was so well lyked that they saide it far surpassed *Damon & Pythias*, then ye whiche nothinge could be better." (Boas, *University Drama*, p. 101.)

Bereblock describes the occasion as follows:

At the approach of night, they came together for the play that has been made ready. Its wonderful setting and its lavish elegance had so filled everybody's minds and ears with its marvellous reputation that a mighty and countless crowd of people gathered together, tremendously and immoderately anxious to see. Moreover, the presence of the Queen, of which they had been deprived for two days now, had added such a great desire for it in the minds of all that the number was far greater and more infinite on that account. Scarcely had the Queen come in, together with the nobles and the chief men, and taken her seat on the lofty throne, when all the approaches to the theatre (this was the hall of the college) were thronged with so great crowd, and the steps were already so filled with people, that by their violent pushing they disturbed the common joy by a frightful accident. A certain wall of great square stones had been built there; it was a bulwark propping each side of a pair of steps to bear the rush of people going up; the crowd becomes too dense, the rush too great, the wall, although quite firm, could not stand the strain; it gives way from the side of the stairs, three men are overwhelmed by the falling mass, as many more wounded. Of those who were overwhelmed the one who survived longest lived not over two days. The wounded, by the application of remedies, soon recovered.

This untoward happening, although touching every one with sadness, could by no means destroy the enjoyment of the occasion. Accordingly, taught by the misfortune of others to be more careful, all turn again to the play. (Durand, *op. cit.*, p. 508. I omit the summary of the plot. For the Latin see Nichols, i, and Plummer, pp. 127-8.)

According to the account from the Wood MSS.,"afterwards the actors performed their parts so well, that the Queen laughed heartily thereat, and gave the author of the play great thanks for his pains." (Nichols, iii.)

Other brief accounts by Robinson, Wood, and Stephens, in the works already cited, add no details of especial interest.

1566. SEPTEMBER 3 (TUESDAY).

The second part of *Palamon and Arcyte* was put off until the following evening. Bereblock says: "No play was given on this night, because the Queen, delayed by the rather long disputation which preceded it, could not be present at the play without some risk to her health." (Durand, *op. cit.*, p. 510, *n.*)

1566. SEPTEMBER 4 (WEDNESDAY). CHRIST CHURCH HALL.

The second part of *Palamon and Arcyte*, acted before the Queen.

At night the Queen was present at the other part of the play of *Palaemon and Arcyte*, which should have been acted the night before, but deferred because it was late when the Queen came from disputations at St. Mary's. When the play was ended, she called for Mr. Edwards, the author, and gave him very great thanks, with praises of reward, for his pains: then making a pause, said to him and her retinue standing about her, this relating to part of the play: "By Palaemon, I warrant he dallieth not in love when he was in love indeed; by Arcyte, he was a right martial Knight, having a swart countenance and a manly face; by Trecatio, God's pity, what a knave it is; by Perithous throwing Sir Edward's rich cloak into the funeral fire, which a stander-by would have stayed by the arm with an oath, Go, fool, he knoweth his part, I warrant". In the said play was acted a cry of hounds in the Quadrant, upon the train of a fox in the hunting of Theseus, with which the young scholars, who stood in the windows, were so much taken (supposing it was real), that they cried out, "Now, now!—there, there! he's caught, he's caught!" All which the Queen merrily beholding, said, "O excellent! Those boys, in very truth, are ready to leap out of the windows, to follow the hounds." This part, it seems, being repeated before certain courtiers, in the lodgings of Mr. Robert Marbeck, one of the canons of Christ Church, by the players in their gowns (for they were all scholars that acted) before the Queen came to Oxford, was by them so well liked, that they said it far surpassed *Damon and Pythias*, than which, they thought, nothing could be better. Likewise some said, that if the author did any more before his death, he would run mad: but this comedy was the last he made; for he died within a few months after. In the acting of the said play, there was a good part performed by the Lady Amelia, who, for gathering her flowers prettily in a garden then represented, and singing sweetly in the time of March, received eight angels for a gracious reward by her Majesty's command. By whom that part was acted I know not, unless by Peter Carew, the pretty boy before mentioned. (Wood's MSS., quoted from Nichols, iii. See also *Athenæ Oxonienses*, ed. by Bliss, i, 354–55.)

I omit Bereblock's account, which consists mainly of a summary of the plot. The writer concludes by saying that at the close of the play the theatre was very full, and that the awarding of the maiden to Palamon "was approved by the throng with a tremendous shout and clapping of hands."

Other brief accounts by Wood, Robinson, and Stephens contribute no new details.

1566. SEPTEMBER 5 (THURSDAY). CHRIST CHURCH HALL.

Progne, a Latin tragedy by Dr. James Calfhill, before the Queen.

After the Queen had refreshed herself with a supper, she, with her nobility, went into Christ Church Hall, where was acted before them a Latin tragedy, called *Progne*, made by Dr. James Calfhill, canon of Christ Church. After which was done, she gave the author thanks; but it did not take half so well as the much-admired play of *Palaemon and Arcyte*. (Wood's MSS., quoted from Nichols, iii.)

Robinson describes the performance as follows:

Afterwards the Queen's Majesty is led into the hall, where the wax candles had been lighted, because eight o'clock had already struck. In the silence of this night there is exhibited on the stage how King Tereus devours his son, slain and prepared by his wife Progne on account of her outraged sister,—all indeed exactly as it should be, with great magnificence and splendor truly regal. (Durand, *op. cit.*, p. 517.)

The story, of course, comes from Ovid. But Calfhill's play, as Durand has pointed out, is probably an adaptation from an earlier Latin play, the *Progne* of Gregorio Corraro, published at Venice in 1558. Again I omit Bereblock's account, which consists mainly of a summary of the plot. Other brief accounts of the performance are given by Wood and Stephens.

This was the last of the plays offered by the University to the Queen for her entertainment. Two days later she departed, leaving behind her, says Wood, "such impressions in the minds of scholars that nothing but emulation was in their studies; and nothing left untouched by them whereby they thought they might be advanced by her, and become acceptable in her eye."

THE SEASON 1566–1567

1566/1566–7. CHRISTMAS.

Two plays before the Queen "this Christmas" by the Children of Paul's (Sebastyan Westcote). Payment £6. 13*s*. 4*d*. each, on warrant dated at Westminster, January 11, 1566–7. (Wallace, *Evol. E. D.*, p. 211. See also Dasent, *Acts*, vii, 322, in which the date is given as January 12; Chalmers, *Apology*, p. 360.)

1566–7. FEBRUARY 9–11 (SHROVETIDE).

A play before the Queen "in Shroftide 1566" by the Children of Westminster (John Taylor). Payment £6. 13*s*. 4*d*., on warrant dated at Westminster, February 13, 1566–7. (Wallace, *Evol. E. D.*, p. 211. See also Dasent, *Acts*, vii, 327; Chalmers, *Apology*, p. 360.)

1566–7. FEBRUARY 11 (SHROVE TUESDAY).

A play before the Queen "at Shroftide laste paste" by the Children of Windsor (Rycharde ffarraunte). Payment £6. 13*s*. 4*d*., on warrant dated February 16, 1566–7. (Wallace, *Evol. E. D.*, p. 212. See also Dasent, *Acts*, vii, 331, in which the warrant is dated February 17, at Westminster, and the date of the play given as "Shrove Tuesday last past.")

1567. APRIL 13 (SUNDAY).

A comedy before the Queen.

On April 14 Guzman de Silva wrote to the King of Spain:

The hatred that this Queen has of marriage is most strange. They represented a comedy before her last night until nearly one in the morning, which ended in a marriage, and the Queen, as she told me herself, expressed her dislike of the woman's part. (*Cal. State Papers, Spanish*, 1558–1567, p. 633.)

THE SEASON 1567–1568

1567/1567–8. JULY 14–MARCH 3.

The titles of the plays performed during the season are given in a warrant issued June 11, 1568, authorizing the payment to "ceartayne Credditours Artifficeares and woorkmen, for stuffe deliuerde and woorke donne" from July 14 to March 3, the sum of £634. 9s. 5d., which had been "ymployed vppon theis playes Tragides and Maskes following":

Imprimis for seven playes, the firste namede *as playne as Canne be*, The seconde *the paynfull plillgrimage*, The thirde *Iacke and Iyll*, The forthe *sixe fooles*, The fivethe callede *witte and will*, The sixte callede *prodigallitie*, The sevoenthe of *Orestes* and a *Tragedie of the kinge of Scottes*, to yᵉ whiche belonged diuers howses, for the setting forthe of the same as Stratoes howse, Gobbyns howse, Orestioes howse Rome, the Pallace of prosperitie Scotlande and a gret Castell one thothere side. (Feuillerat, *Doc.*, p. 119.)

There is record of payment for seven plays, as the following entries show.

Fleay (*Drama*, ii, 294) identifies *Wit and Will* with the *Marriage of Wit and Science*. Of *Prodigality* he asserts, "not *Liberality and Prodigality* of 1602." (*Ibid.*, p. 288.) He regards *Orestes* as a version of the *Horestes* of John Pickering, printed in 1567 as "A Newe Enterlude of Vice Conteyninge, the Historye of Horestes with the cruell reuengment of his Fathers death, vpon his one naturtll Mother." (*Stage*, p. 61.)

1567/1567–8. JULY 14–MARCH 3.

Six masques were prepared, four of which were shown.

The warrant which contains the name of the plays likewise authorizes payment "for the altering and newe makinge of sixe Maskes out of ould stuffe with Torche bearers thervnto wherof iiijᵒʳ hathe byne shewene, before vs, and two remayne vnshewen." (Feuillerat, *Doc.*, p. 119.)

1567/1567–8. Christmas. Whitehall.

A play before the Queen "this laste Christmas" by the Children of Westminster (John Tailer). Payment £6. 13*s*. 4*d*., on warrant dated at Westminster, January 10, 1567–8. (Wallace, *Evol. E. D.*, p. 212. See also Stopes, *Hunnis*, p. 318; Chambers, *M. L. R.*, ii, 3.)

The Queen went to Whitehall on December 23. (Chambers, *Eliz. Stage*, iv, 84.)

1567/1567–8. Christmas. Whitehall.

Two plays before the Queen "this laste Christmas" by Lord Rich's Company. Payment £6. 13*s*. 4*d*. each, on warrant dated January 11, 1567–8. (Wallace, *Evol. E. D.*, p. 212. See also Chambers, *M. L. R.*, ii, 3.)

1567/1567–8. Christmas. Whitehall.

Two plays before the Queen "this laste Christmas" by the Children of Paul's (Sebastian Westecote). Payment £6. 13*s*. 4*d*. each, on warranted dated at Westminster, January 13, 1567–8. (Wallace, *Evol. E. D.*, p. 212. See also Stopes, *Hunnis*, p. 318; Chambers, *M. L. R.*, ii, 3.)

1567–8. February 29–March 2 (Shrovetide).

A play before the Queen "at Shroftyde" by the Children of Windsor (Richarde fferraunte). Payment £6. 13*s*. 4*d*., on warrant dated at Westminster, March 1, 1567–8. (Wallace, *Evol. E. D.*, p. 212. See also Stopes, *Hunnis*, p. 318; Chambers, *M. L. R.*, ii, 3.)

1567–8. February 29–March 2 (Shrovetide).

"A Tragedye" before the Queen "this Shroftyde" by the Children of the Queen's Chapel (William Hunys). Payment £6. 13*s*. 4*d*., on warrant dated at Westminster, March 3, 1567–8. (Wallace, *Evol. E. D.*, p. 212. See also Stopes, *Hunnis*, p. 318; Chambers, *M. L. R.*, ii, 3.)

THE SEASON 1568–1569

That there were masques during the season, as well as plays, is shown by a warrant issued May 10, 1569, for the payment of £453. 5s. 6d. spent in the "furnisshinge of suche playes, Tragidies, and Maskes as hathe byne shewed before vs at Christmas, and Shrovetide Last past in the eleventh year of our Raigne." (Feuillerat, *Doc.*, p. 124.)

1568. DECEMBER 26 (SUNDAY). HAMPTON COURT.

A play before the Queen "on St Stevens Daie at nighte last past" by Lord Rich's Company. Payment £6. 13s. 4d., on warrant dated December 28, 1568. (Wallace, *Evol.*, E. D., p. 212. See also Cunningham, *Revels*, p. xxix, in which the warrant is dated at Hampton Court.)

1568–9. JANUARY 1 (SATURDAY). HAMPTON COURT.

A play before the Queen "on Neweyeares Daye at night 1568" by the Children of Paul's (Sebastian Westcote). Payment £6. 13s. 4d., on warrant dated January 2, 1568–9. (Wallace. *Evol. E. D.*, p. 212. See also Cunningham, *Revels*, p. xxix, in which the date of the warrant is not given; Stopes, *Hunnis*, p. 318.)

1568–9. FEBRUARY 22 (SHROVE TUESDAY).

A play before the Queen "on Shrovetuesday at night laste paste" by the Children of Windsor (Richarde Ferraunte). Payment £6. 13s. 4d., on warrant dated at Westminster, February 25, 1568–9. (Wallace, *Evol. E. D.*, p. 212. See also Cunningham, *Revels*, p. xxix; Stopes, *Hunnis*, p. 318.)

THE SEASON 1569–1570

It is evident that masques were performed during this season also, from the warrant issued July 29, 1570, for the payment of £499. 17s. 6½d. which had been spent in "furnishinge of soche playes, tragedyes and maskes, as hathe bene shewed before vs at

Christmas and Shrovetide Laste paste in the twelvithe yeare of our Raigne." (Feuillerat, *Doc.*, p. 125.)

1569. DECEMBER 27 (TUESDAY). WINDSOR.

A play before the Queen "vpon St Johns daie at nighte laste paste" by the Children of Windsor (Richarde Ferrante). Payment £6. 13*s.* 4*d.*, on warrant dated January 2, 1569–70. (Wallace, *Evol. E. D.*, p. 212. See also Cunningham, *Revels*, p. xxix, in which the warrant is dated at Windsor; Stopes, *Hunnis*, p. 318, in which "2nd June 1569" is given as the date of the warrant.)

1569–70. JANUARY 6 (FRIDAY). WINDSOR.

A play before the Queen "on Twelfe daie at nighte laste paste" by the Children of the Chapel (William Hunys). Payment £6. 13*s.* 4*d.*, on warrant dated January 7, 1569–70. (Wallace, *Evol. E. D.*, p. 213. See also Cunningham, *Revels*, p. xxix, in which the warrant is dated at Windsor; Stopes, *Hunnis*, p. 318.)

1569–70. FEBRUARY 5 (SHROVE SUNDAY). HAMPTON COURT.

A play before the Queen "on Shrovesondaie at nighte laste paste" by Lord Rich's Company. Payment £6. 13*s.* 4*d.*, on warrant dated at Hampton Court, February 7, 1569–70. (Wallace, *Evol. E. D.*, p. 213. See also Cunningham, *Revels*, p. xxix; Stopes, *Hunnis*, p. 319.)

The Queen removed to Hampton Court on January 20. (Chambers, *Eliz. Stage*, iv, 85.)

THE SEASON 1570–1571

No record of masques for the season has been discovered, but in the warrant issued October 23, 1571, for the payment of Revels expenses from Shrovetide 1569–70 to Shrovetide 1570–1, special mention is made of "new making furnishing and setting furth of soundrie Comodies Tragedies Maskes and Showes which were showen before vs this Last Christmas and Shroftyde." (Feuillerat, *Doc.*, p. 126.)

1570. DECEMBER 28 (THURSDAY).

A play before the Queen "vpon Jnnocentes daye last past" by the Children of Paul's (Sebastian Westecote). Payment £6. 13*s*. 4*d*., on warrant dated February 22, 1570–1. (Wallace, *Evol. E. D.*, p. 213. See also Stopes, *Hunnis*, p. 319; Chambers, *M. L. R.*, ii, 4.)

1570–1. FEBRUARY 25–27 (SHROVETIDE).

Three plays before the Queen "at this Shroftyde last past namely Sondaye, Mondaye, and Tewesdaye," by the Children of the Queen's Chapel, the Children of Windsor, and the Children of Paul's (William Honnyes, Richarde Farrante, Sebastian Westcote). Payment £6. 13*s*. 4*d*. each, on warrant dated February ultimo, 1570–1. (Wallace, *Evol. E. D.*, p. 213. See also Stopes, *Hunnis*, p. 319; Chambers, *M. L. R.*, ii, 4.)

THE SEASON 1571–1572

One of the best descriptions to be had from the Revels Accounts of the activities of the Office is found in connection with the plays of this season:

All whiche .vj. playes being chosen owte of many and ffownde to be the best that then were to be had. the same also being often pervsed & necessarely corrected & amended. (by all thafforeseide officers) Then, they being so orderly addressed: were lykewise Throwghly Apparelled, & ffurnished, with sundry kindes, and sutes, of Apparell, & furniture, ffitted and garnished necessarely: & answerable to the matter, person, and parte to be played: Having also apt howses: made of Canvasse, fframed, ffashioned & paynted accordingly: as mighte best serve theier severall purposes. Together with sundry properties incident: ffashioned, paynted, garnished, and bestowed as the partyes them selves required & needed. (Feuillerat, *Doc.* p. 145.)

1570–1/1571–2. DATES UNCERTAIN.

"Maskes vj." (Feuillerat, *Doc.*, p. 146.)

One of the masques "had going before it A Childe gorgeously decked for Mercury, who vttered A speeche: & presented iij fflowers (wroughte in silke & golde) to the Queenes Maiestie signefieng victory, peace, & plenty, to ensue." (*Ibid.*, p. 146.)

Fleay (*Stage*, p. 19) conjectures that a masque was performed on each night after the play.

1571. DECEMBER 26 (WEDNESDAY).

For the play of Sir Robert Lane's Men ascribed in the *Acts of the Privy Council* (viii, 61) to this date, see the following entry.

1571. DECEMBER 27 (THURSDAY).

"*Lady Barbara* showen on Saint Iohns day at nighte by Sir Robert Lanes Men." (Feuillerat, *Doc.*, p. 145.)

£6. 13*s*. 4*d*. was paid, on a warrant dated at Westminster, January 5, 1572 [Wallace regards this date as N. S.], for a play before the Queen "vpon St Johns daie at night last past" by "Lawrence Dutton and his fellowes." (Wallace, *Evol. E. D.*, p. 213. See also Stopes, *Hunnis*, p. 319; Chambers, M. L. R., ii, 4; Dasent, *Acts*, viii, 61, in which the warrant is dated January 12, and the performance December 26; Chalmers, *Apology*, p. 394, in which the warrant is dated 1572–3.)

1571. DECEMBER 27 (THURSDAY).

The *Acts of the Privy Council* (viii, 62) give a play on this date by the Children of Windsor. But the correct date seems to be January 1.

1571. DECEMBER 28 (FRIDAY).

"*Effiginia* A Tragedye showen on the Innosentes daie at nighte by the Children of powles." (Feuillerat, *Doc.*, p. 145.)

£6. 13*s*. 4*d*. was paid, on a warrant dated at Westminster, January 9, 1571–2, for a play before the Queen "vppon Jnnocentes daie at night" by the Children of Paul's (Sebastian Wescot). (Wallace, *Evol. E. D.*, p. 213. See also Stopes, *Hunnis*, p. 319; Chambers, M. L. R., ii, 4; Dasent, *Acts*, viii, 62, in which the warrant is dated January 12 and the performance January 1; Chalmers, *Apology*, p. 394, in which the warrant is dated 1572–3.)

1571–2. JANUARY 1 (TUESDAY).

"*Aiax and vlisses* showen on New yeares daie at nighte by the Children of Wynsor." (Feuillerat, *Doc.*, p. 145.)

£6. 13*s*. 4*d*. was paid, on a warrant dated at Westminster, January 5, 1571–2, for a play before the Queen "vppon Newe yeares daie at night last past" by the Children of Windsor (Richard ffarraunte). (Wallace, *Evol. E. D.*, p. 213. See also Stopes, *Hunnis*, p. 319; Chambers, *M. L. R.*, ii, 4; Dasent, *Acts*, viii, 62, in which the warrant is dated January 12 and the performance December 27; Chalmers, *Apology*, p. 360, in which the date of the warrant is given as 1572–3.)

1571–2. JANUARY 1 (TUESDAY).

For the play by the Children of Paul's ascribed in the *Acts of the Privy Council* (viii, 62) to this date, see the entry for December 28.

1571–2. JANUARY 6 (SUNDAY).

"*Narcisses* showen on Twelfe daye at Nighte by the Children of the Chappell." (Feuillerat, *Doc.*, p. 145.)

Two interesting items from the Revels Accounts throw light on the performance of the play:

Iohn Tryce for mony to him due for Leashes, & Doghookes, with staves, & other necessaries: by him provyded for the hunters that made the crye after the fox (let loose in the Coorte) with their howndes, hornes, and hallowing, in the play of *narcisses*, which crye was made of purpose even as the woordes then in vtterance, & the parte then played, did Requier . . . xxxj*s*. viij*d*. (*Ibid.*, p. 141.)

Iohn Izarde for mony to him due for his device in counterfeting Thunder & Lightning in the playe of *Narcisses* being requested thervnto by the seide Master of this office And for sundry necessaries by him spent therein . . . xxij*s*." (*Ibid.*, p. 142.)

£6. 13*s*. 4*d*. was paid, on the same warrant as that for the play of December 28, for a play before the Queen "on twelf daie at night last past" by the Children of the Chapel (William Hunnys).

(Wallace, *Evol. E. D.*, p. 213. See also Stopes, *Hunnis*, p. 319, in
which the sum is given as £13. 6s. 8d; Chambers, *M. L. R.*, ii, 4,
in which the play is dated January 12; Dasent, *Acts*, viii, 62, in
which the date of the warrant is given as January 12, and the
payee as "John Honnys"; Chalmers, *Apology*, in which the warrant is dated 1572–3.)

1571–2. FEBRUARY 17 (SHROVE SUNDAY).

"*Chloridon and Radiamanta* showen on Shrove sundaye at Nighte
by Sir Robert Lanes Men." (Feuillerat, *Doc.*, p. 145.)

£13. 6s. 8d. was paid, on a warrant dated at Westminster, Feb.
29, 1571–2, for a play "vpon Shrove Sonday at night Last past"
by "Lawrence Dutton and his fellowes." (Wallace, *Evol. E. D.*,
pp. 213–14. See also Dasent, *Acts*, viii, 71; Chalmers, *Apology*, p.
394, in which the warrant is dated 1572–3; Chambers, *M. L. R.*,
ii, 4, in which the payees are given as John Greaves and Thomas
Goughe. In *Eliz. Stage*, iv, 146, the date of the warrant is given
from the Declared Accounts as February 26.)

1571–2. FEBRUARY 19 (SHROVE TUESDAY).

"*Paris and vienna* showen on Shrovetewsdaie at Nighte by the
Children of Westminster." (Feuillerat, *Doc.*, p. 145.)

"Certeine Armour" was hired "for the playe of *parris and
vienna* to furnish the triumphe therein." (*Ibid.*, p. 142.)

£13. 6s. 8d. was paid, on a warrant dated at Westminster,
February 29, 1571–2, for a play before the Queen "vpon Shrove
Tuesday at night Last past" by the Children of Westminster.
(Wallace, *Evol. E. D.*, p. 214. See also Chambers, *M. L. R.*, ii, 4,
in which the company is not specified and the payee given as
John Billingesley; Dasent, *Acts*, viii, 71; Chalmers, *Apology*, p.
360, in which the amount is given as £6. 13s. 4d. and the warrant
dated 1572–3. In the Declared Accounts the warrant is dated
February 26. See *Eliz. Stage*, iv, 146.)

The group of warrants dated January 12 and February 29, 1572–
3, by Chalmers (*Apology*, pp. 360, 394) for plays performed on

December 26, 27, January 1, 6, Shrove Sunday and Shrove Monday, has been a source of confusion, for it has been more than once pointed out that they fit the season 1571–1572 better than that of 1572–1573. A comparison of Chalmers with his source reveals the fact that the warrants appear in the *Acts of the Privy Council* under the date 1571-2. Apparently Chalmers has misdated them by a year.

SUMMER, 1572

1572. JUNE 15 (SUNDAY)? WHITEHALL.

"One Maske showen at White hall before her Maiestie & Duke Mommerancie Embassador for ffraunce." (Feuillerat, *Doc.*, p. 153.)

Stow gives the following account of the arrival and entertainment of the ambassadors:

About the 9. of Iune, Francis duke of Memorencie chiefe Marshall of Fraunce, and Paul de Faix of the priuie counsell to the sayde king, and Bertrande de Saligners, lord de la Mothefenalon, knights of the order of Saint Michaell, ambassadors for the same king, arryued at Douer, and were brought to London.
The 15 day being sunday, the said ambassadors repaired to the White hall, where they were honorably receiued of the Queenes maiestie, with her nobilitie, and there in her graces chappell, about one of the clocke in the afternoone, the articles of treatie, league, or confederacie & sure friendship (concluded at Blois the 19. of Aprill) as is aforeshewed, betwixt the Queenes maiestie, and the French King, being read, the same was by her maiestie and his ambassadors confirmed . . . The rest of that day with great part of the night following was spent in great triumph, with sumptuous banquets . . . The twentie-eyght day of June, the aforenamed Ambassadors departed from London towards France. (Quoted by Feuillerat from Stow, *Annals*, 1615, p. 672.)

Fleay (*Stage*, p. 19) is of the opinion that the devices prepared for the projected masques of 1562 were employed "in a modified form" for this masque; but as Chambers (Malone Soc. *Collections*, I, 1, 144) points out, the interval is ten years and the resemblances "only partial."

THE SEASON 1572–1573

"Sundry playes and Maskes with other sportes & pastymes for her Maiesties Recreacion" were "showen this yeare in Christmas & Shrovetyde at hampton Coorte and at Greenewitche." (Feuillerat, *Doc.*, p. 171.)

1572/1572–3. DATE UNCERTAIN.

The names of two of the plays of the season survive in the record of payment for "ij speares for the *play of Cariclia*" (Feuillerat, *Doc.*, p. 175), and "for drawing of patternes for the *playe of fortune.*" (*Ibid.*, p. 176).

Chambers (*Eliz. Stage*, iv, 88) is of the opinion that a play of Perseus and Andromeda was also presented. This conjecture is based on items in the Accounts referring to the painting of a picture of Andromeda. He would ascribe the performance to Mulcaster's boys, on Shrove Tuesday.

1572–3. CHRISTMAS OR SHROVETIDE.

A double masque.

Three shillings was paid "to henri kellewaye to go to the Coorte abowte the dubble Mask." (Feuillerat, *Doc.*, p. 180.)

"Double Masques, one of Men, another of Ladies, addeth State, and Variety," said Bacon. From various items of expenditure, the masque of men appears to have been of Fishermen. That of women is less certain.

1572/1572–3. CHRISTMAS. HAMPTON COURT.

Three plays before the Queen "in Xpenmas laste" by the Earl of Leicester's Company. Payment £10 each, on a warrant dated at Hampton Court, January 1, 1572–3. (Wallace, *Evol. E. D.*, p. 214. See also Stopes, *Hunnis*, p. 319; *Burbage*, p. 247; Chambers, *M. L. R.*, ii, 5.)

The Revels Accounts record payments for "A Waggen for the first playe of my Lord of Leisters men," and for "the hier of A

Waggon for cariage to the Coorte at the second play of my Lord of Leicesters men." (Feuillerat, *Doc.*, p. 180.)

1572/1572–3. CHRISTMAS. HAMPTON COURT.

A play before the Queen by the Children of Paul's (Sebastian Westecote). Payment £6. 13*s.* 4*d.*, on warrant dated at [Hampton Court, January 7, 1572–3]. (Wallace, *Evol. E. D.*, p. 214. See also Stopes, *Hunnis*, p. 319; Chambers, *M. L. R.*, ii, 5.)

From the Revels Accounts we learn that "ij Squirtes"were bought "for the playe of the children of powles." (Feuillerat, *Doc.*, p. 180.)

1572–3. JANUARY 1 (THURSDAY). HAMPTON COURT.

A play before the Queen "vpon Newyeres daie at night last past" by the Children of Windsor (Richard Pharrante). Payment £6. 13*s.* 4*d.*, on warrant dated at Hampton Court, January 2, 1572–3. (Wallace, *Evol. E. D.*, p. 214. See also Stopes, *Hunnis*, p. 319; Chambers, *M. L. R.*, ii, 5.)

The Revels Accounts record the purchase of "Gloves for the children of Wynsor ij dozen" (Feuillerat, *Doc.*, p. 174), of "a desk for farrantes playe" (*ibid.*, p. 175), and the payment of the "charges & wages of Thomas Lambe for going to wynsor abowte Mr ffarrantes playe by Mr forteskues appointment." (*Ibid.*, p. 180.)

1572–3. [JANUARY 1, THURSDAY.] HAMPTON COURT.

"*The Maske of Ianvs.*" (Feuillerat, *Doc.*, p. 175.)

Doubtless this was the "Maske on New yeres daye." (*Ibid.*, p. 180.)

1572–3. JANUARY 6 (TUESDAY). HAMPTON COURT.

A play before the Queen "on Twelf night last past" by the Children of Eton (Elderton). Payment £6. 13*s.* 4*d.*, on warrant dated at Hampton Court, January 7, 1572–3. (Wallace, *Evol. E. D.*, p. 214. See also Stopes, *Hunnis*, p. 319; Chambers, *M. L. R.*, ii, 5.)

The Office furnished "gloves for the Children of Eaten ij dozen," and paid "Clatterbookes daughter for cloth for Ruffs aporns Neckerchers & Rayles for Eldertons playe." (Feuillerat, *Doc.*, pp. 174, 180.)

1572–3. [FEBRUARY 1–3. SHROVETIDE.] [GREENWICH.]

A play before the Queen by the Earl of Sussex's Company. Payment £6. 13*s.* 4*d.*, on warrant dated February 7, 1572–3. (Wallace, *Evol. E. D.*, p. 215. See also Stopes, *Hunnis*, p. 319; Chambers, *M. L. R.*, ii, 5.)

1572–3. [FEBRUARY 1–3. SHROVETIDE.] [GREENWICH.]

A play before the Queen by the Earl of Lincoln's Company (Laurence Dutton). Payment £6. 13*s.* 4*d.*, on warrant dated February 10, 1572–3. (Wallace, *Evol. E. D.*, p. 214. See also Chambers, *M. L. R.*, ii, 5.)

The Office provided "A tree of Holly for the Duttons playe," "other holly for the forest," and rewarded the "Muzitians that plaide at the proofe" of the play. (Feuillerat, *Doc.*, pp. 175, 176.)

1572–3. FEBRUARY 3 (SHROVE TUESDAY). [GREENWICH.]

A play before the Queen "vpon Shrove Tewsdaie at night" by the Merchant Taylors' School (Mr Monnlcaster). Payment £6. 13*s.* 4*d.*, with "a reward by her ma^{tes} owne comaundem^t" of £13. 6*s.* 8*d.*, on warrant dated February 10, 1572–3. (Wallace, *Evol. E. D.*, p. 215. See also Stopes, *Hunnis*, p. 319; Chambers, *M. L. R.*, ii, 5.)

The Office furnished "cotton to lyne ij paire of hozen for Munkesters playe," and "gloves for Munkesters boyes ij dozen." (Feuillerat, *Doc.*, p. 174.)

SUMMER, 1573

There was evidently a masque at Canterbury during the summer progress, for the officers of the Revels were in attendance, with the "best and most ffyttest ffurniture" of the Office. It is difficult to determine the nature of the performance from the Ac-

counts. Feathers for headpieces, gloves, large silk flowers, tassels
and fringe, chains for the Mariners' knives, twelve vizards for
women, seven Turks' vizards, and stuff for the Monarch's gown
are among the necessaries purchased. See Feuillerat, *Doc.*, pp.
182–85. The performance is dated by Chambers September 7.
(*Eliz. Stage.* iv, 89.)

THE SEASON 1573–1574

The plays of the season had, as usual, been "chosen owte of
many" and subjected to censorship:

Item sundry other tymes for calling together of sundry Players,
and for pervsing, fitting, & Reformyng theier matters (otherwise
not convenient to be showen before her Maiestie). (Feuillerat,
Doc., p. 191.)

Among the expenses of the season is an item of 240 ells of canvas "to paynte for howses for the players & for other properties
as Monsters, greate hollow trees & suche other." (*Ibid.*, p. 197.)

1573. OCTOBER 31–DECEMBER 20. GREENWICH.

"A Mask showen at Grenewitche after the Mariage of
Willyam Drurye esquier." (Feuillerat, *Doc.*, p. 191.)

1573. DECEMBER 26 (SATURDAY). WHITEHALL.

"*Predor: & Lucia.* played by Therle of Leicesters servauntes
vpon Saint stevens daye at nighte at whitehall aforesaide."
(Feuillerat, *Doc.*, p. 193.)

This play, and the five following plays, were "showen at
whytehall," and "all fytted and ffurnyshed with the store of
thoffice." (*Ibid.*, p. 193.)

The Accounts specify "Holly and Ivye for the play of *predor*,"
and "ffyshes Cownterfete for the same viz. whiting, playce,
Mackarell, &c." (*Ibid.*, p. 203.)

£10 each—at this time an unusual sum—was paid "by waye of
speciall rewarde for theyre chardge, cumyng and skill shewed
therein" on a warrant dated at Westminster, January 9, 1573-4,

for two plays "in Xpenmas hollidayes last past" by the Earl of Leicester's Company. (Wallace, *Evol. E. D.*, p. 215. See also Stopes, *Hunnis*, p. 319; *Burbage*, p. 247, in which the author reads "cunnynge" rather than "cumyng"; Dasent, *Acts*, viii, 177, in which the warrant is dated January 8, and the plays are undated; Chalmers, *Apology*, p. 394, in which the warrant is dated January 7. Chambers, *Eliz. Stage*, iv, 147, also reads "cunyng.")

1573. DECEMBER 27 (SUNDAY). WHITEHALL.

"*Alkmeon*, playde by the Children of Powles on Saint Iohns daye at nighte there." (Feuillerat, *Doc.*, p. 193.)

£6. 13*s*. 4*d*. was paid, on a warrant dated at Westminster, January 10, 1573–4, for a play before the Queen "vpon St Johns daye at night last past" by the Children of Paul's (Sebastian Westcote). (Wallace, *Evol. E. D.*, p. 215. See also Stopes, *Hunnis*, p. 319, in which the warrant is dated January 19; Chambers, *M. L. R.*, ii, 5; Dasent, *Acts*, viii, 178, in which the play is dated "this Christmas"; Chalmers, *Apology*, p. 360.)

1573. DECEMBER 27 (SUNDAY). WHITEHALL.

A Masque of "Lanceknightes. vj. in Blew sattyn gaskon cotes & sloppes &c. Torchebearers. vj. in Black & yolo Taffata &c. showen on Saint Iohns daie at nighte." (Feuillerat, *Doc.*, p. 193.)

This masque, and the masques of January 1 and January 6, were "showen at white Hall." (*Ibid.*, p. 193.)

1573. DECEMBER 28 (MONDAY). WHITEHALL.

"*Mamillia*. Playde by therle of Leicesteres seruantes on Innosentes daye at nighte there." (Feuillerat, *Doc.*, p. 193.)

Payment £10, on warrant dated at Westminster, January 9, 1573–4. See the entry for December 26.

1573–4. JANUARY 1 (FRIDAY). WHITEHALL.

"*Truth, ffaythfullness, & Mercye*, playde by the Children of westminster for Elderton vpon New yeares daye at nighte there." (Feuillerat, *Doc.*, p. 193.)

£6. 13s. 4d. was paid, on a warrant dated at Westminster, January 10, 1573–4, for a play before the Queen "on neweyeres daye last paste" by the Children of Westminster (William Elderton). (Wallace, *Evol. E. D.*, p. 215. See also Stopes, *Hunnis*, p. 319; Dasent, *Acts*, viii, 178; Chalmers, *Apology*. p. 394.)

1573–4. JANUARY 1 (FRIDAY). WHITEHALL.

A Masque of "*fforesters or hunters*. vj. in Greene sattyn gaskon cotes & sloppes &c. Torchebearers. vj. attyred in Mosse & Ivye &c. showen on New yeres daye at nighte." (Feuillerat, *Doc.*, p. 193.)

1573–4. JANUARY 3 (SUNDAY). WHITEHALL.

"*Herpetulus the blew knighte & perobia* playde by my Lorde klintons [Earl of Lincoln's] servantes the third of Ianuary being the sunday after Newyeares daye there." (Feuillerat, *Doc.*, p. 193.)

"One Basket with iiij Eares to hang Dylligence in the play of *perobia*." (*Ibid.*, p. 199.)

£6. 13s. 4d. was paid, on a warrant dated at Westminster, January 11, 1573–4, for a play before the Queen "on Sondaye nighte being the thirde of Januarye 1573" by Lord Clinton's Company (Laurence Dutton). (Wallace, *Evol. E. D.*, p. 215. See also Stopes, *Hunnis*, p. 319; Chambers, *M. L. R.*, ii, 5, in which the play is dated "Christmas"; Dasent, *Acts*, viii, 178, in which the play is dated "Christmas" and the warrant January 10; Chalmers, *Apology*, p. 394.)

1573–4. JANUARY 6 (WEDNESDAY). WHITEHALL.

"*Quintus ffabius* playd by the Children of wyndsor ffor Mr ffarrant on Twelfe daye at nighte lykewise at whitehall." (Feuillerat, *Doc.*, p. 193.)

Roger Tyndall received £2. 6s. 8d. "for Lending his Armor and for his seruauntes Attendaunces to arme & vnarme the children in the play of *Quintus ffabivs*." (*Ibid.*, p. 202.) The Office provided four "ffawchions for ffarrantes playe." (*Ibid.*, p. 203.)

£10 (a reward of 66s. 8d. being added to the usual amount "in respecte of his chardges comyng hyther") was paid, on a warrant dated at Westminster, January 10, 1573–4, for a play before the Queen "on Twelfe daye at nighte last past" by the Children of Windsor (Richarde fferrant). (Wallace, *Evol. E. D.*, p. 215. See also Stopes, *Hunnis*, p. 319; Chambers, *M. L. R.*, ii, 5; Dasent, *Acts*, viii, 178, in which the play is dated "this Christmas"; Chalmers, *Apology*, p. 361.)

1573–4. January 6 (Wednesday). Whitehall.

A Masque of "*Sages. vj.* in long gownes of Cownterfet cloth of golde &c. Torchebearers. vj. in Long gownes of Redd damask showen on Twlfe daye at nighte." (Feuillerat, *Doc.*, p. 193.)

1573–4. February 2 (Tuesday). Hampton Court.

"One Playe *Timoclia at the sege of Thebes. by Alexander.* showen at Hampton Coorte before her Maiestie by Mr Munkesters Children." (Feuillerat, *Doc.*, p. 206.)

£13. 6s. 8d. (the usual amount being doubled by way of "her ma^tes especiall rewarde for suche Costes and chardges as he was at for the same") was paid, on a warrant dated at Greenwich, March 18, 1573–4, for a play before the Queen on "Candlemas daye last past" by the Merchant Taylors' School (Richarde Moncaster). (Wallace, *Evol. E. D.*, p. 216. See also Stopes, *Hunnis*, p. 320; Dasent, *Acts*, viii, 210; Chalmers, *Apology*, p. 395.)

1573–4. February 2 (Tuesday). Hampton Court.

"One Maske of Ladies with lightes being *vj vertues* likewyse prepared & brought thither in Redynesse but not showen for the Tediusnesse of the playe that nighte." (Feuillerat, *Doc.*, p. 206.)

The item, "The skrivener for writing in fayer Text the speches viij delivered to her Maiestie" (*ibid.*, p. 209), is probably to be connected with the masque.

1573–4. February 21 (Shrove Sunday). Hampton Court.

A play before the Queen "the xxjth of February" by the Earl of Leicester's Company. Payment £10 (a reward of 66s. 8d. being added to the usual payment "forther by waye of her highnes Rewarde for such chardges as they had bene at for the furniture of the same"), on warrant dated at Hampton Court, February 22, 1573–4. (Wallace, *Evol. E. D.*, pp. 215–16. See also Stopes, *Hunnis*, p. 320, in which the play is dated February 20; *Burbage*, p. 247, in which the error is corrected; Dasent, *Acts*, viii, 198; Chalmers, *Apology*, p. 395.)

1573–4. February 22 (Shrove Monday). Hampton Court.

"*Philemon & philecia* play by the Earle of Lecesters men on Shrove Mundaye nighte." (Feuillerat, *Doc.*, p. 213.)

The Shrovetide plays were "Playde at Hampton Coorte," and "Throughly furnished garnished & fytted with the store of thoffice and provisions following." (*Ibid.*, p. 213.)

No warrant for payment has been discovered for this play. It is probable, as Wallace suggests, that "Mundaye" is an error of the scribe for "Sunday." See the preceding entry.

1573–4. February 23 (Shrove Tuesday). Hampton Court.

"*Percius & Anthomiris* playde by Munkesters Children on Shrovetewsdaye at Nighte." (Feuillerat, *Doc.*, p. 213.)

£13. 6s. 8d. was paid, on the same warrant as that for the play of February 2, for a play before the Queen "on Shroveteusdaye" by the Merchant Taylors' School (Richarde Moncaster). In each case the usual amount was doubled by way of "her ma^{tes} especiall rewarde for suche Costes and chardges as he was at for the same." (Wallace, *Evol. E. D.*, p. 216. See also Stopes, *Hunnis*, p. 320; Dasent, *Acts*, viii, 210–11; Chalmers, *Apology*, p. 395.)

Feuillerat says of Malone's conjecture that "Anthomiris" was an ignorant blunder for "Andromeda" by the man who made out the accounts, "This is most probable."

1573–4. FEBRUARY 23 (SHROVE TUESDAY). HAMPTON COURT.

A Masque of "*Warriers vij* with one shippmaster that vttered speche. Torchebearers vj. the warriers had hargabusses." (Feuillerat, *Doc.*, p. 213.)

The two Shrovetuesday masques were "showen at Hampton Coorte." (*Ibid.*, p. 213.)

1573–4. FEBRUARY 23 (SHROVE TUESDAY). HAMPTON COURT.

A Masque of "*Ladyes. vij.* with one that vttered a speeche. Torchebearers .vj. both which Maskes were showen on Shrovetewsdaye nighte." (Feuillerat, *Doc.*, p. 213.)

SUMMER, 1574

1574. JULY. WINDSOR, READING.

Italian players followed the Queen's progress and "made pastyme first at Wynsor and afterwardes at Reading." (Feuillerat, *Doc.*, p. 225.)

Feuillerat points out the fact that the preparations suggest a pastoral, either a masque or a play, and adds, "This is very important, especially if we remember that Tasso's *Aminta* was performed at Ferrara on July 31, 1573, and that the pastoral before the Queen was shown by Italian players."

According to Chambers (*Eliz. Stage*, iv, 90) the Queen was at Windsor July 11–13, and at Reading July 15–23.

THE SEASON 1574–1575

Thomas Blagrave, who had been in charge of the Office since the death of Tylney in 1572, seems for this season to have engaged assistance in selecting and censoring plays. Forty shillings were "paid by Dodmer by the speciall appoyntment of the said Mr Blagrave" to a person whose name was not recorded "for his paynes in pervsing and Reformyng of playes svndry tymes as neede required for her Maiesties Lyking." (Feuillerat, *Doc.*, p. 242.)

Expenses of rehearsals are entered in the Accounts as follows:

14° Decembris. The expences & charges where my Lord Chamberlens players did show the history of *Phedrastus & Phigon and Lucia* together amounteth vnto ix^s. iiij^d. (*Ibid.*, p. 238.)

18° Decembris. The expences and charges wheare my Lord of Leicesters menne showed theier matter of *Panecia.* x^s. (*Ibid.*, p. 238.)

20° Die. The Charges and expences where my Lord Clyntons players rehearsed a matter called *pretestus.* xiij^s. (*Ibid.*, p. 238.)

21° Die. The Charges and expences where the showed ij other playes with iiij^s for torches & iiij^d for an howerglasse xiij^s iiij^d. (*Ibid.*, p. 238.)

The Christmas and Candlemas festivities were held at Hampton Court, as various expenses for attendance and barge hire show.

1574/1574–5. CHRISTMAS. HAMPTON COURT.

A Masque of Pedlers.

"Mirors or lookingglasses" were provided "for the pedlers Mask" (Feuillerat, *Doc.*, p. 238), and 6s. 8d. was entered, under date of December 29, for "ffayer wryting of pozies for the Mask." (*Ibid.*, p. 239.)

1574. DECEMBER 26 (SUNDAY). HAMPTON COURT.

A play before the Queen "vppon St Stephens daie then laste past" by the Earl of Leicester's Company. Payment £10, on warrant dated January 9, 1574–5. (Wallace, *Evol. E. D.*, p. 216. See also Cunningham, *Revels*, p. xxx; Stopes, *Hunnis*, p. 320; *Burbage*, p. 247.)

"25° Decembris. Cariage of iiij Lodes of Tymber for the Rock (which Mr Rosse made for my Lord of Leicesters menns playe) & for other frames for players howses ij^s. iiij^d." (Feuillerat, *Doc.*, p. 244.)

The following entry occurs in the Revels Accounts:

27° Decembris. The same Thomas Blagrave for mony by him disbursed for Gloves for my Lord of Lesters boyes y^t plaied at the coorte ij^s. for Cariage of theier stuf & for the Carters attendaunce that night xvj^d. (Feuillerat, *Doc.*, p. 239.)

Nothing is known of a company of "boyes" under the patronage of the Earl of Leicester.

1574. December 27 (Monday). Hampton Court.

A play before the Queen "vppon St Johns daie" by Lord Clinton's Company. Payment £6. 13*s*. 4*d*., on warrant dated January 11, 1574-5. (Wallace, *Evol. E. D.*, p. 216. See also Cunningham, *Revels*, p. xxx; Stopes, *Hunnis*, p. 320.)

On December 27 a wagon was hired "to carry a Lode of stvf to the Coorte for the Duttons playe." (Feuillerat, *Doc.*, p. 244.)

One of the two plays by Lord Clinton's company may have been *Pretestus*, which was rehearsed on December 20.

1574-5. January 1 (Saturday). Hampton Court.

A play before the Queen "vppon Newyers daie at night then laste paste" by the Earl of Leicester's Company. Payment £6. 13*s*. 4*d*., on warrant dated January 9, 1574-5. (Wallace, *Evol. E. D.*, p. 216. See also Cunningham, *Revels*, p. xxx; Stopes, *Hunnis*, p. 320.)

1574-5. January 2 (Sunday). Hampton Court.

A play before the Queen "vppon Sondaie beinge the second of January then last" by Lord Clinton's Company. Payment £10, on warrant dated January 11, 1574-5. (Wallace, *Evol. E. D.*, p. 216. See also Cunningham, *Revels*, p. xxx, in which the sum is given as £6. 13*s*. 4*d*.; Stopes, *Hunnis*, p. 320. Chambers, *Eliz. Stage*, iv, 148, likewise gives the smaller payment.)

1574-5. January 6 (Thursday). Hampton Court.

A play before the Queen "vppon Twelveth night then last past" by the Children of Windsor (Richard ffarraunte). Payment

£13. 6s. 8d., on warrant dated at Hampton Court, January 23, 1574–5. (Wallace, *Evol. E. D.*, p. 216. See also Cunningham, *Revels*, pp. xxx–xxxi; Stopes, *Hunnis*, p. 320.)

This play apparently required an unusual amount of "perusing." Under the date of November 26 we find "Horshyer and charges by the waye at Wynsor stayeng there ij dayes in November iiij daies for pervzing & Reformyng of ffarrantes playe &c.," and again under December 5, "Horshyer to hampton Coorte to conferr with my Lord Chamberlayne the Lord Howard, & Mr Knevett upon certayne devices & to pervze ffarrantes playe there again iij daies." (Feuillerat, *Doc.*, p. 238.)

"Roger Tyndall tharmerer" was paid "for Lending of Armor for ffarrantes playe and for attending the same." (*Ibid.*, p. 240.) The Office also provided "Wax for A Cake in ffarrantes playe" (p. 240), "A perwigg of Heare for king xerxces syster in ffarrantes playe," and "ij ells of Canvas to make frenge for the players howse in ffarrantes play." (*Ibid.*, p. 244.)

1574–5. FEBRUARY 2 (WEDNESDAY). HAMPTON COURT.

A play before the Queen "on Candlemas daie at night then last past" by the Children of Paul's (Sebastian Westcote). Payment £13. 6s. 8d., on warrant dated February 16, 1574–5. (Wallace, *Evol. E. D.*, p. 217. See also Cunningham, *Revels*, p. xxxi; Stopes, *Hunnis*, p. 320.)

The Revels Office provided "A cote, A hatt, & Buskins all over covered with ffethers of cvllers for vanytie in sabastians playe" (Feuillerat, *Doc.*, p. 241), "skynnes to furr the hoods in sabastians playe," and "ffor making of ij sarcenet hooddes for Cyttyzens in the same playe." (*Ibid.*, p. 244.)

1574–5. FEBRUARY 2 (WEDNESDAY). HAMPTON COURT.

A play before the Queen "on Candlemas-day at night," by the Earl of Leicester's Company. Payment £10, on warrant dated December 29, 1575. (Chalmers, *Apology*, p. 395.)

There is possibly an error here. I have not discovered the warrant in the *Acts of the Privy Council*.

1574–5. FEBRUARY 2 (WEDNESDAY). HAMPTON COURT.

For the play by the Lord Chamberlain's Company seemingly assigned to this date in the *Acts of the Privy Council* (Dasent, ix, 81), see the following year.

1574–5. FEBRUARY 13 (SHROVE SUNDAY). RICHMOND.

A play before the Queen "vppon Shrove sonday then last past" by the Children of the Queen's Chapel (William Hunys). Payment £13. 6s. 8d., "by waie of her ma^{tes} guifte," on warrant dated at Richmond, February 16, 1574–5. (Wallace, *Evol. E. D.*, p. 216. See also Cunningham, *Revels*, p. xxxi; Stopes, *Hunnis*, p. 320, in which the date of the warrant is given as February 17. Cf. the two following entries.)

The expenses for the play include, on February 1, "Holly, Ivye, firr poles & Mosse for the Rock in M^r hvnnyes playe," "Hornes iij, Collers iij, Leashes iij & dogghookes iij with Bawdrickes for the hornes in hvnnyes playe," on February 13 the "Cariage of Tymber woork for the same M^r hvnnyes his playe downe to the watersyde" (Feuillerat, *Doc.*, p. 244), and a generous reward to "the french woman for her paynes and her Dawghters paynes that went to Richemond & there attended vpon M^r hunnyes his Children & dressed theier heades &c. when they played before her Majestye." (*Ibid.*, p. 241.)

1574–5. FEBRUARY 13 (SHROVE SUNDAY)? RICHMOND.

A play before the Queen "on Shrove Sondaie then last paste" by the Earl of Warwick's Company. Payment £10, on warrant dated at Richmond, February 16, 1574–5. (Wallace, *Evol. E. D.*, p. 216. See also Cunningham, *Revels*, p. xxxi, in which the date is given as "Shrovemonday"; Stopes, *Hunnis*, p. 320.)

1574–5. FEBRUARY 13 (SHROVE SUNDAY)? RICHMOND.

A play before the Queen "vppon Shrovesondaie" by the Merchant Taylors' School (Richard Moncaster). Payment £13. 6s. 8d., the usual amount being doubled by way of "a reward gyven by her heighnes," on warrant dated at Richmond, February 22, 1574–5. (Wallace, *Evol. E. D.*, p. 216. See also Stopes, *Hunnis*, p. 320, in which the warrant is dated February 17; Chambers, *M. L. R.*, ii, 5; *Eliz. Stage*, iv, 149, in which the warrant is dated February 17.)

Probably, as Wallace suggests, there is an error in one or more of the Shrove Sunday dates. Three plays on one occasion are unusual.

1574–5. FEBRUARY 14 (SHROVE MONDAY).

For the play by the Earl of Warwick's Company dated by Cunningham (*Revels*, p. xxxi) Shrove Monday, see the second entry for February 13.

SUMMER, 1575

1575. JULY 17 (SUNDAY). KENILWORTH.

A play before the Queen.

All that is known of this play, with which Leicester entertained the Queen, is found in Robert Laneham's *Letter:*

Thus, though the day took an eend, yet slipt not the night all sleeping away; for az neyther offis nor obsequie ceassed at any time too the full, to perform the plot hiz Honor had appoynted: so after supper was thear a Play prezented of a very good theam, but so set foorth, by the Actoorz well handling, that pleazure and mirth made it seem very short, though it lasted too good oourz and more. (Nichols, i. See also *Laneham's Letter*, ed. Furnivall, p. 32.)

1575. JULY 17 (SUNDAY). KENILWORTH.

A masque prepared for presentation before the Queen, but not shown.

Laneham, in his letter cited above, continues:

After the Play, oout of hand folloed a most deliciouz and (if I may so terme it) ambrosiall banket. . . . Untoo this banket thear waz appoynted a Mask; for riches of aray, of an incredibl cost; but the time so far spent, and very late in the night noow, waz cauz that it cam not foorth to the sheaw.

1575. September 20 (Thursday). Woodstock.

A comedy acted before the Queen on "the 20 day of the same moneth" which "was as well thought of, as anye thing ever done before her Maiestie," as a part of the entertainment at Woodstock. For a discussion of the date and circumstances, see Chambers, *Eliz. Stage*, iii, 400–402.

THE SEASON 1575–1576

1575. December 26 (Monday). Hampton Court.

A play before the Queen "on St Stephens daie at night" by the Earl of Warwick's Company (John Dutton, Lawrence Dutton, Jerome Savage). Payment £10, on warrant dated at Hampton Court, January 2, 1575–6. (Wallace, *Evol. E. D.*, p. 217. See also Chambers, *M. L. R.*, ii, 5; Dasent, *Acts*, ix, 68; Chalmers, *Apology*, p. 395.)

According to Nichols, the Queen kept Christmas at Hampton Court.

1575. December 27 (Tuesday). Hampton Court.

A play before the Queen "vppon St Johns daie at night then last past" by the Children of Windsor (Richard ffarraunte). Payment £10, on warrant dated at Hampton Court, December 30, 1575. (Wallace, *Evol. E. D.*, p. 217. See also Stopes, *Hunnis*, p. 320; Dasent, *Acts*, ix, 67, in which the warrant is dated December 29; Chalmers, *Apology*, p. 361.)

1575. December 28 (Wednesday). Hampton Court.

A play before the Queen "vppon St Jnnocentes daye at night anno xix dicte Domine Re^{ne}" by the Earl of Leicester's Company. Payment £10, on warrant dated at Hampton Court, December 30, 1575. (Wallace, *Evol. E. D.*, p. 217. See also Stopes, *Hunnis*, p. 320; *Burbage*, p. 248; Dasent, *Acts*, ix, 68, in which the warrant is dated December 29.)

Evidently there is an error in the regnal year. The nineteenth regnal year began November 17, 1576.

1575–6. JANUARY 1 (SUNDAY). HAMPTON COURT.

A play before the Queen "on Neweyeres daie at nighte then last past" by the Earl of Warwick's Company. Payment £10, on the same warrant as that for the play of December 26. (Wallace, *Evol. E. D.*, p. 217. See also Chambers, *M. L. R.*, ii, 5; Dasent, *Acts*, ix, 68; Chalmers, *Apology*, p. 395.)

1575–6. JANUARY 6 (FRIDAY). HAMPTON COURT.

A play before the Queen "vpon Twelf night last past" by the Children of Paul's (Sebastean Westcott). Payment £10, on warrant dated at Hampton Court, January 7, 1575–6. (Wallace, *Evol. E. D.*, p. 217. See also Stopes, *Hunnis*, p. 320, in which the warrant is dated February 7; Dasent, *Acts*, ix, 71; Chalmers, *Apology*, p. 361.)

1575–6. FEBRUARY 2 (THURSDAY). [HAMPTON COURT.]

A play before the Queen "vpon Candlemas daie last past" by the Lord Chamberlain's Company (John Adams). Payment £10, on warrant dated at Hampton Court, February 4, 1575–6. (Wallace, *Evol. E. D.*, p. 217. See also Chambers, *M. L. R.*, ii, 5.)

In the *Acts of the Privy Council* (Dasent, ix, 81) there is given a warrant for £10 dated at Hampton Court "January —," 1575–6, for a play "on Candelmas Day at night" by the Lord Chamberlain's Company. In Chalmers (*Apology*, p. 395) the date is given as January 7. Since this warrant is found nowhere else, and since Candlemas of the preceding year is provided with at least one play, the date may perhaps be regarded as an error for that of the warrant given above.

1575–6. February 26 (Sunday). Whitehall.

A play before the Queen "vpon Sondaye before Shrovetyde last" by the Earl of Leicester's Company (Burbage). Payment £10, on warrant dated at Westminster, March 14, 1575–6. (Wallace, *Evol. E. D.*, p. 217. See also Stopes, *Hunnis*, p. 320; *Burbage*, p. 248; Chambers, *M. L. R.*, ii, 6, in which the play is dated Shrove Sunday. Cf. *Eliz. Stage.* iv, 150.)

The Queen removed to Whitehall on February 6. (*Journal of Sir Francis Walsingham*, ed. by Martin, p. 25.)

1575–6. February 27 (Monday). Whitehall.

A play before the Queen on "the xxvij[th] of februarye last past" by "Alfruso Ferrabolle and the rest of the Italian players." Payment £10, on warrant dated at Whitehall, March 12, 1575–6. (Wallace, *Evol. E. D.*, p. 218. See also Stopes, *Hunnis*, p. 320; Chambers, *M. L. R.*, ii, 5.)

1575–6. March 4 (Shrove Sunday).

For the Merchant Taylors' play dated Shrove Sunday in the *Acts of the Privy Council* (ix, 94), see the entry for March 6, Shrove Tuesday.

1575–6. March 5 (Shrove Monday). Whitehall.

A play before the Queen "vpon Shrove Mounday at night last past" by the Earl of Warwick's Company (Laurence Dutton). Payment £10, on warrant dated March 8, 1575–6. (Wallace, *Evol. E. D.*, p. 217. See also Dasent, *Acts*, ix, 95, in which the warrant is dated at Westminster, March 11, and "Lawrence Dutton and John Dutton" named as payees; Chalmers, *Apology*, p. 395.)

1575–6. March 6 (Shrove Tuesday). Whitehall.

A play before the Queen "on Shrovetuisdaie last past" by the Merchant Taylors' School (Richarde Moulcaster). Payment £10, on warrant dated at Westminster, March 11, 1575–6. (Wallace, *Evol. E. D.*, p. 217. See also Dasent, *Acts*, ix, 94, in which the play is dated "Shrove Sonday"; Chalmers, *Apology*, p. 395.)

1576. MAY 10–12 (THURSDAY–SATURDAY). OSTERLEY
HOUSE.

A play by Thomas Churchyard acted before the Queen at
Osterley House [Sir Thomas Gresham's].

"Among the publications of Churchyard, one (which unluckily
we cannot now recover) was 'The Devises of Warre, and a Play
at Austerley, her Highness being at Sir Thomas Gresham's'."
(Nichols, *Progresses Elizabeth*, ii.) According to *The Journal of Sir
Francis Walsingham* (p. 25), the Queen was at Sir Thomas Gresham's May 10–12.

THE SEASON 1576–1577

Two items may be quoted from the Revels Accounts regarding
the season's entertainments. One records "the hier of a horse
from London to Hampton Court the xxiiij of December for the
warrant and carying a note to the Chamberleyn of alteracion of
the plaies and retornyng on the morow." (Feuillerat, *Doc.*, p. 267.)

The other, from the Shrovetide expenses, is "ffor the Cariadge
of the partes of ye well counterfeit from the Bell in gracious
strete to St Iohns to be performed for the play of *Cutwell*." (*Ibid.*,
p. 277.) This item probably refers to the rehearsal of the play.
There is no record of its performance.

1576. DECEMBER 26 (WEDNESDAY). HAMPTON COURT.

"*The Paynters daughter* showen at Hampton Court on St Stevens
daie at night, enacted by the'erle of warwickes seruauntes."
(Feuillerat, *Doc.*, p. 256.)

Kelsey was paid 2*s.* 6*d.* "for vsing of his Dromme in the Duttons plaie." (*Ibid.*, p. 269.) But the expenses are related mainly
to the transportation of "stuff": "ffor a barge to carry stuffe to
the Court 26: Decembris for therle of warwick his mens plaie";
"ffor one waggon 26° Decembris to cary stuff to the Court for the
Earle of Warwick his mens plaie"; "ffor a waggon two or three
daies after (for that their plaie was deferred vntill the Sundaie
folowing) to bring their stuff to the Revelles." (*Ibid.*, p. 266.)

Feuillerat conjectures that the last item refers, by error of the scribe, to the play of Leicester's men on Sunday, December 30.

£16. 13*s*. 4*d*. was paid, on a warrant dated at Hampton, January 20, 1576–7, for a play before the Queen "in Xpenmas hallidaies last past" by the Earl of Warwick's Company. (Wallace, *Evol. E. D.*, p. 218. See also Dasent, *Acts*, ix, 270; Chalmers, *Apology*, pp. 395–6.)

1576. DECEMBER 27 (THURSDAY). HAMPTON COURT.

"*Toolie* showen at Hampton Court on St Iohns daie at night enacted by the Lord Howardes seruauntes." (Feuillerat, *Doc.*, p. 256.)

Two wagons were hired on December 27 "for the Cariadge of stuff for the Lord Howardes seruauntes." (*Ibid.*, p. 266.)

£10 was paid, on a warrant dated at Hampton Court, January 12, 1576–7, for a play before the Queen "on St Johns daie in Xpenmas last past" by Lord Howard's Company. (Wallace, *Evol. E. D.*, p. 218.)

1576. DECEMBER 30 (SUNDAY). HAMPTON COURT.

"*The historie of the Collyer* showen at Hampton Court on the Sundaie folowing enacted by th'erle of Leicesters men." (Feuillerat, *Doc.*, p. 256.)

A "paynted cloth and two frames" for this play were carried to the Court by water on December 28. (*Ibid.*, p. 266.)

£16. 13*s*. 4*d*. was paid, on a warrant dated at Hampton Court, January 20, 1576–7, for a play before the Queen "in Xpenmas Hallydaies last past" by the Earl of Leicester's Company. (Wallace, *Evol. E. D.*, p. 219. See also Stopes, *Burbage*, p. 248; Dasent, *Acts*, ix, 270; Chalmers, *Apology*, pp. 395–6.)

1576–7. JANUARY 1 (TUESDAY). HAMPTON COURT.

"*The historie of Error* showen at Hampton Court on Newyeres daie at night, enacted by the Children of Powles." (Feuillerat, *Doc.*, p. 256.)

A horse was hired "the 29: of December for 2: daies last before at xx^d the daie, to the Court and back for the plaie of Powles on Newyeres daie." (*Ibid.*, p. 267.)

£16. 13*s*. 4*d*. was paid, on a warrant dated at Hampton Court, January 20, 1576–7, for a play before the Queen "in Xpenmas hallidaies last past" by the Children of Paul's (Sebastian West-cote). (Wallace, *Evol. E. D.*, p. 218. See also Dasent, *Acts*, ix, 270; Chalmers, *Apology*, p. 361, in which the payment is given as £6. 13*s*. 4*d*. plus a reward of £2. 10*s*.)

1576–7. JANUARY 6 (SUNDAY). HAMPTON COURT.

"*The historye of Mutius Sceuola* showen at Hampton Court on Twelf daie at night, enacted by the Children of windsore and the Chappell." (Feuillerat, *Doc.*, p. 256.)

The expense of "a barge to cary two fframes to the Court for the Children of windsours plaie on Twelf daie" (*ibid.*, p. 266), and of the "Cariadge of stuff for fferrantes playe, and furnyture for the lightes to Hampton Court on Twelf daie by Tilt bote" (*ibid.*, p. 268) is noted in the Accounts.

£16. 13*s*. 4*d*. was paid, on a warrant dated at Hampton Court, January 20, 1576–7, for a play before the Queen "in Xpenmas Hallydaies last past" by the Children of the Chapel (Richard ffarrante). (Wallace, *Evol. E. D.*, p. 218. See also Dasent, *Acts*, ix, 270; Chalmers, *Apology*, p. 361, in which the payment is given as £6. 13*s*. 4*d*. plus a reward of £2. 10*s*.)

When the First Blackfriars was opened, the Children of the Chapel Royal under William Hunnis were united with the Children of Windsor in order to form a company of adequate size for the new theatre. Hunnis was not displaced, but Farrant was recognized as the head of the new company. See Adams, *Shakespearean Playhouses*, pp. 102–3.

1576–7. JANUARY 6 (SUNDAY).

A masque was intended, but deferred. See the entry for February 19.

The masque was evidently put off at the last moment. Among the expenses are items "ffor two Waggons to carie stuff for the

Mask, and to carie the Children that shold have served in the Maske," and for the pains of Nicholas Newdigate "in hearing and trayninge of the ⁷boyes that should have spoken the speeches in the Mask, and for their charges and Cariadge back againe." (Feuillerat, *Doc.*, pp. 266, 268.)

1576–7. FEBRUARY 2 (SATURDAY). HAMPTON COURT.

"*The historye of the Cenofalles* [Cenocephali] showen at Hampton Court on Candlemas day at night, enacted by the Lord Chamberleyn his men." (Feuillerat, *Doc.*, p. 256.)

Expenses are recorded "for vj feltes for the Cenofalles heade-peeces," "for a houndes heade mowlded for a Cenofall" (*ibid.*, p. 265), and "ffor a waggon to cary stuffe to Hampton Court for the Lord Chamberleyn his mens plaie on Candlemas daie." (*Ibid.*, p. 266.)

£16. 13s. 4d. was paid, on a warrant dated at Hampton Court, February 3, 1576–7, for a play before the Queen "on Candlemas daie at night last past" by the Earl of Sussex's [Chamberlain's] Company. (Wallace, *Evol. E. D.*, p. 218; See also Dasent, *Acts*, ix, 280; Chalmers, *Apology*, p. 396.)

1576–7. FEBRUARY 17 (SHROVE SUNDAY). WHITEHALL.

"*The Historie of the Solitarie knight* showen at whitehall on Shrovesundaie at night, enacted by the Lord Howardes seruauntes." (Feuillerat, *Doc.*, p. 270.)

John Edwyn was paid "for the lone of certeine Armour with a base and Targettes which the Lord Howardes seruauntes vsed in their plaie of *the Solytarye knyght.*" (*Ibid.*, p. 275.) The Office furnished "two glasse voyalles for the Lord Howardes seruauntes on Shrovesunday" (*ibid.*, p. 275), and "breade which was vsed in *the Historie of the Solitarye knight,*" and hired "a Car from the Revelles to the waterside to cary stuff for the Lord Howardes seruauntes." (*Ibid.*, p. 276.)

£10 was paid, on a warrant dated at Westminster, February 20, 1576–7, for a play before the Queen "at white hall on Shrove sondaie at night" by the Lord Howard's Company. (Wallace, *Evol. E. D.*, p. 218. See also Dasent, *Acts*, ix, 293, in which the company is given as the Lord Chamberlain's. Thomas Ratcliffe, third Earl of Sussex, was at this time Lord Chamberlain, but Lord Charles Howard seems occasionally to have acted as his deputy. This fact probably explains the attribution of the play to the Chamberlain's Company. For a full discussion of the subject see E. K. Chambers, "The Elizabethan Lords Chamberlain," Malone Soc. *Collections*, I, i. Chalmers, *Apology*, p. 396, of course follows the Council Registers.)

1576–7. FEBRUARY 17 (SHROVE SUNDAY).

For the play by the Children of Paul's assigned by the Declared Accounts to Shrove Sunday, see the entry for February 19.

1576–7. FEBRUARY 18 (SHROVE MONDAY). WHITEHALL.

"*The Irisshe Knyght* showen at Whitehall on Shrove-mundaie at night enacted by the Earle of warwick his seruauntes." (Feuillerat, *Doc.*, p. 270.)

The following expenses for transportation are recorded in the Accounts: "ffor a Carr to cary stuff for the Earle of Warwick his men" (*ibid.*, p. 276), "ffor the Cariadge of the Earle of Warwick his mens stuffe from the Revelles to Whitehall and back againe to recyte before my Lord Chamberleyn," "ffor the hier of a barge the 14: of ffebruarie for the Cariadge of the Earle of warwick his men and stuff for them to the Court and back againe for the 14: and 16: of ffebruarie for recytall of playes, and the 17: and 18: for the playes before ye Quene." (*Ibid.*, p. 277.)

£10 was paid, on a warrant dated at Westminster, February 20, 1576–7, for a play before the Queen "at Whitehall on Shroue Mondaie at night last past" by the Earl of Warwick's Company. (Wallace, *Evol. E. D.*, p. 219. See also Dasent, *Acts*, ix, 293; Chalmers, *Apology*, p. 396.)

1576–7. FEBRUARY 19 (SHROVE TUESDAY). WHITEHALL.

"The historye of Titus and Gisippus showen at whitehall on Shrovetuysdaie at night, enacted by the Children of Pawles." (Feuillerat, *Doc.*, p. 270.)

The Revels Office supplied "two formes for the Senatours in *the historie of Titus and Gisippus"* (*ibid.*, p. 276), six "Senatours Cappes of Crymsen Taffita" (*ibid.*, p. 275), and hired "two Carres to Cary stuff for the Mask and for the Children of Powles from the Courte to St Iohns." (*Ibid.*, p. 276.)

£10 was paid, on a warrant dated at Westminster, February 20, 1576–7, for a play before the Queen "on Shrove sondaie at night" by the Children of Paul's (Sebastian Westcote). (Wallace, *Evol. E. D.*, p. 218. See also Dasent, *Acts*, ix, 293, in which the exact date of the play is not given, and Chalmers, *Apology*, p. 361. Chalmers tacitly assigns the play to Shrove Tuesday by assuming that Chamberlain's and Warwick's men played on the other two days of Shrovetide. I have followed the date given in the Revels Accounts.)

1576–7. FEBRUARY 19 (SHROVE TUESDAY). WHITEHALL.

"A longe Maske of murrey satten crossed all over with silver lace with sleves of gold tyncell, with headepeeces full of pipes of white silver lawne laid bias very rich, prepared for Twelf night, with a device of 7: speeches framed correspondent to the daie. Their Torchebearers vj: had gownes of crysmen Damask, and headepeeces new furnished, showen on Shrovetuysdaie night, without anie speeche." (Feuillerat, *Doc.*, p. 270.)

THE SEASON 1577–1578

1577. DECEMBER 26 (THURSDAY). HAMPTON COURT.

A play before the Queen "vpon St Stephens Daye" by the Earl of Leicester's Company. Payment £10, on warrant dated at Hampton Court, January 9, 1577–8. (Wallace, *Evol. E. D.*, p. 219. See also Dasent, *Acts*, x, 138, in which the play is dated "in the

Christemas hollidaies"; Chalmers, *Apology*, p. 396; Stopes, *Hunnis*, p. 320, in which the warrant is dated "1587"; *Burbage*, p. 249; Chambers, *M. L. R.*, ii, 6, in which the play is incorrectly dated December 25; the error is corrected in *Eliz. Stage*, iv, 152.)

The Queen removed from Windsor to Hampton Court on Dec. 10. (*Journal of Sir Francis Walsingham*, p. 33.) There is no record of further removal until February 25. (*Ibid.*, p. 35.)

1577. DECEMBER 27 (FRIDAY). HAMPTON COURT.

A play before the Queen "vpon St Johns Day at night in the Christmas Hollidayes 1577" by the Children of the Chapel (Richard Farrant). Payment £10, on warrant dated at Hampton Court, January 20, 1577–8. (Wallace, *Evol. E. D.*, p. 220. See also Stopes, *Hunnis*, p. 320; Chambers, *M. L. R.*, ii, 6.)

1577. DECEMBER 28 (SATURDAY). HAMPTON COURT.

A play before the Queen "on Childermas Day at night" by the Earl of Warwick's Company. Payment £10, on warrant dated at Hampton Court, January 12, 1577–8. (Wallace, *Evol. E. D.*, p. 219. See also Stopes, *Hunnis*, p. 320; Chambers, *M. L. R.*, ii, 6.)

1577. DECEMBER 29 (SUNDAY). HAMPTON COURT.

A play before the Queen "the xxixth of December" by the Children of Paul's (Sebastian Westcote). Payment of £10, on warrant dated at Hampton Court, January 31, 1577–8. (Wallace, *Evol. E. D.*, p. 220. See also Stopes, *Hunnis*, p. 320; Chambers, *M. L. R.*, ii, 6, and *Eliz. Stage*, iv, 153, in which the play is dated December 30.)

1577–8. JANUARY 5 (SUNDAY). HAMPTON COURT.

A play before the Queen "on Sundaye beinge the fifte daye of January last past" by the Lord Howard's Company. Payment £10, on warrant dated at Hampton Court, January 9, 1577–8. (Wallace, *Evol. E. D.*, p. 220. See also Chambers, *M. L. R.*, ii, 6, in which the date is given as January 1; *Eliz. Stage*, iv, 153, in which the error is corrected; Dasent, *Acts*, x, 138, in which the play is undated; Chalmers, *Apology*, p. 396.)

1577–8. January 6 (Monday). Hampton Court.

A play before the Queen "on twelfe day at night" by the Earl of Warwick's Company. Payment £10, on warrant dated at Hampton, January 12, 1577–8. (Wallace, *Evol. E. D.*, p. 219. See also Stopes, *Hunnis*, p. 320; Chambers, *M. L. R.*, ii, 6.)

1577–8. February 2 (Sunday). Hampton Court.

A play before the Queen "vppon Candlemas daye at night last paste" by the Lord Chamberlain's Company. Payment £10, on warrant dated at Greenwich, March 15, 1577–8. (Wallace, *Evol. E. D.*, p. 219. See also Dasent, *Acts*, x, 185, in which the warrant is dated March 14; Chalmers, *Apology*, p. 396; Stopes, *Hunnis*, p. 320; Chambers, *M. L. R.*, ii, 6.)

The warrant for this play exists in duplicate. See Wallace, p. 220, and Chambers, p. 6.

Fleay (*Stage*, pp. 26, 33) assigns the play to the Lord Charles Howard's Men. But the Earl of Sussex was Lord Chamberlain at this time, as Chambers (Malone Soc. *Collections*, I, i) has shown.

1577–8. February 9 (Shrove Sunday). Hampton Court.

A play before the Queen "on Shrovesonday at night" by the Earl of Warwick's Company. Payment £10, on warrant dated at Hampton Court, February 18, 1577–8. (Wallace, *Evol. E. D.*, p. 219. See also Stopes, *Hunnis*, p. 319; Chambers, *M. L. R.*, ii, 6.)

1577–8. February 10 (Shrove Monday).

For the play of the Children of Windsor, given only by Chalmers (*Apology*, p. 361), see the corresponding entry for 1578–9.

1577–8. February 11 (Shrove Tuesday). Hampton Court.

A play intended by the Earl of Leicester's Company. £6. 13*s.* 4*d.* was paid them on a warrant dated at Hampton Court, February 18, 1577–8, "for makinge theire Repaire to the Courte wth theire whole Companye and furniture to present A play before her ma^tie vpon Shrove-twesday at night in Consideracion of theire Chardges for that purpose althoughe the place by her ma^ties Comandm^t was supplyed by others." (Wallace, *Evol. E. D.*, p. 219. See also Stopes, *Hunnis*, p. 320; *Burbage*, p. 249; Chambers, *M. L. R.*, ii, 6.)

1577–8. February 11 (Shrove Tuesday). Hampton Court.

A play before the Queen "on Shrovetwesday at night" by the Countess of Essex's Company. Payment £10, on warrant dated at Hampton Court, February 14, 1577–8. (Wallace, *Evol. E. D.*, p. 219. See also Chambers, *M. L. R.*, ii, 6.)

Chambers (*M. L. R.*, ii, 6–7) writes: "No company under Lady Essex's name is on record, but Essex's men was one of six companies which the Lord Mayor was directed by the Privy Council on December 24, 1578, to allow to exercise for Christmas in the City. Walter, Earl of Essex, died in 1576, and his son Robert was a boy of ten in February, 1577–8. The Company did not appear at Court in 1578–9, or ever again. Lady Essex was disgraced in the summer of 1579, owing to the discovery of her secret marriage to Leicester."

SUMMER, 1578

1578. July 27 (Sunday). Audley End.

A play prepared by the University of Cambridge for presentation before the Queen?

On July 27, when the Queen was at Audley End, "the University of Cambridge waited upon her, with speeches and disputations made before her." In the account by Nichols there is no mention of a play. But Boas has discovered among the University expenses connected with this visit a payment "to the musitians at rehearsing the Comedy." (*University Drama*, p. iii, *n.*)

1578. August 21 (Thursday). Norwich.

A masque, by Henry Goldingham, before the Queen.

The nexte night, beyng Thursdaye, there was an excellent princely maske brought before hir after supper, by Mayster Goldingham, in the Privie Chamber; it was of gods and goddesses, both strangely and richly apparelled. (Nichols, *Progresses Eliza-beth*, ii.)

The masque was probably presented in the Bishop's house, where, says Nichols, "hir Majestie kepte the time she continued in Norwich."

THE SEASON 1578–1579

On December 24, 1578, a letter was sent to the Lord Mayor of London by the Privy Council "requiring him to suffer the Children of her Majesties Chappell, the servauntes of the Lord Chamberlaine, therle of Warwicke, the Erle of Leicester, the Erle of Essex and the Children of Powles, and no companies els, to exercise playeng within the Cittie, whome their Lordships have onlie allowed thereunto by reason that the companies aforenamed are appointed to playe this tyme of Christmas before her Majestie." (Dasent, *Acts*, x, 436.)

No play is recorded as by the Earl of Essex's Company.

The Lord Chamberlain took an especially active part in selecting the plays and masques of the season, and in supervising the details of the performances. Some of the more interesting of the items may be quoted from the Revels Accounts:

Boate hier to and from the courte to carry the stuffe for the children of the chappell to Recite before my Lord Chamberleyne. (Feuillerat, *Doc.*, p. 297.)

Boate hier to the courte to carry my Lord Chamberleyne Patorns of the maske. (*Ibid.*, p. 297.)

ffor A Carre the next daie to carry ij Baskettes of stuffe to Barmesey to shewe my Lord Chamberleyne. (*Ibid.*, p. 297.)

The Sixte of Ianuary for m^r Blagraves bote hier to and from the courte being sent for by my Lord Chamberlayne. (*Ibid.*, pp. 298–99.)

1578. DECEMBER 26 (FRIDAY). RICHMOND.

"An Inventyon or playe of *the three Systers of Mantua* shewen at Richmond on St Stephens daie at night enacted by thearle of warwick his servauntes furnished in this office with sondrey thinges as was requisite for the same." (Feuillerat, *Doc.*, p. 286.)

The Office furnished "A rope A pulley," and "A basket" for "the Earle of warwickes men plaie." (*Ibid.*, p. 296.)

£10 was paid, on a warrant dated January 16, 1578–9, for a play before the Queen "on S^ct Stephens daie at night" by the Earl of Warwick's Company. (Wallace, *Evol. E. D.*, p. 220. See also Chambers, *M. L. R.*, ii, 7; Dasent, *Acts*, xi, 21, in which the warrant is dated at Richmond, the play not dated, and no sum mentioned; Chalmers, *Apology*, p. 396.)

1578. DECEMBER 27 (SATURDAY). RICHMOND.

"The *historie of* ———— shewen at Richmond on St Iohns daie at night enacted by the children of the Quenes maiesties chappell furnished in this office with verie manie thinges aptly fitted for the same." (Feuillerat, *Doc.*, p. 286.)

Among the expenses of the season are items "ffor tape occupied when the children of the chappell plaid before the Queene" (*ibid.*, p. 295), and "The same daie [December 27] for cariage of the stuffe that served the plaie for the children of the chappell to the courte and back agayne." (*Ibid.*, p. 298.)

The Declared Accounts give no play by the Children of the Chapel on December 27, but record one on January 6: £10 was paid, on a warrant dated January 16, 1578–9, for a play before the Queen "on Twelfe daye at night" by the Children of the Queen's Chapel (M^r fferaunte). (Wallace, *Evol. E. D.*, p. 220. See also Chambers, *M. L. R.*, ii, 7; Dasent, *Acts*, xi, 21, in which the warrant is dated at Richmond, play not dated, and no sum mentioned; Chalmers, *Apology*, p. 361.)

Feuillerat and Wallace regard the date in the Revels Accounts as the correct one. It seems to be confirmed by the record of the transportation of "stuff" on December 27.

1578. DECEMBER 28 (SUNDAY). RICHMOND.

"*An history of the creweltie of A Stepmother* shewen at Richmond on Innocentes daie at night enacted by the Lord Chamberlaynes servauntes furnished in this office with sondrey thinges." (Feuillerat, *Doc.*, p. 286.)

The "cariadge of the stuffe from the courte by water the 27th of December that served in my Lord Chamberleynes men plaie" is noted among the season's expenses. (*Ibid.*, p. 298.)

£10 was paid, on a warrant dated January 16, 1578–9, for a play before the Queen "on Sondaye the xxviij^th of Decemb er 1578" by the Lord Chamberlain's Company. (Wallace, *Evol. E. D.* p. 220. See also Chambers, *M. L. R.*, ii, 7; Dasent, *Acts*, xi, 21, in which the warrant is dated at Richmond, the play not dated, and no sum mentioned; Chalmers, *Apology*, p. 396.)

1578–9. JANUARY 1 (THURSDAY). RICHMOND.

"*A Morrall of the marryage of Mynde and Measure* shewen at Richmond on the sondaie next after Newe yeares daie enacted by the Children of Pawles furnished somethinges in this office." (Feuillerat, *Doc.*, p. 286.)

An item in the Revels Accounts, "The ffirste of Ianuarie for cariage of A frame for master Sebastian to the Courte" (*ibid.*, p. 298), suggests a confusion of dates. The Declared Accounts give no payment for a play by the Children on Sunday after New Year's [January 4]. But £10 was paid on a warrant dated January 16, 1578–9, for a play before the Queen "on Newyers day at night" by the children of Paul's. (Wallace, *Evol. E. D.*, pp. 220–221. See also Chambers, *M. L. R.*, ii, 7; Dasent, *Acts*, xi, 21, in which the warrant is dated at Richmond, the play not dated, and no sum mentioned; Chalmers, *Apology*, p. 361.)

Since the Earl of Leicester's Company played "on the sondaie next after Newe yeares daie" (see the following entry), it seems likely that January 1 is correct for the Children of Paul's. Feuillerat suggests that the error may be explained by supposing that the scribe was making up his list from a rough copy, and inadvertently reproduced a part of the entry for the Earl of Leicester's Company, which immediately follows it.

1578–9. JANUARY 4 (SUNDAY). RICHMOND.

"*A pastorell or historie of A Greeke maide* shewen at Richmond on the sondaie next after Newe yeares daie enacted by the Earle of Leicester his servauntes furnished with some thinges in this office." (Feuillerat, *Doc.*, p. 286.)

The Revels Office furnished "Three yardes of gray cloth to make my Lord of Leicesters men A fishermans coat" (*ibid.*, p. 295), "holly and Ivie for my Lord of Leicesters servauntes," and, on January 4, provided for "the hier of A horsse ij daies to the courte to ffurnishe my Lord of Leicesters players the ffrost being so greate no bote could goe." (*Ibid.*, p. 298.)

£10 was paid, on a warrant dated January 16, 1578–9, for a play before the Queen "on Sonday iiij^to Januarij 1578" by the Earl of Leicester's Company. (Wallace, *Evol.*, E. D. p. 221. See also Stopes, *Hunnis*, p. 321; *Burbage*, p. 249; Chambers, *M. L. R.*, ii, 7; Dasent, *Acts*, xi, 21, in which the warrant is dated at Richmond, the play not dated, and no sum mentioned; Chalmers, *Apology*, p. 396.)

1578–9. JANUARY 6 (TUESDAY). RICHMOND.

"*The historie of the Rape of the second Helene* shewen at Richmond on Twelf daie at night well furnished in this office with manie thinges for them." (Feuillerat, *Doc.*, p. 286.)

On January 6 seven shillings was paid "for cariage of the Revells stuffe to the courte and back agayne that served my Lord Chamberleynes players second plaie." (*Ibid.*, p. 299.)

£10 was paid, on a warrant dated January 16, 1578–9, for a play before the Queen "on Twelfe daye at night" by the Lord Chamberlain's Company. (Wallace, *Evol. E. D.*, p. 220. See also Chambers, *M. L. R.*, ii, 7; Dasent, *Acts*, xi, 21, in which the warrant is dated at Richmond, the play not dated, and no sum mentioned.)

Although the Revels Accounts do not give the name of the company, it seems likely that *The Rape of the Second Helen* was "my Lord Chamberleynes players second plaie." The Declared Accounts give a performance by the Children of the Chapel on January 6, but this seems to be an error for December 27.

Murray (*English Dramatic Companies*, i, 37 and *n.*), following Fleay (*Stage*, p. 26) and relying on Chalmers (who gives two plays by Leicester's Company and only one by the Lord Chamberlain's), assigns the play to Leicester's Men. But Chalmers seems to be in error. *The Acts of the Privy Council* (Dasent, xi, 21) gives two plays by Chamberlain's and one by Leicester's men. This is confirmed, as we have seen, by the Revels Accounts, and by the Declared Accounts.

1578–9. JANUARY 6 (TUESDAY).

For the play by the Children of the Chapel dated January 6 in the Declared Accounts, see the entry for December 27.

1578–9. JANUARY 11 (SUNDAY).

"*A Maske of Amasones*." (Feuillerat, *Doc.*, p. 286.)

One of the Amazons, "with A speech to the Quenes maiestie," delivered "A Table with writinges vnto her highnes." (*Ibid.*, pp. 286–87.) Among the expenses we find the following item:

To Patruchius Vbaldinas by the comaundment of the Lord chamberleyne for the translating of certen speaches into Italian to be vsed in the maske the making the Tables for them the writing faire in the same Tables and for his chardges in travelling About the same xlij^s ij^d. (*Ibid.*, p. 301.)

This masque, which with the one following constituted a "doble maske" (*ibid.*, p. 296), was "shewen before her maiestie the ffrench Imbassadour being presente the sonday night after Twelfdaie." (*Ibid.*, p. 287.)

The resident French Ambassador was M. de Mauvissière. But Feuillerat thinks that the reference is to Simier, the envoy of Alençon, who arrived early in January.

1578–9. JANUARY 11 (SUNDAY).

"An other *Maske of knightes.*" (Feuillerat, *Doc.*, p. 287.)

1578–9. FEBRUARY 2 (MONDAY). WHITEHALL.

"*The history of* ————— provided to have been shewen at Whitehall on candlemas daie at nighte by the Earle of Warwickes servantes furnished in this office with sondrey garmentes and properties Being in redines At ye place to have enacted the same. But the Quenes maiestie wold not come to heare the same and therefore put of." (Feuillerat, *Doc.*, p. 303.)

The Office furnished "ij li. of Sises" and hired "iij vizars that should have served that night." (*Ibid.*, p. 308.)

£6. 13s. 4d. was paid, on a warrant dated March 11, 1578–9, "to Jerome Savage & his company servauntes to Therle of Warwicke in consideracion of a playe wch was in a reddynes to haue bene presented before her ma^tie one Candlemas night last past." (Wallace, *Evol. E. D.*, p. 221. See also Stopes, *Hunnis*, p. 321, in which the date of the play is given as "1st March 1578"; Chambers, *M. L. R.*, ii, 7; Dasent, *Acts*, xi, 81, in which the payee is not given and the warrant is dated March 18; Chalmers, *Apology*, p. 397.)

1578–9. MARCH 1 (SHROVE SUNDAY). WHITEHALL.

"*The history of the Knight in the Burnyng Rock* shewen at Whitehall on shrovesondaie at night enacted by the Earle of warwickes servauntes furnished in this office with sondrey garmentes and properties." (Feuillerat, *Doc.*, p. 303.)

The Accounts show that the staging of this play required an unusual amount of attention. The items of expense tell a fairly complete story. "Long sparre poles of ffurre," "peeces of Elme cutt compasse"; "Dobble quarters . . . single quarters . . . Deale bourdes . . . Elme bordes. 153. foote . . . in all" (*ibid.*, p. 206), and nails of various sizes were employed in the construction of the Rock. Its size is further indicated by the item "for mending A scalling Ladder that serued at the Rock." (*Ibid.*, p.

307.) The frame work was probably covered with canvas and painted. Sixpence was paid "ffor Coales at the courte to drie the Painters worke on the Rock." (*Ibid.*, p. 307.)

It was decorated with "Ivie and holly." "Aquavite to burne in the same Rock . . . Rosewater to Alay the smell thereof," and "glasses to carry the same and other for the vse thereof" (*ibid.*, p. 308) were supplied.

Two shillings and sixpence worth of lead was employed "for the chaire of the burnyng Knight." (*Ibid.*, p. 307.)

Payments for "Cariage of the rock from Bridewell to the court the first of March. 1578," to "John Rose seniour . . . ffor his bote hier to the courte to take measure of the bignes of the Rock" (*ibid.*, p. 309); and "ffor cariage of them two frames and the rock from the court in two Carres" (*ibid.*, p. 310) complete the account of this unusually large property.

A "cloud" was employed in the same play. Ten shillings was paid "ffor A hoope and blewe Lynnen cloth to mend the clowde that was Borrowed and cut to serve the rock in the plaie of *the burnyng knight* and for the hire therof and setting vpp the same where it was borrowed." (*Ibid.*, p. 308.) There are also items "for nayles of sondry sortes vsed about the Clowde and drawing it vpp and downe," and "for A coard and pullies to drawe vpp the clowde." (*Ibid.*, p. 307.)

£10 was paid, on a warrant dated March 13, 1578–9, for a play before the Queen "on Shrove sonday laste paste" by the Earl of Warwick's Company. (Wallace, *Evol. E. D.*, p. 221. See also Stopes, *Hunnis*, p. 321; Dasent, *Acts*, xi, 75, in which the warrant is dated at Westminster; Chalmers, *Apology*, p. 397.)

1578–9. MARCH 2 (SHROVE MONDAY). WHITEHALL.

"*The history of Loyaltie and bewtie* shewen at Whitehall on Shrove monday at night enacted by the children of the Quenes maiesties chappell furnished in this office with verie manie Riche garmentes and properties aptly fitted for the same." (Feuillerat, *Doc.*, p. 303.)

The properties and other provisions for this play noted in the Accounts are "an Iron for the wagon that serued in the play of *Loyaltie and bewtie*," "for the wagon of *Loyaltie and bewtie*" (*ibid.*, p. 307), "Gloves for the children of the chappell xviij^ten paire," and "A garland of grapes and Leaves for Baccus and other of roses for   vsed in the play of *Loyaltie and Bewtie*." (*Ibid.*, p. 308.)

£10 was paid, on a warrant dated March 12, 1578-9, for a play before the Queen "on Shrove Monday" by the Children of the Chapel (Richard ffarrante). (Wallace, *Evol. E. D.*, p. 221. See also Stopes, *Hunnis*, p. 321; Dasent, *Acts*, xi, 70, in which the warrant is dated at Westminster; Chalmers, *Apology*, p. 361, in which what appears to be the same warrant is dated 1577-8.)

1578-9. MARCH 3 (SHROVE TUESDAY). WHITEHALL.

"*The history of murderous mychaell* shewen at Whitehall on shrovetuesdaie at night enacted by the Lord Chamberleynes servauntes furnished in this office with sondrey thinges." (Feuillerat, *Doc.*, p. 303.)

The Office furnished "ffurre poles xxj. wherof xiiij. for altering the lightes on Shrovetuesdaie and the rest for the frames" (*ibid.*, p. 306), and "Doble x^d. nayles to alter the lightes in the hall on shrovetuesdaie and to have lightes in the presence and for setting vpp of the frames." (*Ibid.*, p. 307.) Sixpence was given "to the painters on shrove tuesday to send for victualls because they should not go from their worke"; Roger Atkinson was paid four shillings "for carying Stuffe at two seuerall tymes that served the children of the Quenes chapell and my Lord Chamberleynes men to the court and back agayne." (*Ibid.*, p. 310.)

£10 was paid, on a warrant dated March 13, 1578-9, for a play before the Queen "on Shrovetewsday last paste" by the Lord Chamberlain's Company. (Wallace, *Evol. E. D.*, p. 221. See also Stopes, *Hunnis*, p. 321; Dasent, *Acts*, xi, 75, in which the play is dated "Shrove Sunday," and the warrant at Westminster; Chalmers, *Apology*, p. 396-7.)

1578–9. MARCH 3 (SHROVE TUESDAY).

A *"mores maske"* intended.

Four shillings was paid "for ffyne Cullers gold and silver for patorns for *the mores maske* that should have served on Shrovetuesday." (Feuillerat, *Doc.*, p. 308.)

THE SEASON 1579–1580

Ten plays were selected for the season's performances by Edmund Tylney, the newly-appointed Master of the Revels, as the following entry from the Accounts shows:

Edmonde Tylney . . . ffor his Chardges with the Chardges of the players the Carriage and recariage of their stuffe for examynynge and Rehersinge of dyuers plaies and Choise makinge of x of them to be showen before her Maiestie at Christmas twelfetide Candelmas and Shrovetide and their sondry rehersalls afterwardes till to be presented before her Maiestie x^{li}. (Feuillerat, *Doc.*, pp. 325–326.)

One porter and three other attendants were each paid 12*d.* a day "for their Attendaunce and service at the rehersalls and Choise makinge of the said x plaies." (*Ibid.*, p. 326.)

The "choise makinge" ended December 19, "at which tymes the workes began." (*Ibid.*, p. 320.) The most important of the "workes" described is the preparation against Christmas of "vij Cities one villadge one Cuntrey howse one Battlement iiij axes a Braunche lillyes and a mount." (*Ibid.*, p. 328.)

1579. DECEMBER 26 (SATURDAY). WHITEHALL.

"*A history of the Duke of Millayn and the Marques of Mantua* shewed at Whitehall on St Stephens daie at nighte enacted by the lord Chamberlaynes seruauntes wholie furnyshed in this offyce some newe made and moche altered whereon was Imployed for iiij^{or} newe head Attyers with traynes Scarfes, garters and other Attyres, xiij Ells of Sarcenett a countrie howse a Cyttye and vij paire of gloves." (Feuillerat, *Doc.*, p. 320.)

£10 was paid, on a warrant dated at Whitehall, February 25, 1579–80, for a play before the Queen "vpon s^t Stephens daye last past" by the Lord Chamberlain's Company. (Wallace, *Evol. E. D.*, p. 221. See also Stopes, *Hunnis*, p. 321, in which the warrant is dated February 26; Dasent, *Acts*, xi, 377, in which the warrant is dated January 25, and the play is undated; Chalmers, *Apology*, p. 397.)

1579. DECEMBER 27 (SUNDAY). WHITEHALL.

"*A history of Alucius*. shewed at white hall on St Iohns daie at nighte enacted by the Children of her Maiesties Chappell wholly furnyshed in this offyce with many garmentes newe made manye altered and translated whereon was Imployed for head Attyers sleeves Canyons cases for hoase skarfes garters and other reparacions tenne Ells of Sarcenett A Cittie a Battlement and xviij paire of gloves." (Feuillerat, *Doc.*, p. 320.)

£10 was paid, on a warrant dated at Whitehall, January 25, 1579–80, for a play before the Queen "vpon St Johns day laste paste" by the Children of the Chapel (Richard ffarrant). (Wallace, *Evol. E. D.*, p. 221. See also Stopes, *Hunnis*, p. 321; Dasent, *Acts*, xi, 377, in which the play is undated; Chalmers, *Apology*, pp. 361–2.)

1579. DECEMBER 28 (MONDAY). WHITEHALL.

"*A historye of* ———— provided to haue bene shewen at Whitehall on Innocentes daie at nighte by the Earle of Leicesters seruauntes beinge in Readynes in the place to haue enacted the same whollye furnyshed with sondrye thinges in this offyce. But the Queenes Maiestie coulde not come forth to heare the same therefore put of." (Feuillerat, *Doc.*, p. 320.)

1579–80. JANUARY 1 (FRIDAY). WHITEHALL.

"*A history of the foure sonnes of ffabyous* shewed at Whithall on Newe Yeares daie at [ni]ghte enacted by the Earle of Warwickes servauntes wholie furnyshed in this offyce with garmentes some

new some altered and repaired whereon was Imployed for newe
lynynge translatinge and alteringe of the Senatours gownes iij
head Attyres with traynes for womens skarfes and girdles xiij ells
of Sarcenett A Cytie a Mounte & vj paire of gloves." (Feuillerat,
Doc., p. 320.)

Sixpence each was paid for ten "ffurre poles to make Rayles for
the battlementes and to make the prison for my Lord of Warwickes men." (*Ibid.*, p. 327.)

£10 was paid, on a warrant dated at Whitehall, January 25,
1579-80, for a play before the Queen "one Newyeresday laste" by
the Earl of Warwick's Company. (Wallace, *Evol. E. D.*, p. 222.
See also Stopes, *Hunnis*, p. 321; Dasent, *Acts*, xi, 377, in which
the play is undated; Chalmers, *Apology*, p. 397.)

1579-80. JANUARY 3 (SUNDAY). WHITEHALL.

"*The history of Cipio Africanus* shewen at whitehall the sondaye
night after newe yeares daie enacted by the Children of Pawles
furnyshed in this Offyce with sondrie garmentes and tryumphant
ensignes & banners newe made and their head peeces of white
sarcenett scarfes and garters whereon was ymployed   ells
of Sarcenett A Citie a Battlement and xviij^{ne} payre of gloues."
(Feuillerat, *Doc.*, p. 321.)

£10 was paid, on a warrant dated at Whitehall, January 25,
1579-80, for a play before the Queen "vpon sonday the iijth of
this present" by the Children of Paul's (Sebastian Wescote).
(Wallace, *Evol. E. D.*, p. 222. See also Stopes, *Hunnis*, p. 321;
Dasent, *Acts*, xi, 377, in which the play is undated; Chalmers,
Apology, p. 362.)

1579-80. JANUARY 6 (WEDNESDAY). WHITEHALL.

"*The history of* ————— shewen at white hall on Twelvedaye
at nighte by the Earl of Leicesters seruauntes furnished in this
offyce with many garmentes vtensells and properties some made
newe some translated and made fitt whereon was ymployed for

head Attyers scarfes and garters   ells of Sarcenett, A Citie a Countrye house and vij paire of gloves." (Feuillerat, *Doc.*, p. 321.)

Single and double "Quarters" were employed "to enlardge the Scaffolde in the hall one Twelfe night." (*Ibid.*, p. 327.)

£10 was paid, on a warrant dated at Whitehall, January 25, 1579–80, for a play before the Queen "on Twelf day laste paste" by the Earl of Leicester's Company. (Wallace, *Evol. E. D.*, p. 222. See also Stopes, *Hunnis*, p. 321, *Burbage*, p. 249; Dasent, *Acts*, xi, 377, in which the play is undated; Chalmers, *Apology*, p. 397.)

1579–80. FEBRUARY 2 (TUESDAY). WHITEHALL.

"*The history of Portio and demorantes* shewen at whitehall on Candlemas daie at nighte enacted by the Lord Chamberleyns seruauntes wholly furnyshed in this offyce whereon was ymployed for scarfes garters head Attyers for women & Lynynges for hattes vj ells of Sarcenett A Cytie a towne & vj payre of gloves." (Feuillerat, *Doc.*, p. 321.)

£10 was paid, on a warrant dated at Whitehall, February 23, 1579–80, for a play before the Queen "vpon Candlemas day last paste" by the Lord Chamberlain's Company. (Wallace, *Evol. E. D.*, p. 222. See also Stopes, *Hunnis*, p. 321; Dasent, *Acts*, xi, 398; Chalmers, *Apology*, p. 397.)

1579–80. FEBRUARY 14 (SHROVE SUNDAY). WHITEHALL.

"*The history of the Soldan and the Duke of* ————— shewen at Whitehall on Shrovesondaye at nighte enacted by the Earle of Derby his seruauntes wholly furnyshed in this offyce whereon was ymployed for two Robes of blacke sarcenett, head Attyers and scarfes   ells of Sarcenett A Citie and xij payre of gloves." (Feuillerat, *Doc.*, p. 321.)

£10 was paid, on a warrant dated at Whitehall, February 23, 1579–80, for a play before the Queen "vpon sonday the xiiij[th] of this present monethe" by the Earl of Derby's Company. (Wallace, *Evol. E. D.*, p. 222. See also Dasent, *Acts*, xi, 398; Chalmers, *Apology*, p. 397.)

1579–80. February 16 (Shrove Tuesday). Whitehall.

"*The history of Serpedon* shewen at whitehall on Shrovetwesdaye
at nighte enacted by the Lord Chamberleyns seruauntes wholly
furnyshed in this offyce whereon was ymployed for head Attyers
for women and Scarfes xj ells of Sarcenett a greate Citie a wood,
A wood A Castell and vj payre of gloves." (Feuillerat, *Doc.*,
p. 321.)

£10 was paid, on a warrant dated at Whitehall, February 23,
1579–80, for a play before the Queen "vpon shrove tewesdaye at
night" by the Lord Chamberlain's Company. (Wallace, *Evol.
E. D.*, p. 222. See also Stopes, *Hunnis*, p. 321; Dasent, *Acts*, xi,
398; Chalmers, *Apology*, p. 397.)

THE SEASON 1580–1581

1580. December 26 (Monday). Whitehall.

"The Earle of Leicesters men. A Comodie called *delighte* shewed
at white hall on St Stephens daie at nyght wheron was ymployed
newe, one cittie, one battlement and .xij. paire of gloves."
(Feuillerat, *Doc.*, p. 336.)

£10 was paid, on a warrant dated at Whitehall, January 14,
1580–1, for a play before the Queen "on St Stevens day at night
laste past" by the Earl of Leicester's Company. (Wallace, *Evol.
E. D.*, p. 222. See also Stopes, *Hunnis*, p. 321; Dasent, *Acts*, xii,
321, in which the warrant is dated January 30; Chalmers, *Apology*,
p. 398, in which it is dated January 20.)

Fleay (*Stage*, p. 28) identifies *Delight* with the *Play of Plays*
mentioned by Gosson in the *School of Abuse* (1579).

1580. December 27 (Tuesday). Whitehall.

"The Earle of Sussex men. *A storie of* ————— enacted on S^t
Iohns daie at night wheron was Imploied newe one howse on
battlement and thirtene paire of gloves." (Feuillerat, *Doc.*, p. 336.)

£10 was paid, on a warrant dated at Westminster, January 14, 1580–1, for a play before the Queen "on Ste Johns daye at night laste paste" by the Earl of Sussex's Company. (Wallace, *Evol. E. D.*, p. 222. See also Stopes, *Hunnis*, p. 321; Dasent, *Acts*, xii, 321; Chalmers, *Apology*, p. 398.)

1580–1. JANUARY 1 (SUNDAY). WHITEHALL.

"The Earle of Derbies men. *A storie of* ———— shewed at white hall on newe yeres daye at nyght wheron was ymployed newe one cittie one battlement and .xiij. paire ofgloves."(Feuillerat, *Doc.*, p. 336.)

£10 was paid, on a warrant dated at Westminster, January 20, 1580–1, for a play before the Queen "on Newyers daie at night laste paste" by the Earl of Derby's Company. (Wallace, *Evol. E. D.*, p. 222. See also Stopes, *Hunnis*, p. 321; Dasent, *Acts*, xii, 321; Chalmers, *Apology*, p. 398.)

1580–1. JANUARY 6 (FRIDAY). WHITEHALL.

"The children of Pawles. *A storie of Pompey* enacted in the hall on twelf nighte wheron was ymploied newe one great citty, a senate howse and eight ells of dobble sarcenet for curtens and .xviij. paire of gloves." (Feuillerat, *Doc.*, p. 336.)

£10 was paid, on a warrant dated at Westminster, January 18, 1580–1, for a play before the Queen "on Tewsday at night" by the Children of Paul's (Sebastian Westcote). (Wallace, *Evol. E. D.*, p. 223. See also Stopes, *Hunnis*, p. 321; Dasent, *Acts*, xii, 321, in which the play is dated "Twelfte Daye at night"; Chalmers, *Apology*, p. 362, in which the warrant is dated January 30.)

January 6 is probably the correct date, since the Revels Accounts and the Council Register agree.

1580–1. FEBRUARY 2 (THURSDAY).

"The earle of Sussex men. *A storie of* ———— shewed on Candlemas daie at night wheron was ymploied newe, one cittie, one battlement and xij. paire of gloves besides other furniture out of thoffice." (Feuillerat, *Doc.*, p. 336.)

£10 was paid, on a warrant dated at Whitehall, February 13, 1580–1, for a play before the Queen "vppon Candlemas daye at night" by the Lord Chamberlain's [Sussex's] Company. (Wallace, *Evol. E. D.*, p. 223. See also Stopes *Hunnis*, p. 321; Dasent, *Acts*, xii, 330, in which it is dated February 14; Chalmers, *Apology*, p. 398, in which it is dated February 13.)

1580–1. FEBRUARY 5 (SHROVE SUNDAY). WHITEHALL.

"The children of the Quenes maiesties chappell. *A Storie of* ————— enacted on shrovesondaie night wheron was ymployed .xij. newe sutes of apparrell .ij. new hates of velvet xx^{tie} Ells of single sarcenet for facinges bandes scarfes and girdles one citty, one pallace and xviij. paire of gloves." (Feuillerat, *Doc.*, p. 336.)

£10 was paid, on a warrant dated at Whitehall, February 14, 1580–1, for a play before the Queen "at Whitehaule vppon Shrovesoundaie at night laste past" by the Children of the Chapel. (Wallace, *Evol. E. D.*, p. 223. See also Stopes, *Hunnis*, p. 321; Dasent, *Acts*, xii, 330; Chalmers, *Apology*, p. 362, in which the warrant is dated February 13.)

1580–1. FEBRUARY 7 (SHROVE TUESDAY).

"The Earle of Leicesters men. *A Storie of* ————— shewed on shrovetuesdaie at night in the hall wheron was ymploied one great citty and .xij. paire of gloves." (Feuillerat, *Doc.*, p. 336.)

£10 was paid, on a warrant dated at Whitehall, January [evidently an error for February] 14, 1580–1, for a play before the Queen "on Shrove Tewsdaye laste past" by the Earl of Leicester's Company. (Wallace, *Evol. E. D.*, p. 222. See also Stopes, *Burbage*, p. 250; *Hunnis*, p. 321; Dasent, Acts, xii, 330; Chalmers, *Apology*, p. 398.)

1581. APRIL 20–JUNE 14.

Masques were prepared in honor of the French Commissioners who came to treat of a marriage between Elizabeth and the Duke of Alençon. At least one of them seems not to have been shown.

In the Revels Accounts there is a record of "Attendaunce given and worke done betwixt the xviijth daie of marche and the firste of Aprill Anno predicto at the Comaundement of the Lord Chamberleyne for setting downe of paterns for maskes and making up of some of the same for the Receaving of the ffrench Comissioners with the provision of certeyne stuffe properties and making of modells for A mownte and for the edifying of the greate parte of the said mounte The particularities wherof herafter ensueth." (Feuillerat, *Doc.*, p. 340.)

The mount, however, was "not vsed." Nor was "A paire of winges of Estrichfeathers." (*Ibid.*, p. 341.)

The Commissioners, according to Chambers (*Eliz. Stage*, iv, 98), were in London from April 20 to June 14.

THE SEASON 1581–1582

According to the Declared Accounts, "v Playes twoe Maskes & one fightinge at Barriers with diuerse Devises" were "shewed before her maiestie" during the year which began November 1, 1581, and ended October 31, 1582. (Feuillerat, *Doc.*, Table II.) The most important properties provided were "a Mount with a Castle vpon the toppe of it, a Dragon & a Artificiall Tree" which cost £100; an "artificiall Lyon & a horse made of wood," and three painted cloths. (*Ibid.*)

On December 3, 1581, the Privy Council, upon the petition of "certayne companyes of players," removed the prohibition against acting on account of the decrease in number of deaths from the plague, and also "for that they are to present certayne playes before the Quenes Majestie for her solace in the Christmas tyme nowe following." (Dasent, *Acts*, xiii, 269–70.)

Payments are recorded for three plays by children's companies, as the following entries show. Christmas and Shrovetide were probably kept at Whitehall. (See *Journal of Sir Francis Walsingham*, p. 44.)

1581. DECEMBER 26 (TUESDAY). WHITEHALL.

A play before the Queen "on St Stephens daie last past" by the Children of Paul's. Payment £10, on warrant dated at Westminster, April 14, 1582. (Wallace, *Evol. E. D.*, p. 223. See also Stopes, *Hunnis*, p. 321; Dasent, *Acts*, xiii, 393, in which the warrant is dated from Greenwich; Chalmers, *Apology*, p. 362, in which the warrant is dated April 24.)

1581. DECEMBER 31 (SUNDAY). WHITEHALL.

A play before the Queen on "the laste daie of december" by the Children of the Chapel. Payment £10, on warrant dated at Greenwich, April 1, 1582. (Wallace, *Evol. E. D.*, p. 223. See also Stopes, *Hunnis*, p. 321; Dasent, *Acts*, xiii, 374; Chalmers, *Apology*, p. 362.)

1581–2. FEBRUARY 27 (SHROVE TUESDAY). WHITEHALL.

A play before the Queen on "shrovetuesdaie" by the Children of the Queen's Chapel. Payment £10, on the same warrant as that for the play of December 31. (Wallace, *Evol. E. D.*, p. 223. See also Stopes, *Hunnis*, p. 321; Dasent, *Acts*, xiii, 374; Chalmers, *Apology*, p. 362.)

THE SEASON 1582–1583

1582. DECEMBER 26 (TUESDAY). WINDSOR.

"A Comodie or Morrall devised on A game of the Cardes shewed on St Stephens daie at night before her maiestie at Wyndesor Enacted by the Children of her maiesties Chapple, furnished with many thinges within this Office, whereof some were translated, and some newe made, and Imploied therein viz. Twoe clothes of canvas xx^tie Ells of sarcenet for iiij^or pavilions and girdles for the Boyes and viij. paire of gloves." (Feuillerat, *Doc.*, p. 349.)

£10 was paid, on a warrant dated at Richmond, February 17, 1582–3, for a play before the Queen on "St Steuens day last at windsor" by the Children of the Chapel (William Hunnys). (Wallace, *Evol. E. D.*, p. 224. See also Stopes, *Hunnis*, p. 322.)

As Cunningham points out, this play is mentioned by Sir John Harrington in his *Brief Apologie of Poetrie* (1591):

Or, to speake of a London Comedie, How much good matter, yea and matter of state, is there in that Comedie cald *the play of the Cards*, in which it is showed how foure Parasiticall knaues robbe the foure principall vocations of the Realme, *videl.* the vocation of Souldiers, Schollers, Marchants, and Husbandmen? Of which Comedie I cannot forget the saying of a notable wise counseller that is now dead, who when some (to sing *Placebo*) aduised that it should be forbidden, because it was some what too plaine, and indeed as the old saying is, *sooth boord is no boord*, yet he would haue it allowed, adding it was fit that *They which doe that they should* not should heare that they would not. (Quoted from G. Gregory Smith, *Elizabethan Critical Essays*, ii, 210.)

1582. DECEMBER 27 (WEDNESDAY). WINDSOR.

"*A Comodie of Bewtie and Huswyfery* shewed before her maiestie at Wyndesor on St Iohns daie at night enacted by the lord of Hundesdons servauntes, for which was prepared newe one Cloth and one Battlement of Canvas, iij. Ells of sarcenet and Eight paire of gloves with sondrey other thinges out of this office." (Feuillerat, *Doc.*, p. 349.)

£10 was paid, on a warrant dated at Richmond, February 17, 1582–3, for a play before the Queen "on St Johns day last at Windsor" by Lord Hundson's Company. (Wallace, *Evol. E. D.*, p. 224. See also Stopes, *Hunnis*, p. 322; *Burbage*, p. 250.)

1582. DECEMBER 30 (SUNDAY). WINDSOR.

"*A Historie of Loue and ffortune* shewed before her maiestie at Wyndesor on the sondaie at night next before newe yeares daie Enacted by the Earle of Derbies servauntes. ffor which newe provision was made of one Citty and one Battlement of Canvas iij Ells of sarcenet A   of canvas, and viij. paire of gloves with sondrey other furniture in this office." (Feuillerat, *Doc.*, p. 349.)

£10 was paid, on a warrant dated at Richmond, February 17, 1582–3, for a play before the Queen "vppon the Sunday after Xpenmas day at Windsor" by the Earl of Derby's Company. (Wallace, *Evol. E. D.*, p. 224. See also Stopes, *Hunnis*, p. 322.)

1582–3. JANUARY 5 (SATURDAY). WINDSOR.

"A maske of Ladies presented them selues before her maiestie at wyndesor at Twelf Eve at night, wherevnto was prepared and Imployed (beside the stuff of this office) xv yardes of black and white Lawne or Cipres for head Attires & vizardes xj. ells of Sarcenet. viij paire of gloves for boyes and Torchbearers, and one paire of white shoes." (Feuillerat, *Doc.*, p. 349.)

1582–3. JANUARY 6 (SUNDAY). WINDSOR.

"*A historie of fferrar* shewed before her maiestie at wyndesor on Twelf daie at night Enacted by the Lord Chamberleynes serv-auntes furnished in this office with diverse new thinges As one Citty, one Battlement of canvas, iij Ells of sarcenet and .x. paire of gloves, and sondrey other thinges in this office whereof some were translated for fitting of the persons &c." (Feuillerat, *Doc.*, p. 350.)

£10 was paid, on a warrant dated at Richmond, February 17, 1582–3, for a play before the Queen "on the Twelveth day at night last past at Windsor" by the Lord Chamberlain's Com-pany. (Wallace, *Evol. E. D.*, pp. 223–4; Stopes, *Hunnis*, p. 322.)

There have been various conjectures about this play. Boswell conjectured that it was a play by George Ferrers. Collier (i, 240) says: "Probably the same piece as *The History of Error*, mentioned under the date of 1576–7 . . . It is, no doubt, a mere mistake in the title by the clerk who made out the account, and who wrote by his ear, and not by his copy." Feuillerat, however, asserts that "it is, on the contrary, most probable that he wrote by his copy and not by his ear. It is more simple and more natural to suppose that 'Ferrar' may have been one of the principal dramatis personae."

1582–3. FEBRUARY 10 (SHROVE SUNDAY). RICHMOND.

"*A historie of Telomo* shewed before her maiestie at Richmond on Shrovesondaie at night Enacted by the Earle of Leicesters servauntes, for which was prepared and Imployed, one Citty, one Battlement of canvas iij. Ells of sarcenet and viij. paire of gloves. And furnished with sondrey other garmentes of the store of the office &c." (Feuillerat, *Doc.*, p. 350.)

£10 was paid, on a warrant dated at Richmond, February 17, 1582–3, for a play before the Queen "vppon Shrouesunday last at Richmonde" by the Earl of Leicester's Company. (Wallace, *Evol. E. D.*, p. 224. See also Stopes, *Hunnis*, p. 322; *Burbage*, p. 250.)

Fleay identifies this play with the *Ptolemy* mentioned by Gosson in the *School of Abuse* (1579) as having been acted at the Red Bull.

1582–3. FEBRUARY 12 (SHROVE TUESDAY). RICHMOND.

"*A historie of Ariodante and Geneuora* shewed before her maiestie on Shrovetuesdaie at night enacted by m^r Mulcasters children, ffor which was newe prepared and Imployed, one Citty, one battlement of Canvas, vij Ells of sarcenet, and ij. dozen of gloves. The whole furniture for the reste was of the store of this office, whereof sondrey garmentes for fytting of the Children were altered & translated." (Feuillerat, *Doc.*, p. 350.)

£10 was paid, on a warrant dated February 17, 1582–3, for a play before the Queen "on Shroue Twesday last at Richmonde" by the Merchant Taylors' School (Richarde Mulcaster). (Wallace, *Evol. E. D.*, p. 223. See also Stopes, *Hunnis*, p. 321.)

1582–3. SHROVETIDE?

"*A Maske of Sixe Seamen* prepared to have ben shewed, but not vsed." (Feuillerat, *Doc.*, p. 350.)

This masque was probably intended for Shrovetide.

THE SEASON 1583–1584

According to the Declared Accounts, "vj histories, one Comedie one Maske and other devises" were "shewed before hir Maiestie" during the year which began November 1, 1583, and ended October 31, 1584. (Feuillerat, *Doc.*, Table III.)

Payments for seven plays are recorded, as the following entries show. Christmas was kept at Whitehall. (See Chambers, *Eliz. Stage*, iv, 100.)

1583. DECEMBER 26 (THURSDAY). WHITEHALL.

A play before the Queen "vpon St Stevens daie at night" by the Queen's Company. £6. 12*s*. 4*d*. was paid, on May 9, 1584, on a warrant dated at Westminster, March 12, 1583–4. (Wallace, *Evol. E. D.*, p. 224. See also Stopes, *Burbage*, p. 251, in which the plays are undated; Chambers, *M. L. R.*, ii, 7.)

1583. DECEMBER 29 (SUNDAY). WHITEHALL.

A play before the Queen "vpon the sondaie following" by the Queen's Company. £6. 13*s*. 4*d*. was paid, on May 9, 1584, on the same warrant as that for the preceding play. (Wallace, *Evol. E. D.*, p. 224. See also Stopes, *Burbage*, p. 251; Chambers, *M. L. R.*, ii, 7.)

1583–4. JANUARY 1 (WEDNESDAY). WHITEHALL.

Campaspe, Played beefore the Queenes Maiestie on newyeares day at night, by her Maiesties Children, and the Children of Paules. London. 1591.

£10 was paid, November 25, 1584, on the warrant dated at Westminster, March 12, 1583–4, for a play "vpon newyeresdaie at nighte" by the Earl of Oxford's Company (John Lilie). (Wallace, *Evol. E. D.*, p. 224. See also Stopes, *Burbage*, p. 251; Chambers, *M. L. R.*, ii, 7.)

When the Earl of Oxford bought the lease of Blackfriars from Henry Evans, he presented it to his secretary, John Lyly, and proceeded to form a new troupe of child-actors by adding the

Children of Paul's to Hunnis's Children of the Chapel. Lyly wrote his first play for the new organization. For a full discussion, see Adams, *Shakespearean Playhouses*, pp. 108–109.

The title-page of another issue of this edition of the play gives the date of the court performance as "twelfe day at night."

1583–4. JANUARY 6 (MONDAY). WHITEHALL.

A play before the Queen "vpon Twelfedaie at night" by the Children of the Queen's Chapel. £7. 10s. was paid, on May 29, 1584, on the warrant dated at Westminster, March 12, 1583–4. (Wallace, *Evol. E. D.*, p. 224. See also Stopes, *Burbage*, p. 251; Chambers, *M. L. R.*, ii, 7.)

1583–4. FEBRUARY 2 (SUNDAY).

A play before the Queen "on Candlemas daie at night" by the Children of the Queen's Chapel. £7. 10s. was paid, on May 29, 1584, on the same warrant as that for the preceding play. (Wallace, *Evol. E. D.*, p. 224. See also Stopes, *Burbage*, p. 251; Chambers, *M. L. R.*, ii, 7.)

1583–4. MARCH 3 (SHROVE TUESDAY).

A play before the Queen "on shrovetuesdaie" by the Queen's Company. £6. 13s. 4d. was paid, on May 9, 1584, on the same warrant as that for the play of December 26. (Wallace, *Evol. E. D.*, p. 224. See also Stopes, *Burbage*, p. 251.)

1583–4. MARCH 3 (SHROVE TUESDAY).

Sapho and Phao, Played beefore the Queenes Maiestie on Shrouetews-day, by her Maiesties Children, and the Boyes of Paules. London. 1584.

£10 was paid, on November 25, 1584, on the same warrant as that for the play of New Year's, for a play before the Queen "on shrovetuesdaie at nighte" by the Earl of Oxford's Company. (Wallace, *Evol. E. D.*, p. 224.)

For an explanation of the union of the two companies under the Earl of Oxford's patronage, see the entry for January 1.

THE SEASON 1584–1585

No masques have been recorded for the season. But mention is made of "maskes" in the customary preamble to the Accounts for "Crystmas Twelftyde & Shrouetyde." (Feuillerat, *Doc.*, p. 365.) And there are charges between February 25, 1584-5, and the last of October for airing and safe-bestowing of garments "both for maskers and players." (*Ibid.*, p. 372.)

1584. DECEMBER 26 (SATURDAY). GREENWICH.

"*A pastorall of phillyda & Choryn* presented and enacted before her maiestie by her highnes servauntes on St Stephens daie at night at Grenewich wheron was ymployed   yardes of Buffyn for Shepherdes coates xxx^{tie} ells of sarcenet for fower matachyne sutes one greate curteyne and scarfes for the nymphes one mounttayne and one great cloth of canvas and vj peeces of buccram." (Feuillerat, *Doc.*, p. 365.)

£10 was paid, on a warrant dated at Greenwich, March 14, 1584-5, for a play "vppon St Steuensday at nighte last" by the Queen's Company (Roberte Willson). (Wallace, *Evol. E. D.*, pp. 224-5. See also Chambers, *M. L. R.*, ii, 8.)

1584. DECEMBER 27 (SUNDAY). GREENWICH.

"*The history of Agamemnon & Vlisses* presented and enacted before her maiestie by the Earle of Oxenford his boyes on St Iohns daie at night at Grenewich." (Feuillerat, *Doc.*, p. 365.)

£6. 13s. 4d. was paid, on a warrant dated at Greenwich, April 7, 1585, for a play "on St John the Evangelistes daye last past at nighte" by the Children of the Earl of Oxford (Henrye Evans). (Wallace, *Evol. E. D.*, p. 225.)

1584-5. JANUARY 3 (SUNDAY). GREENWICH.

"*The history of felix & philiomena.* shewed and enacted before her highnes by her maiesties servauntes on the Sondaie next after newe yeares daye at nighte at Grenewiche wheron was ymployed one battlement & a howse of canvas." (Feuillerat, *Doc.*, p. 365.)

£10 was paid, on the same warrant as that for the play of December 26, for a play "vppon the Sondaye after Newyeres day" by the Queen's Company. (Wallace, *Evol. E. D.*, pp. 224-5. See also Chambers, *M. L. R.*, ii, 8.)

1584-5. JANUARY 6 (WEDNESDAY). GREENWICH.

"An Inuention called *ffiue playes in one* presented and enacted before her maiestie on Twelfe daie at nighte in the hall at Grene-wiche by her highnes servauntes wheron was ymployed a greate cloth and a battlement of canvas and canvas for a well and a mounte .xv ells of sarcenet .ix yardes of sullen cloth of gold purple." (Feuillerat, *Doc.*, p. 365.)

£10 was paid, on the same warrant as that for the play of December 26, for a play "vppon yᵉ Twelveth day" by the Queen's Company. (Wallace, *Evol. E. D.*, pp. 224-5. See also Chambers, *M. L. R.*, ii, 8.)

Fleay (*Stage*, p. 67, *Drama*, ii, 259) identifies this play with the first part of Tarleton's *Seven Deadly Sins*.

1584-5. FEBRUARY 21 (SHROVE SUNDAY).

"An Inuention of *three playes in one* prepared to haue been shewed before her highnes on Shroue sondaye at night and to haue ben enacted by her maiesties servauntes at Somerset place. But the Quene came not abroad that night. yet was ymployed on the same one howse & a battlement." (Feuillerat, *Doc.*, p. 365.)

Fleay identifies this play with the second part of Tarleton's *Seven Deadly Sins*.

1584-5. FEBRUARY 23 (SHROVE TUESDAY). SOMERSET.

"An Antick playe & a comodye shewed presented and enacted before her highnes on Shrouetewsdaie at nighte at Somerset place by her maiesties servauntes wheron was ymployed one howse." (Feuillerat, *Doc.*, p. 365.)

£10 was paid, on the same warrant as that for the play of December 26, for a play "vppon Shroue Twesdaye last" by the Queen's Company. (Wallace, *Evol. E. D.*, pp. 224–5. See also Chambers, *M. L. R.*, ii, 8.)

THE SEASON 1585–1586

It appears from diplomatic correspondence that the Court was at Greenwich during Christmas and Shrovetide.

1585. DECEMBER 26 (SUNDAY). GREENWICH.

A play by the Queen's Company. Payment £10, on warrant dated at Greenwich, January 31, 1585–6. (Chambers, *Eliz. Stage*, iv, 161. See also *M. L. R.*, ii, 8; Stopes, *Hunnis*, p. 322.)

1585. DECEMBER 27 (MONDAY). GREENWICH.

A play by the Admiral's Company. Payment £10, on warrant dated at Greenwich, January 31, 1585–6. (Chambers, *Eliz. Stage*, iv, 161. See also *M. L. R.*, ii, 8; Stopes, *Hunnis*, p. 322.)

1585–6. JANUARY 1 (SATURDAY). GREENWICH.

A play by the Queen's Company. Payment £10, on warrant dated at Greenwich, January 31, 1585–6. (Chambers, *Eliz. Stage*, iv, 161. See also *M. L. R.*, ii, 8; Stopes, *Hunnis*, p. 322.)

1585–6. JANUARY 6 (THURSDAY). GREENWICH.

A play by "the Servantes of the lo: admirall and the lo Chamberlaine." Payment £10, on warrant dated at Greenwich, January 31, 1585–6. (Chambers, *Eliz. Stage*, iv, 161. See also *M. L. R.*, ii, 8; Stopes, *Hunnis*, p. 322; Halliwell–Phillipps, *Illustrations*, p. 31.)

1585–6. JANUARY 6 (THURSDAY).

A play "on Twelfth Day last past" by the Queen's Company. Payment £10, on warrant dated January 31, 1585–6. (Stopes, *Hunnis*, p. 322.)

Possibly there is some error here. No one else prints this warrant.

1585–6. FEBRUARY 13 (SHROVE SUNDAY). GREENWICH.

A play by the Queen's Company. Payment £10, on warrant dated at Greenwich, February 28, 1585–6. (Chambers, *Eliz. Stage*, iv, 161. See also *M. L. R.*, ii, 9; Stopes, *Hunnis*, p. 322. Dasent, *Acts*, xiv, 20, in which the date of the warrant is given as March 6; Chalmers, *Apology*, p. 399.)

SUMMER, 1586

Possibly the following dispatch refers to court performances. At any rate, it gives, if true, an interesting glimpse of the way in which anti-Spanish feeling was being displayed. On July 20, 1586, Hieronimo Lippomano, Venetian Ambassador in Spain, wrote to the Doge and Senate:

But what has enraged him [the King of Spain] more than all else, and has caused him to show a resentment such as he has never before displayed in all his life, is the account of the masquerades and comedies which the Queen of England orders to be acted at his expense. His Majesty has received a summary of one of these which was recently represented, in which all sorts of evil is spoken of the Pope, the Catholic religion, and the King, who is accused of spending all his time in the Escurial with the monks of St. Jerome, attending only to his buildings, and a hundred other insolences which I refrain from sending to your Serenity. (*Calendar State Papers, Venetian*, viii, 182.)

THE SEASON 1586–1587

1586. DECEMBER 26 (MONDAY). GREENWICH.

A play by the Queen's Company. Payment £10, on warrant dated at Greenwich, March 18, 1586–7. (Chambers, *Eliz. Stage*, iv, 161. See also *M. L. R.*, ii, 9; Stopes, *Hunnis*, p. 322.)

Christmas was kept at Greenwich. (Chambers, *Eliz. Stage*, iv, 102.)

1586. DECEMBER 27 (TUESDAY). GREENWICH.

A play by the Earl of Leicester's Company. Payment £10, on warrant dated at Greenwich, March 31, 1586–7. (Chambers,

Eliz. Stage, iv, 161. See also *M. L. R.*, ii, 9; Stopes, *Hunnis*, p. 322; Burbage, p. 251.)

1586–7. JANUARY 1 (SUNDAY). GREENWICH.

A play by the Queen's Company. Payment £10, on the same warrant as that for the play of December 26. (Chambers, *Eliz. Stage*, iv, 161. See also *M. L. R.*, ii, 9; Stopes, *Hunnis*, p. 322.)

1586–7. JANUARY 6 (FRIDAY). GREENWICH.

A play by the Queen's Company. Payment £10, on the same warrant as that for the play of December 26. (Chambers, *Eliz. Stage*, iv, 161. See also *M. L. R.*, ii, 9; Stopes, *Hunnis*, p. 322.)

1586–7. FEBRUARY 26 (SHROVE SUNDAY). GREENWICH.

A play by the Children of Paul's (Thomas Giles). Payment £10, on warrant dated at Greenwich April 9, 1587. (Chambers, *Eliz. Stage*, iv, 161. See also *M. L. R.*, ii, 9; Dasent, *Acts*, xv, 24. Chalmers, *Apology*, p. 362, assigns the play to 1587–8. In dating the play the clerk of the Council evidently used New Style.)

It appears from correspondence that the Court was still at Greenwich during the latter days of February.

1586–7. FEBRUARY 28 (SHROVE TUESDAY). GREENWICH.

A play by the Queen's Company. Payment £10, on the same warrant as that for the play of December 26. (Chambers, *Eliz. Stage*, iv, 161. See also *M. L. R.*, ii, 9; Stopes, *Hunnis*, p. 322.)

THE SEASON 1587–1588

According to the Revels Accounts, "The Quenes Maiestie beinge At Grenewich ther were showed presented and enacted before: her highnes betwixte Christmas & Shrouetid vij playes besides feattes of Activitie And other shewes by the Children of Poles her Maiesties owne servantes & the gentlemen of grayes In on whom was Imployed dyverse remnanttes of Clothe of goulde & other stuffe oute of the Store." (Feuillerat, *Doc.*, p. 378.)

1587. DECEMBER 26 (TUESDAY). GREENWICH.

A play by the Queen's Company. Payment £6. 13s. 4d., on
warrant dated at Greenwich, March 20, 1587-8. (Chambers,
Eliz. Stage, iv, 161. See also *M. L. R.*, ii, 9; Stopes, *Hunnis*, p. 322;
Dasent, *Acts*, xv, 425, in which warrant and plays are undated;
Chalmers, *Apology*, p. 399, in which the date of the warrant is
given as March 4.)

1587-8. JANUARY 1 (MONDAY). GREENWICH.

A play by the Children of Paul's (Thomas Giles). Payment £10,
on warrant dated at Greenwich, February 29, 1587-8. (Chambers,
Eliz. Stage, iv, 162. See also *M. L. R.*, ii, 9.)

It is generally agreed that this play was Lyly's *Galathea*,
entered on the Stationers' Register October 4, 1591, and printed
in 1592 "As it was played before the Quenes Maiestie at Green-
wiche, on Newyeeres day at night. By the Chyldren of Paules."
See Fleay, *Drama*, ii, 40; Bond, *Works*, ii, 230; Feuillerat, *John
Lyly*, p. 575.

1587-8. JANUARY 6 (SATURDAY). GREENWICH.

A play by the Queen's Company. Payment £6. 13s. 4d., on the
same warrant as that for the play of December 26. (Chambers,
Eliz. Stage, iv, 161. See also *M. L. R.*, ii, 9; Stopes, *Hunnis*, p. 322;
Dasent, *Acts*, xv, 425; Chalmers, *Apology*, p. 399.)

1587-8. FEBRUARY 2 (FRIDAY). GREENWICH.

A play by the Children of Paul's. Payment £10, on the same
warrant as that for the play of January 1. (Chambers, *Eliz. Stage*,
iv, 162. See also *M. L. R.*, ii, 9.)

1587-8. FEBRUARY 18 (SHROVE SUNDAY). GREENWICH.

A play by the Queen's Company. Payment £6. 13s. 4d., on the
same warrant as that for the play of December 26. (Chambers,
Eliz. Stage, iv, 161. See also *M. L. R.*, ii, 9; Stopes, *Hunnis*, p.
322; Dasent, *Acts*, xv, 425; Chalmers, *Apology*, p. 399.)

For the play by the Children of Paul's which Chalmers assigns to this date, see the entry for 1586–7, February 26.

1587–8. FEBRUARY 28 (WEDNESDAY). GREENWICH.

The Misfortunes of Arthur, a tragedy by Thomas Hughes and others, was one of "Certaine deuises and shewes presented to her Maiestie by the Gentlemen of Grayes-Inne at her Highnesse Court in Greenwich, the twenty-eighth day of Februarie in the thirtieth yeare of her Maiesties most happy Raigne," printed in 1587–8.

THE SEASON 1588–1589

The Revels Accounts furnish the following particulars of the season's performances:

The Queenes Maiestie being at Richemonde at Christmas Newyearstide & Twelftide there were shewed presented & enacted before her highnes ffyve playes & her Maiestie being at white hall at Shrovetide there were shewed & presented before her twoe plaies All which playes were enacted by her Maiesties owne servantes the children of Paules & the Lord Admiralls men besides sondry feates of actyvity tumbling & Matichives shewed before her highnes within the tyme & at the places aforesaide. (Feuillerat, *Doc.*, p. 388.)

1588. DECEMBER 26 (THURSDAY). RICHMOND.

A play by the Queen's Company. Payment £10, on warrant dated at Westminster, March 16, 1588–9. (Chambers, *Eliz. Stage*, iv, 162. See also Stopes, *Hunnis*, p. 322; Dasent, *Acts*, xvii, 109, in which the warrant is dated at Whitehall; Chalmers, *Apology*, p. 399.)

1588. DECEMBER 27 (FRIDAY). RICHMOND.

A play by the Children of Paul's (Tho Gyles). Payment £10, on warrant dated at Westminster, March 23, 1588–9. (Chambers, *Eliz. Stage*, iv, 162. See also *M. L. R.*, ii, 9; Stopes, *Hunnis*, p. 322, in which the amount is given as £6. 13*s.* 4*d.*; Dasent, *Acts*, xvii, 115; Chalmers, *Apology*, p. 362.)

1588. DECEMBER 29 (SUNDAY). RICHMOND.

A play by the Lord Admiral's Company. Payment [£6. 13*s*. 4*d*.], on warrant dated at Westminster, February 29, 1588–9. (Chambers, *Eliz. Stage*, iv, 162. See also *M. L. R.*, ii, 9; Stopes, *Hunnis*, p. 322, in which the payees, William Gascoigne and William Spencer, are given; Dasent, *Acts*, xvii, 90; Chalmers, *Apology*, in which the date of the warrant is given as February 27.)

1588–9. JANUARY 1 (WEDNESDAY). RICHMOND.

A play by the Children of Paul's. Payment £10, on the same warrant as that for the play of December 27. (Chambers, *Eliz. Stage*, iv, 162. See also *M. L. R.*, ii, 9; Stopes, *Hunnis*, p. 322; Dasent, *Acts*, xvii, 115; Chalmers, *Apology*, p. 362.)

1588–9. JANUARY 12 (SUNDAY). [RICHMOND.]

A play by the Children of Paul's. Payment £10, on the same warrant as that for the play of December 27. (Chambers, *Eliz. Stage*, iv, 162. See also *M. L. R.*, ii, 9; Stopes, *Hunnis*, p. 322; Dasent, *Acts*, xvii, 115; Chalmers, *Apology*, p. 362.)

1588–9. FEBRUARY 9 (SHROVE SUNDAY). WHITEHALL.

A play by the Queen's Company. Payment £10, on the same warrant as that for the play of December 26. (Chambers, *Eliz. Stage*, iv, 162. See also Stopes, *Hunnis*, p. 322; Dasent, *Acts*, xvii, 109; Chalmers, *Apology*, p. 399.)

1588–9. FEBRUARY 11 (SHROVE TUESDAY). WHITEHALL.

A play by the Admiral's Company. Payment £6. 13*s*. 4*d*., on the same warrant as that for the play of December 29. (Chambers, *Eliz. Stage*, iv, 162. See also *M. L. R.*, ii, 9. The play is dated February 9 in Stopes, *Hunnis*, p. 322; Dasent, *Acts*, xvii, 90, and Chalmers, *Apology*, p. 399.)

THE SEASON 1589–1590

1589. DECEMBER 26 (FRIDAY). RICHMOND.

A play by the Queen's Company (John Dutton and John Lanham). Payment £10, on warrant dated March 15, 1589–90. (Chambers, *Eliz. Stage*, iv, 163. See also Stopes, *Hunnis*, p. 323; Dasent, *Acts*, xviii, 420, in which the warrant is dated at Greenwich; Chalmers, *Apology*, p. 399.)

Christmas was probably celebrated at Richmond. (See Chambers, *Eliz. Stage*, iv, 104.)

1589. DECEMBER 28 (SUNDAY). RICHMOND.

A play during "Christide" by the Children of Paul's (Thomas Giles). Payment £10, on warrant dated March 10, 1589–90. (Chambers, *Eliz. Stage*, iv, 163. See also Stopes, *Hunnis*, p. 322; Dasent, *Acts*, xviii, 410, in which the play is dated "on Sondaie after Christemas Daie," and the warrant at Greenwich; Chalmers, *Apology*, p. 362.)

1589–90. JANUARY 1 (THURSDAY). RICHMOND.

A play by the Children of Paul's. Payment £10, on the same warrant as that for the play of December 28. (Chambers, *Eliz. Stage*, iv, 163. See also Stopes, *Hunnis*, p. 322; Dasent, *Acts*, xviii, 410; Chalmers, *Apology*, p. 362.)

1589–90. JANUARY 6 (TUESDAY). RICHMOND.

A play by the Children of Paul's. Payment £10, on the same warrant as that for the play of December 28. (Chambers, *Eliz. Stage*, iv, 163. See also Stopes, *Hunnis*, p. 322; Dasent, *Acts*, xviii, 410; Chalmers, *Apology*, p. 362.)

1589–90. MARCH 1 (SHROVE SUNDAY). GREENWICH.

A play by the Queen's Company. Payment £10, on the same warrant as that for the play of December 26. (Chambers, *Eliz. Stage*, iv, 163. See also Stopes, *Hunnis*, p. 323; Dasent, *Acts*, xviii, 420; Chalmers, *Apology*, p. 399.)

On January 23 or 24 the Court removed to Greenwich. (Chambers, *Eliz. Stage*, iv, 104.)

1589–90. MARCH 3 (SHROVE TUESDAY). GREENWICH.

A play by the Lord Admiral's Company. Payment £10, on a warrant dated at Greenwich, March 10, 1589–90. (Chambers, *Eliz. Stage*, iv, 163. See also Stopes, *Hunnis*, p. 322; Dasent, *Acts*, xviii, 410; Chalmers, *Apology*, p. 399.)

THE SEASON 1590–1591

1590. DECEMBER 26 (SATURDAY). RICHMOND.

A play before the Queen "on St. Steuens day" by the Queen's Company (Lawrence Dutton and John Dutton). Payment £10, on warrant dated March 7, 1590–1. (Cunningham, *Revels*, p. xxxii. See also Chambers, *Eliz. Stage*, iv, 163; Stopes, *Hunnis*, p. 323, in which no dates are given; Dasent, *Acts*, xx, 327, in which the payees are not named and the warrant is dated at Greenwich, March 5; Chalmers, *Apology*, p. 399.)

The Court removed to Richmond about November 24. (Chambers, *Eliz. Stage*, iv, 105.)

1590. DECEMBER 27 (SUNDAY).

For the play ascribed in the *Acts of the Privy Council* (xx, 328) to the Admiral's Company, see the following entry.

1590. DECEMBER 27 (SUNDAY). RICHMOND.

A play by Lord Strange's Company (George Ottewell). Payment £10, on warrant dated March 7, 1590–1. (Chambers, *Eliz. Stage*, iv, 163. See also *M. L. R.*, ii, 10; Dasent, *Acts*, xx, 328, in which the warrant is dated at Greenwich, March 5, and the play ascribed to the Admiral's Company; Chalmers, *Apology*, p. 400.)

1590–1. JANUARY 1 (FRIDAY). RICHMOND.

A play before the Queen "on Newe yeres day last past" by the Queen's Company (John Laneham). Payment £10, on warrant dated March 7, 1590–1. (Cunningham, *Revels*, p. xxxii. See also Chambers, *Eliz. Stage*, iv, 163; Stopes, *Hunnis*, p. 323; Dasent, *Acts*, xx, 328, in which the date is given as March 5; Chalmers, *Apology*, p. 400.)

1590–1. JANUARY 3 (SUNDAY). RICHMOND.

A play before the Queen "the Sonday after Newyeres daye" by the Queen's Company. Payment £10, on the same warrant as that for the play of December 26. (Cunningham, *Revels*, p. xxxii; Chambers, *Eliz. Stage*, iv, 163. See also Stopes, *Hunnis*, p. 323; Dasent, *Acts*, xx, 327; Chalmers, *Apology*, p. 399.)

1590–1. JANUARY 6 (WEDNESDAY). RICHMOND.

A play before the Queen on "Twelueth day" by the Queen's Company. Payment £10, on the same warrant as that for the play of December 26. (Cunningham, *Revels*, p. xxxii. See also Chambers, *Eliz. Stage*, iv, 163; Stopes, *Hunnis*, p. 323; Dasent, *Acts*, xx, 327; Chalmers, *Apology*, p. 399.)

1590–1. FEBRUARY 14 (SHROVE SUNDAY). GREENWICH.

A play before the Queen on "Shroue Sondaye last" by the Queen's Company. Payment £10, on the same warrant as that for the play of December 26. (Cunningham, *Revels*, p. xxxii. See also Chambers, *Eliz. Stage*, iv, 163; Stopes, *Hunnis*, p. 323; Dasent, *Acts*, xx, 327; Chalmers, Apology, p. 399.)

The Court removed to Greenwich February 11–13. (Chambers, *Eliz. Stage*, iv, 105.)

1590–1. FEBRUARY 16 (SHROVE TUESDAY).

For the play ascribed in the *Acts of the Privy Council* (xx, 328), to the Admiral's Company, see the following entry.

1590–1. FEBRUARY 16 (SHROVE TUESDAY). GREENWICH.

A play by Lord Strange's Company. Payment £10, on the same warrant as that for the play of December 27. (Chambers, *Eliz.*

Stage, iv, 163. See also *M. L. R.*, ii, 10; Dasent, *Acts*, xx, 327, in which the play is ascribed to the Admiral's Men; Chalmers, *Apology*, p. 400.)

THE SEASON 1591–1592

Christmas and Shrovetide were kept at Whitehall, according to the Council's warrant for the six plays by Lord Strange's Company. (Dasent, *Acts*, xxii, 264.)

1591. DECEMBER 26 (SUNDAY). WHITEHALL.

A play by the Queen's Company. Payment £10, on warrant dated at Westminster, February 29, 1591-2. (Chambers, *Eliz. Stage*, iv, 163. See also Stopes, *Hunnis*, p. 323; Dasent, *Acts*, xxii, 286, in which the warrant is dated February 27, at Whitehall; Chalmers, *Apology*, p. 400. Mrs. Stopes, evidently in error, places the notices of this season's plays under the heading "32-33 Eliz.")

Possibly the play performed on this occasion was Greene's *Orlando Furioso*, written probably in 1591, and published in 1594 as having been "plaid before the Queenes Maiestie." In the opinion of Greg (*Two Elizabethan Stage Abridgements*, p. 129), it is unlikely that the court performance would have followed the seemingly unsuccessful public presentation in February, 1591-2.

1591. DECEMBER 27 (MONDAY). WHITEHALL.

A play by Lord Strange's Company. Payment £10, on warrant dated at Westminster, February 24, 1591-2. (Chambers, *Eliz. Stage*, iv, 164. This play and the play following are dated, evidently through typographical error, December 7 and 8. See also Stopes, *Hunnis*, p. 323; Dasent, *Acts*, xxii, 264, in which the play is dated "St. John's daie," and the warrant February 20, at Whitehall; Chalmers, *Apology*, p. 400.)

1591. DECEMBER 28 (TUESDAY). WHITEHALL.

A play by Lord Strange's Company. Payment £10, on the same warrant as that for the preceding play. (Chambers, *Eliz. Stage*, iv,

164. See also Stopes, *Hunnis*, p. 323; Dasent, *Acts*, xxii, 264, in which the play is dated "Inocents daie"; Chalmers, *Apology*, p. 400.)

1591–2. JANUARY 1 (SATURDAY). WHITEHALL.

A play by Lord Strange's Company. Payment £10, on the same warrant as that for the play of December 27. (Chambers, *Eliz. Stage*, iv, 164. See also Stopes, *Hunnis*, p. 323; Dasent, *Acts*, xxii, 264; Chalmers, *Apology*, p. 400.)

1591–2. JANUARY 2 (SUNDAY). WHITEHALL.

A play by the Earl of Sussex's Company. Payment £10, on warrant dated at Westminster, February 20, 1591–2. (Chambers, *Eliz. Stage*, iv, 164. See also Dasent, *Acts*, xxii, 264, in which the warrant is dated at Whitehall; Chalmers, *Apology*, p. 400.)

1591–2. JANUARY 6 (THURSDAY). WHITEHALL.

A play by the Earl of Hertford's Company. Payment £10, on warrant dated at Westminster, February 28, 1591–2. (Chambers, *Eliz. Stage*, iv, 164. See also Stopes, *Hunnis*, p. 323; Dasent, *Acts*, xxii, 263–4, in which the warrant is dated February 20, at Whitehall; Chalmers, *Apology*, p. 400.)

1591–2. JANUARY 9 (SUNDAY). WHITEHALL.

A play by Lord Strange's Company. Payment £10, on the same warrant as that for the play of December 27. (Chambers, *Eliz. Stage*, iv, 164. See also Stopes, *Hunnis*, p. 323; Dasent, *Acts*, xxii, 264; Chalmers, *Apology*, p. 400.)

1591–2. FEBRUARY 6 (SHROVE SUNDAY). WHITEHALL.

A play by Lord Strange's Company. Payment £10, on the same warrant as that for the play of December 27. (Chambers, *Eliz. Stage*, iv, 164. See also Stopes, *Hunnis*, p. 323; Dasent, *Acts*, xxii, 264; Chalmers, *Apology*, p. 400.)

1591–2. February 8 (Shrove Tuesday). Whitehall.

A play by Lord Strange's Company. Payment £10, on the same warrant as that for the play of December 27. (Chambers, *Eliz. Stage*, iv, 164. See also Stopes, *Hunnis*, p. 323; Dasent, *Acts*, xxii, 264; Chalmers, *Apology*, p. 400.)

OXFORD, SEPTEMBER, 1592

For a general account of the Queen's second visit to Oxford, and of the plays presented before her, see F. S. Boas, *University Drama in the Tudor Age*, pp. 252–67.

1592. September 24 (Sunday). Christ Church Hall.

Bellum Grammaticale, probably by Leonard Hutten, acted before the Queen.

Only two plays were provided for the Queen's second visit to the University. And, according to Philip Stringer's grudging account, these two were "but meanely performed." Stringer, however, was a Cambridge man, and could not be expected to view the efforts of Oxford with an approving eye. It is not likely, as Boas shows, that pains were spared in preparing for the plays. The Office of the Revels was called on to help provide "furniture." On September 2 the Vice Chancellor wrote to Sir Francis Dorset: "We have sent up two to procure furniture for our plays, with your lordship's letter to the Master of the Revels, whom we understood not to be in London." (*MSS. of Earl de la Warr, Hist. MSS. Com., Ap. to Fourth Report*, p. 300.)

Stringer writes:

At night there was a comedy acted before hir Highnes in the hall of that colledge; and one other on Tuesday at night, being both of them but meanely performed (as we thought), and yet most graciouslye, and with great patience, heard by hir Majestie. The one being called *Bellum Grammaticale*, and the other intituled *Rivales*. (Nichols, *Progresses Elizabeth*, ii.)

1592. September 26 (Tuesday). Christ Church Hall.

Rivals, by William Gager, acted before the Queen.

For Philip Stringer's brief account, see the note to the preceding entry.

THE SEASON 1592–1593

On December 2, 1592, the Vice-Chamberlain wrote to the two universities requesting that each prepare a comedy in English to be acted before the Queen during Christmas. Two days later Dr. John Still, the Vice-Chancellor of Cambridge, and six Heads of Houses replied, in a letter which betrays extreme reluctance to comply with the request at all, that if they "must needes vndertake the business, and that with conveniencie it may be grunted; These two things" they "would gladly desire, some further limitacion of time for due preparacion, And liberty to play in latyn." (See Malone Soc. *Collections*, I, 2, pp. 198–200.) The reply of Oxford has not been preserved. But there is no record that the students of either university played before the Queen during the season.

1592. December 26 (Tuesday). Hampton Court.

A play before the Queen by the Earl of Pembroke's Company. Payment £10, on warrant dated at St. James's, March 11, 1592–3. (Chambers, *Eliz. Stage*, iv, 164. See also Stopes, *Hunnis*, p. 323; Dasent, *Acts*, xxiv, 113, in which the play is dated December 27; Chalmers, *Apology*, pp. 400–401.)

Pembroke's Men acted again on Twelfth Night. "On one of these dates," writes Professor J. Q. Adams (*Life of Shakespeare*, p. 143), "we may suppose, they acted Shakespeare's new comedy [*Love's Labour's Lost*], which obviously had been composed with the audience at Court in mind."

1592. December 27 (Wednesday). Hampton Court.

A play by Lord Strange's Company. Payment £10, on warrant dated at St. James's, March 7, 1592–3. (Chambers, *Eliz. Stage*, iv, 164. See also Stopes, *Hunnis*, p. 323, in which the payment is incorrectly given; Dasent, *Acts*, xxiv, 102; Chalmers, *Apology*, p. 400.)

According to the Council's warrant, the three plays by Lord Strange's Company, on December 27, 31, and January 1, were presented "before her Majestie at Hampton Courte."

1592. DECEMBER 31 (SUNDAY). HAMPTON COURT.

A play by Lord Strange's Company. Payment £10, on the same warrant as that for the preceding play. (Chambers, *Eliz. Stage*, iv, 164. See also Stopes, *Hunnis*, p. 323; Chalmers, *Apology*, p. 400.)

1592–3. JANUARY 1 (MONDAY). HAMPTON COURT.

A play by Lord Strange's Company. Payment £10, on the same warrant as that for the play of December 27. (Chambers, *Eliz. Stage*, iv, 164. See also Stopes, *Hunnis*, p. 323; Dasent, *Acts*, xxiv, 102; Chalmers, *Apology*, p. 400.)

1592–3. JANUARY 6 (SATURDAY). HAMPTON COURT.

A play by the Earl of Pembroke's Company. Payment £10, on the same warrant as that for their play of December 26. (Chambers, *Eliz. Stage*, iv, 164. See also Stopes, *Hunnis*, p. 323; Dasent, *Acts*, xxiv, 113; Chalmers, *Apology*, pp. 400–1.)

THE SEASON 1593–1594

1593–4. JANUARY 6 (WEDNESDAY). HAMPTON COURT.

A play by the Queen's Company. Payment £10, on warrant dated January 31, 1593–4. (Chambers, *Eliz. Stage*, iv, 164. See also *M. L. R.*, ii, 10; Stopes, *Hunnis*, p. 323; *Jahrbuch*, xxxii, 183.)

The performance is mentioned in the following letter quoted by Chambers (*Eliz. Stage*, iv, 108, *n. 14*):

Mr. [Anthony] Standen was at the play and dancing on twelfth-night, which lasted till one after midnight, more by constraint than by choice, the earl of Essex having committed to him the placing and entertaining of certain Germans. The queen appeared there in a high throne, richly adorned, and "as beautiful," says he, "to my old sight, as ever I saw her; and next to her chair the earl, with whom she often devised in sweet and favourable manner."

Christmas was probably celebrated at Hampton, whither the Queen removed on December 1. (Chambers, *Eliz. Stage*, iv, 108.)

THE SEASON 1594–1595

1594. DECEMBER 26 (THURSDAY). GREENWICH.

A play before the Queen "upon St. Stephens daye" by the Lord Chamberlain's Company (William Kempe, William Shakespeare and Richarde Burbage). Payment £10, on warrant dated at Whitehall, March 15, 1594–5. (Halliwell-Phillipps, *Illustrations*, p. 31. See also Stopes, *Hunnis*, p. 323; *Burbage*, pp. 251–2; Chambers, *M. L. R.*, ii, 11; *Eliz. Stage*, iv, 164.)

The Company acted again the following evening. The names of the plays presented have not come down to us. But one of them, writes Professor J. Q. Adams (*Life of Shakespeare*, p. 209), "may well have been *The Two Gentlemen of Verona*, the courtly style of which would render it highly suitable for performance before Her Majesty. The other, we may guess, was *The Comedy of Errors*, just rewritten by Shakespeare for a great Christmas celebration to be held by the members of Gray's Inn."

The Court was at Greenwich. In the Accounts of the Treasurer of the Chamber are two items, one "for making ready at Grenewich for the Qu. Majestie against her Highnes coming thether, by the space of viij. daies mense Decembr. 1594," and another "to Tho: Sheffielde, under keaper of her Majesties house at Grenewich for thallowaunce of viij. Labourers there three severall nightes, at xij *d.* the man, by reason it was night woorke, for making cleane the greate chamber, the Presence, the galleries and clossettes, mense Decembr. 1594." (Halliwell-Phillipps, *Illustrations*, p. 33.)

1594. DECEMBER 27 (FRIDAY). GREENWICH.

A play before the Queen on "Innocentes daye" by the Lord Chamberlain's Company. Payment £10, on the same warrant as that for the preceding play. (Halliwell-Phillipps, *Illustrations*, p. 31. See also Stopes, *Hunnis*, p. 323; *Burbage*, pp. 251–2; Chambers, *M. L. R.*, ii, 11; *Eliz. Stage*, iv, 161).

"Innocentes daye" is usually regarded as an error for St. John's day, December 27. For the Court was at Greenwich, and we know that on December 28 the Chamberlain's Men acted at Gray's Inn. "The truth seems to be that the Chamberlain's Company performed before the Queen at Greenwich on December 26 and 27, and returned to London for their performance at Gray's Inn on December 28." (Adams, *Life of Shakespeare*, p. 208. *n.*)

1594. DECEMBER 28 (SATURDAY). GREENWICH.

A play by the Admiral's Company (Edwarde Allen, Richarde Jones, John Synger.) Payment £10, on warrant dated at Westminster, March 15, 1595–6. (Chambers, *M. L. R.*, ii, 10; *Eliz. Stage*, iv, 165.)

Three plays by the Admiral's Men are recorded during the season. On two occasions Henslowe enters in his *Diary* the expenditure of 1*s.* 4*d.* which was "Layd owt for my Lorde Admeralle seruantes" in 1594; one item is "for gowinge & cominge to somerset howe for iiij tymes," and the other for "goinge up & downe to corte twise." (*Diary*, ed. by Greg, p. 198.)

1594–5. JANUARY 1 (WEDNESDAY). GREENWICH.

A play by the Admiral's Company. Payment £10, on the same warrant as that for the play of December 28. (Chambers, *Eliz. Stage*, iv, 165; *M. L. R.*, ii, 10).

1594–5. JANUARY 6 (MONDAY). GREENWICH.

A play by the Admiral's Company. Payment £10, on the same warrant as that for the play of December 28. (Chambers, *Eliz. Stage*, iv, 165; *M. L. R.*, ii, 10).

1594–5. JANUARY 26 (SUNDAY). GREENWICH.

Two masques before the Queen at the marriage of William Earl of Derby to Lady Elizabeth Vere?

Arthur Throgmorton, who was out of favor with the Queen, wrote to Robert Cecil:

If I may I mind to come in a masque, brought in by the nine muses, whose music, I hope, shall so modify the easy softened mind of her Majesty as both I and mine may find mercy. The song, the substance I have herewith sent you, myself, whilst the singing, to lie prostrate at her Majesty's feet till she says she will save me. Upon my resurrection the song shall be delivered by one of the muses, with a ring made for a wedding ring set round with diamonds, and with a ruby like a heart placed in a coronet, with this inscription, *Elizabetha potest*. I durst not do this before I had acquainted you herewith, understanding her Majesty had appointed the masquers, which resolution made me the unreadier: yet, if this night I may know her Majesty's leave and your liking, I hope not to come too late, though the time be short for such a show and my preparations posted for such a presence. I desire to come in before the other masque, for I am sorrowful and solemn, and my stay shall not be long. I rest upon your resolution, which must be for this business tonight or not at all. (Quoted from Chambers, *Eliz. Stage*, i, 168.)

1594–5. MARCH 3 OR 4 (SHROVE MONDAY OR TUESDAY). WHITEHALL.

The *Masque of Proteus*, by Gray's Inn. Printed in *Gesta Grayorum: or, the History of the High and mighty Prince, Henry*, "as it was presented (by His Highness's Command) for the Entertainment of Q. Elizabeth; who, with the Nobles of both Courts, was present thereat."

The speeches were written by Francis Davison and others. It is certain from the text that the masque was presented at Shrovetide; but it is difficult to say whether on Monday or Tuesday. For the text see Nichols, *Progresses Elizabeth*, ii; *Gesta Grayorum*, ed. W. W. Greg, Malone Soc. Reprints, 1914.

THE SEASON 1595–1596

1595. DECEMBER 26 (FRIDAY). RICHMOND.

A play before the Queen "on St. Stephens daye at nighte" by Lord Hunsdon's Company (John Hemynge and George Bryan, servauntes to the late Lorde Chamberlayne and now servauntes to the Lord Hunsdon). Payment £10, on warrant dated at Whitehall, December 21, 1596. (Halliwell-Phillipps, *Illustrations*, p. 30. See also Stopes, *Hunnis*, p. 323, in which the date of the warrant is given as December 23; *Burbage*, p. 252; Chambers, *Eliz. Stage*, iv, 165, in which the warrant is dated at Westminster).

The Court removed to Richmond on December 23. (Chambers, *Eliz. Stage*, iv, 110.)

1595. DECEMBER 27 (SATURDAY). RICHMOND.

A play before the Queen on "St. Johns daye" by Lord Hunsdon's Company. Payment £10, on the same warrant as that for the preceding play. (Halliwell-Phillipps, *Illustrations*, p. 30. See also Stopes, *Hunnis*, p. 323; *Burbage*, p. 252; Chambers, *Eliz. Stage*, iv, 165.)

1595. DECEMBER 28 (SUNDAY). RICHMOND.

A play before the Queen on "the sondaye nighte following" by Lord Hunsdon's Company. Payment £10, on the same warrant as that for the play of December 26. (Halliwell-Phillipps, *Illustrations*, p. 30. See also Stopes, *Hunnis*, p. 323; *Burbage*, p. 252; Chambers, *Eliz. Stage*, iv, 165.)

1595–6. JANUARY 1 (THURSDAY). RICHMOND.

A play by the Lord Admiral's Company (Edwarde Allen and Martyn Slater). Payment £10, on warrant dated at Westminster, December 13, 1596. (Chambers, *Eliz. Stage*, iv, 165. See also *M. L. R.*, ii, 11; Stopes, *Hunnis*, p. 323).

1595–6. JANUARY 4 (SUNDAY). RICHMOND.

A play by the Lord Admiral's Company. Payment £10, on the same warrant as that for the preceding play. (Chambers, *Eliz. Stage*, iv, 165. See also *M. L. R.*, ii, 11; Stopes, *Hunnis*, p. 323.)

1595–6. JANUARY 6 (TUESDAY). RICHMOND.

A play before the Queen on "Twelfe Nighte" by Lord Hunsdon's Company. Payment £10, on the same warrant as that for the play of December 26. (Halliwell-Phillipps, *Illustrations*, p. 30. See also Stopes, *Hunnis*, p. 323; *Burbage*, p. 252; Chambers, *Eliz. Stage*, iv, 165.)

1595–6. FEBRUARY 22 (SHROVE SUNDAY).

A play by the Lord Admiral's Company. Payment £10, on the same warrant as that for the play of January 1. (Chambers, *Eliz. Stage*, iv, 165. See also *M. L. R.*, ii, 11; Stopes, *Hunnis*, p. 323.)

1595–6. FEBRUARY 22 (SHROVE SUNDAY).

A play before the Queen "on Shrovesunday at nighte laste" by Lord Hunsdon's Company. Payment £10, on the same warrant as that for the play of December 26. (Halliwell-Phillipps, *Illustrations*, p. 30. See also Stopes, *Hunnis*, p. 323; *Burbage*, 252; Chambers, *Eliz. Stage*, iv, 165.)

1595–6. FEBRUARY 24 (SHROVE TUESDAY).

A play by the Lord Admiral's Company. Payment £10, on the same warrant as that for the play of January 1. (Chambers, *Eliz. Stage*, iv, 165. See also *M. L. R.*, ii, 11; Stopes, *Hunnis*, p. 323.)

THE SEASON 1596–1597

1596. DECEMBER 26 (SUNDAY). WHITEHALL.

A play by the Lord Chamberlain's Company (Thomas Pope and John Hemynges). Payment £10, on warrant dated at Westminster, November 27, 1597. (Chambers, *Eliz. Stage*, iv, 165. See also *M. L. R.*, ii, 11; Stopes, *Hunnis*, p. 323; *Burbage*, p. 252;

Dasent, *Acts*, xxviii, 151, in which dates for the six plays covered by the warrant are not given; Chalmers, *Apology*, p. 401.)

At the time of the performances the Company was really Lord Hunsdon's, as Chambers points out. George Lord Hunsdon became Lord Chamberlain April 17, 1597.

Christmas was probably kept at Whitehall. (Chambers, iv, 110.)

1596. DECEMBER 27 (MONDAY). WHITEHALL.

A play by the Lord Chamberlain's Company. Payment £10, on the same warrant as that for the preceding play. (Chambers, *Eliz. Stage*, iv, 165. See also M. L. R., ii, 11; Stopes, *Hunnis*, p. 323; *Burbage*, p. 252; Dasent, *Acts*, xxviii, 151; Chalmers, *Apology*, p. 401.)

1596–7. JANUARY 1 (SATURDAY). WHITEHALL.

A play by the Lord Chamberlain's Company. Payment £10, on the same warrant as that for the play of December 26. (Chambers, *Eliz. Stage*, iv, 165. See also M. L. R., ii, 11; Stopes, *Hunnis*, p. 323; *Burbage*, p. 252; Dasent, *Acts*, xxviii, 151; Chalmers, *Apology*, p. 401.)

1596–7. JANUARY 6 (THURSDAY). WHITEHALL.

A play by the Lord Chamberlain's Company. Payment £10, on the same warrant as that for the play of December 26. (Chambers, *Eliz. Stage*, iv, 165. See also M. L. R., ii, 11; Stopes, *Hunnis*, p. 323; *Burbage*, p. 252; Dasent, *Acts*, xxviii, 151; Chalmers, *Apology*, p. 401.)

1596–7. FEBRUARY 6 (SHROVE SUNDAY). WHITEHALL.

A play by the Lord Chamberlain's Company. Payment £10, on the same warrant as that for the play of December 26. (Chambers, *Eliz. Stage*, iv, 165. See also M. L. R., ii, 11; Stopes, *Hunnis*, p. 323; *Burbage*, p. 252; Dasent, *Acts*, xxviii, 151; Chalmers, *Apology*, p. 401.)

1596–7. FEBRUARY 8 (SHROVE TUESDAY). WHITEHALL.

A play by the Lord Chamberlain's Company. Payment £10, on the same warrant as that for the play of December 26 (Chambers, *Eliz. Stage*, iv, 165. See also *M. L. R.*, ii, 11; Stopes, *Hunnis*, p. 323; *Burbage*, p. 252; Dasent, *Acts*, xxviii, 151, in which the performance is dated Shrove Monday; Chalmers, *Apology*, p. 401.)

THE SEASON 1597–1598

1597. DECEMBER 26 (MONDAY). WINDSOR.

A play by the Lord Chamberlain's Company (John Heminges and Thomas Pope). Payment £10, on warrant dated at Westminster, December 3, 1598. (Chambers, *Eliz. Stage*, iv, 165; See also *M. L. R.*, ii, 11; Dasent, *Acts*, xxix, 324; Chalmers, *Apology*, p. 401.)

Professor Adams (*Life of Shakespeare*, p. 232) suggests that the two parts of *Henry IV*, then new, were probably presented before the Queen by the Lord Chamberlain's men during the Christmas festivities, which were held at Windsor. It is possible, too, he adds (pp. 232–3) that the *Merry Wives of Windsor*, which according to tradition was written in two weeks at the command of the Queen, was completed in order to be presented as a part of the season's festivities.

According to the title-page of the quarto of 1598, *Love's Labour's Lost* "was presented before her Highnes this last Christmas. Newly corrected and augmented By W. Shakespeare."

Payment was made, as the entries show, to the Chamberlain's Company for four plays. It is possible that all these were by Shakespeare.

1597. DECEMBER 27 (TUESDAY). WINDSOR.

A play by the Earl of Nottingham's [Admiral's] Company. (Robert Shawe and Thomas Downton). Payment £10, on warrant dated at Westminster, December 3, 1598. (Chambers, *Eliz. Stage*, iv, 165. See also *M. L. R.*, ii, 11; Dasent, *Acts*, xxix, 325; Chalmers, *Apology*, p. 401.)

1597–8. JANUARY 1 (SUNDAY). WINDSOR.

A play by the Lord Chamberlain's Company. Payment £10, on the same warrant as that for the play of December 26. (Chambers, *Eliz. Stage*, iv, 165. See also *M. L. R.*, ii, 11; Dasent, *Acts*, xxix, 324; Chalmers, *Apology*, p. 401.)

1597–8. JANUARY 6 (FRIDAY). WINDSOR.

A play by the Lord Chamberlain's Company. Payment £10, on the same warrant as that for the play of December 26. (Chambers, *Eliz. Stage*, iv, 165. See also *M. L. R.*, ii, 11; Dasent, *Acts*, xxix, 324; Chalmers, *Apology*, p. 401.)

1597–8? JANUARY 6 (FRIDAY).

A Masque of the Nine Passions, performed at Court by the gentlemen of the Middle Temple.

The masque is described by Sir Benjamin Rudyerd in *Noctes Templariae*, an account of the Christmas festivities of the Middle Temple, dated "anno ab aula condita 27":

Wednesday, the Prince's Excellence [the Lord of Misrule] was invited to the Lord Mayor's, and expected; but hee deferd his comming because of the preparation for barriers and a mask to the Court. Thursday was also spent in that business. Uppon Friday, being twelf day, att night there went to the Court 11 Knights and 11 Squires, 9 maskers, 9 torch-bearers; theyr setting forth was with a peale of ordinance, a noyse of trumpets allways sounding before them; the heralds next; after, 2 Squires and 2 Knights; the Knights for theyr upper parts in bright armour, theyr hose of cloth of gold and cloth of silver; the Squires in jerkins laced with gold and silver, and theyr hose as faire; all uppon greate horses, all richly furnished. Then came the maskers by couples, on velvet foote-cloths, theyr short cloaks and doublets, and those of cloth of gold and silver of the several colours, representing 9 several passions; to every masker a torch bearer on a foote-cloth, carrying his device, besides a 100 torches borne by servants. Never any Prince in this kingdome, or the like, made soe glorious, soe rich a shew.

When they came to Court, the Knights brake every man his lance and two swords; the 9 maskers like passions issued out of a hart: all was fortunately performed, and received great commendations." (J. A. Manning, *Memoirs of Sir Benjamin Rudyerd*, p. 14.)

There is some difficulty in the date. Since the hall of the Middle Temple was built in 1572, Rudyerd seems to be referring to the festivities of 1599–1600. But Twelfth Night of this season fell on Sunday, not Friday. And the Court was at Richmond. The year 1597–8 fits the week-day, but the Court was at Windsor.

1597–8. FEBRUARY 26 (SHROVE SUNDAY).

A play by the Lord Chamberlain's Company. Payment £10, on the same warrant as that for the play of December 26. (Chambers, *Eliz. Stage*, iv, 165. See also *M. L. R.*, ii, 11; Dasent, *Acts*, xxix, 324; Chalmers, *Apology*, p. 401.)

1597–8. FEBRUARY 28 (SHROVE TUESDAY).

A play by the Earl of Nottingham's [Admiral's] Company. Payment £10, on the same warrant as that for the play of December 27. (Chambers, *Eliz. Stage*, iv, 165. See also *M. L. R.*, ii, 11; Dasent, *Acts*, xxix, 325; Chalmers, *Apology*, p. 401.)

On January 3, 1597–8, Henslowe "layd owt for my lord admeralles meane" 29*s*. for copper lace and a veil "for the boye a geanste the playe of *dido & enevs*," and on January 8 "lent vnto the company when they fyrst played *dido* at nyght the some of" 30*s*. (*Diary*, ed. by Greg, p. 83.) Possibly these items indicate a court performance. But neither date on which the Admiral's Men are known to have acted at Court this season is appropriate.

THE SEASON 1598–1599

1598. SEPTEMBER. CROYDON.

A play before the Queen by the Admiral's Company?

On September 27 Henslowe lent 5*s*. to William Borne [Birde] "when he Reade to croyden to ther lorde when the quene came thether." (*Diary*, ed. by Greg, p. 72.)

"It appears," says Greg (ii, 95) "that the Queen was at Croyden and that on 27 Sept. the company rode down to 'ther lorde,' i. e. Nottingham, presumably for the purpose of giving a performance." No mention of the Queen's being at Croydon at this time, however, has been discovered.

1598. DECEMBER 26 (TUESDAY). WHITEHALL.

A play before the Queen "on St. Stephens daye at night" by the Lord Chamberlain's Company (John Heming and Thomas Pope). Payment £10, on warrant dated at Nonesuch, October 2, 1599. (Cunningham, *Revels*, p. xxxii. See also Stopes, *Burbage*, p. 252; Chambers, *Eliz. Stage*, iv, 166.)

"The Queene is resolved to kepe Christmas at Whitehall," wrote Chamberlain to Carleton, December 20, 1598. (*Letters*, ed. by Williams, p. 33.)

1598. DECEMBER 27 (WEDNESDAY). WHITEHALL.

A play by the Earl of Nottingham's [Admiral's] Company (Robert Shawe and Thomas Downton). Payment £6. 13s. 4d., on warrant dated at Nonesuch, October 2, 1599. (Chambers, *Eliz. Stage*, iv, 166. See also *M. L. R.*, ii, 11.)

The Admiral's Men acted also on January 6, and again on February 18. Possibly on one of these occasions they presented *Robin Hood* [*The Downfall of Robert, Earl of Huntingdon*]. On November 25 Henslowe gave Henry Chettle xs. "for mendinge of *Roben hood* for the corte." (*Diary*, ed. by Greg, p. 99.)

1598–9. JANUARY 1 (MONDAY). WHITEHALL.

A play before the Queen on "Newyears daye at night" by the Lord Chamberlain's Company. Payment £10, on the same warrant as that for the play of December 26. (Cunningham, *Revels*, p. xxxii. See also Stopes, *Burbage*, p. 252; Chambers, *Eliz. Stage*, iv, 166.)

1598–9. JANUARY 6 (SATURDAY). WHITEHALL.

A play by the Earl of Nottingham's [Admiral's] Company. Payment £6. 13s. 4d., on the same warrant as that for the play of December 27. (Chambers, *Eliz. Stage*, iv, 166.)

1598–9. FEBRUARY 18 (SHROVE SUNDAY). RICHMOND.

A play by the Earl of Nottingham's [Admiral's] Company. Payment £6. 13s. 4d., on the same warrant as that for the play of December 27. (Chambers, *Eliz. Stage*, iv, 166. See also *M.L.R.*, ii, 11.)

"The Quene removed to Richmont on Satterday last," wrote Chamberlain to Carleton, February 15, 1598–9. (*Letters*, ed. by Williams, p. 45.)

1598–9. FEBRUARY 20 (SHROVE TUESDAY). RICHMOND.

A play before the Queen on "Shrouetewsday at night last past" by the Lord Chamberlain's Company. Payment £10, on the same warrant as that for the play of December 26. (Cunningham, *Revels*, p. xxxii. See also Stopes, *Burbage*, p. 252; Chambers, *Eliz. Stage*, iv, 166.)

1599. APRIL 7 (SATURDAY).

A play at Court by the Admiral's Company?

Henslowe lent Thomas Towne and Richard Allen 10s. "to go to the corte vpon ester euen." (*Diary*, ed. by Greg, p. 104.)

THE SEASON 1599–1600

Christmas, and probably Shrovetide, were kept at Richmond. The warrant from the Earl of Nottingham for the building of the Fortune Theatre, in which is mentioned the "acceptable Service" of the Admiral's Company to the Queen "aswell this last Christmas as att sondrie other tymes" is dated "att the Courte at Richmond the xij^th of Januarye 1599." Diplomatic correspondence shows that the Court was still at Richmond on March 2. See Winwood, *Memorials of Affairs of State* (1725), i, 157.

1599. DECEMBER 26 (WEDNESDAY). RICHMOND.

A play before the Queen "on St Stephens daye at night" by the Lord Chamberlain's Company (John Heming). Payment £10, on warrant dated at Richmond, February 17, 1599–1600. (Cunningham, Revels, pp. xxxii-xxxiii. See also Stopes, *Burbage*, p. 252; Chambers, *Eliz. Stage*, iv, 166; Dasent, *Acts*, xxx, 89, in which the warrant is dated February 18; Chalmers, *Apology*, p. 401.)

1599. DECEMBER 27 (THURSDAY). RICHMOND.

The Pleasant Comedie of Old Fortunatus. As it was plaied before the Queenes Maiestie this Christmas, by the Right Honourable the Earle of Nottingham, Lord high Admirall of England his Seruants. London. 1600.

This play was thoroughly revised by Thomas Dekker in November and December. For the last alteration, "for the eande of *fortewnatus* for the corte at the a poynment of Robarte shawe" he received 40s. (*Henslowe's Diary*, ed. by Greg, p. 116.) Shortly before, Downton had received £10 from Henslowe "for the vse of the Companye . . . ffor to by thinges for *ffortunatus*" (*ibid.*, p. 115), probably for the court performance.

£10 was paid, on a warrant dated at Richmond, February 18, 1599–1600, for a play before the Queen "on S[t]. Johnes daye at night" by the Earl of Nottingham's Company (Robert Shaw). (Cunningham, *Revels*, p. xxxiii. See also Chambers, *Eliz. Stage*, iv, 166; Dasent, *Acts*, xxx, 89, in which the name of the payee is given as "John Shawe"; Chalmers, *Apology*, p. 401.)

Since only two plays by the Admiral's Men are recorded, and the *Shoemaker's Holiday* was given on New Year's, it is probable that *Old Fortunatus* was performed on December 27.

1599–1600. JANUARY 1 (TUESDAY). RICHMOND.

The Shomakers Holiday. Or The Gentle Craft. With the humorous life of Simon Eyre, shoomaker, and Lord Maior of London. As it was acted before the Queenes most excellent Maiestie on New yeares day at night last, by the right honourable the Earle of Notingham, Lord high Admirall of England, his seruants. London. 1600.

£10 was paid, on the same warrant as that for the play of December 27, for a play before the Queen on "Newyeares daye at night last" by the Earl of Nottingham's Company. (Cunningham, *Revels*, p. xxxiii. See also Chambers, *Eliz. Stage*, iv, 166; Dasent, *Acts*, xxx, 89; Chalmers, *Apology*, p. 401.)

1599–1600. JANUARY 6 (SUNDAY). RICHMOND.

A play before the Queen on "Twelfdaye at night" by the Lord Chamberlain's Company. Payment £10, on the same warrant as that for the play of December 26. (Cunningham, *Revels*, pp. xxxii-xxxiii. See also Chambers, *Eliz. Stage*, iv, 166; Stopes, *Burbage*, p. 252; Dasent, *Acts*, xxx, 89; Chalmers, *Apology*, p. 401.)

1599–1600. FEBRUARY 3 (SHROVE SUNDAY). [RICHMOND.]

A play before the Queen on "Shrouesonday at night last past" by the Lord Chamberlain's Company. Payment £10, on the same warrant as that for the play of December 26. (Cunningham, *Revels*, pp. xxxii-xxxiii. See also Stopes, *Burbage*, p. 252; Chambers, *Eliz. Stage*, iv, 166; Dasent, *Acts*, xxx, 89; Chalmers, *Apology*, p. 401.)

1599–1600. FEBRUARY 5 (SHROVE TUESDAY). [RICHMOND.]

A play before the Queen "on Shrove Tuesday at night" by the Earl of Derby's Company (Robert Browne). Payment £10, on warrant dated February 18, 1599–1600. (Dasent, *Acts*, xxx, 89. See also Chalmers, *Apology*, pp. 401–2; Chambers, *Eliz. Stage*, iv, 166, in which the date is given as February 3.)

1600. APRIL 27 (SUNDAY). WINDSOR.

A play by the Admiral's Company?

Henslowe lent the Admiral's Company 50s "to goo winswarth to the installinge the 27. of Aprell 1600." (*Diary*, ed. by Greg, p. 120.) This, says Greg, "presumably indicates a performance at Windsor on the occasion of an installation of Knights of the Garter." According to Sir N. H. Nicholas (*History of the Order of Knighthood*, 1842, i, 209) there was no installation in 1600.

SUMMER, 1600

1600. JUNE 16 (MONDAY). BLACKFRIARS.

A Masque of Muses, at the marriage of the Lady Anne Russell to Henry Lord Herbert.

Chamberlain wrote to Carleton, June 13: "We shall have the great marriage on Monday at the Lady Russells, where it is saide the Quene will vouchsafe her presence." Again on June 24 he wrote: "I doubt not but you have heard of the great marriage at the Lady Russells, where the Quene was present, being carried from the water side in a curious chaire and lodged at the Lord Cobham's; and of the maske of the Muses that came to seeke one of their fellowes." (*Letters*, ed. by Williams, pp. 79, 83.)

There is a confusion of dates in the court correspondence. Rowland White, writing to Sir Robert Sidney on June 14, speaks of the marriage as having taken place "this day se'night." (Nichols, ii.)

THE SEASON 1600–1601

1600. DECEMBER 26 (FRIDAY). WHITEHALL.

A play before the Queen "on St Stephens day at night" by the Lord Chamberlain's Company (John Hemynges and Richard Cowley). Payment £10, on warrant dated at Whitehall, March 31, 1601. (Cunningham, *Revels*, p. xxxiii. See also Chambers, *Eliz. Stage*, iv, 166, in which the warrant is dated at Westminster; Stopes, *Burbage*, p. 252; Dasent, *Acts*, xxxi, 217, in which the warrant is dated March 11, and the plays which it covers "Christmas last"; Chalmers, *Apology*, p. 402.)

On December 22, 1600, Chamberlain wrote from London to Carleton, "The Court is settled here for all Christmas." (*Letters*, ed. by Williams, p. 97.)

1600. DECEMBER 28 (SUNDAY). WHITEHALL.

A play before the Queen "On Innocents day at night" by the Lord Admiral's Company (Edwarde Allen). Payment £10, on warrant dated at Whitehall, March 31, 1601. (Cunningham, *Revels*, p. xxxiii. See also Chambers, *Eliz. Stage*, iv, 166, in which the warrant is dated at Westminster.)

1600–1. JANUARY 1 (THURSDAY). WHITEHALL.

A play by the Earl of Derby's Company (Roberte Browne). Payment £10, on warrant dated at Westminster, March 31, 1601. (Chambers, *Eliz. Stage*, iv, 166. See also *M. L. R.*, ii, 12.)

1600–1. JANUARY 1 (THURSDAY). WHITEHALL.

A play by the Children of Paul's (Edwarde Peers). Payment £10, on warrant dated at Greenwich, June 24, 1601. (Chambers, *Eliz. Stage*, iv, 166. See also Dasent, *Acts*, xxxi, 453; Chalmers, *Apology*, p. 363.)

1600–1. JANUARY 6 (TUESDAY). WHITEHALL.

A play before the Queen on "Twelfth day at night" by the Lord Chamberlain's Company. Payment £10, on the same warrant as that for the play of December 26. (Cunningham, *Revels*, p. xxxiii. See also Chambers, *Eliz. Stage*, iv, 166; Stopes, *Burbage*, p. 252; Dasent, *Acts*, xxxi, 217; Chalmers, *Apology*, p. 402.)

Besides three plays, the Queen had also on Twelfth Night, unless the records are in error, "a show wth musycke and speciall songs prepared for ye purpose on Twelfth day at night" by the Children of the Chapel, for which they were paid £5 on May 4, 1601. (Cunningham, *op. cit.*, p. xxxiii; See also *Chambers*, iv, 166.)

Chambers is of the opinion that *Cynthia's Revels* was presented by them on this occasion. He writes: "I feel little doubt that the play was the subject of the Chapel presentation on 6 Jan. 1601, and the description of this by the Treasurer of the Chamber as including a 'show,' which puzzled Small, is explained by the presence of a full-blown Court mask in v. vii-x." (*Eliz. Stage*, iii, 364.)

1600–1. JANUARY 6 (TUESDAY). WHITEHALL.

A play before the Queen on "Twelfth day at night" by the Lord Admiral's Company. Payment £10, on the same warrant as that for the play of December 28. (Cunningham, *Revels*, p. xxxiii. See also Chambers, *Eliz. Stage*, iv, 166.)

The Admiral's Men played again on Candlemas day. On one of these occasions it is likely that they presented *Phaeton*. Dekker had been paid £2, December 14–22, for altering the play "for the corte," and on January 2 Henslowe lent William Birde xxs. "for diuers thinges a bowt the playe of *fayeton* for the corte." (*Diary*, ed. by Greg, pp. 124, 125.)

1600–1. JANUARY 6 (TUESDAY). WHITEHALL.

A play by the Earl of Derby's Company. Payment £10, on the same warrant as that for the play of January 1. (Chambers, *Eliz. Stage*, iv, 166. See also *M. L. R.*, ii, 12.)

1600–1. FEBRUARY 2 (MONDAY). WHITEHALL.

A play before the Queen on "Candelmas day at night last paste" by the Lord Admiral's Company. Payment £10, on the same warrant as that for the play of December 28. (Cunningham, *Revels*, p. xxxiii. See also Chambers, *Eliz. Stage*, iv, 166.)

1600–1. FEBRUARY 22 (SHROVE SUNDAY). WHITEHALL.

A play before the Queen "on Shrouesondaye at night" by the Children of the Chapel (Nathaniel Gyles). Payment £10, on warrant dated at Whitehall, May 4, 1601. (Cunningham, *Revels*, p. xxxiii. See also Chambers, *Eliz. Stage*, iv, 166, in which the warrant is dated at Westminster.)

1600–1. FEBRUARY 24 (SHROVE TUESDAY). WHITEHALL.

A play before the Queen on "Shrovetuesday at night" by the Lord Chamberlain's Company. Payment £10, on the same warrant as that for the play on December 26. (Cunningham, *Revels*, p. xxxiii. See also Stopes, *Burbage*, p. 252; Chambers, *Eliz. Stage*, iv, 166; Dasent, *Acts*, xxxi, 217; Chalmers, *Apology*, p. 402.)

THE SEASON 1601–1602

1601. DECEMBER 26 (SATURDAY). WHITEHALL.

A play by the Lord Chamberlain's Company (John Hemyng). Payment £10, on warrant dated at Richmond, February 28,

1601–2. (Chambers, *Eliz. Stage*, iv, 167. See also *M. L. R.*, ii, 12.)

Christmas was kept at Whitehall. On December 29 Chamberlain wrote from London to Carleton: "There has been such a small court this Christmas that the guard were not troubled to keep doors at the plays and pastimes." (*Cal. State Papers, Domestic*, 1601–1603, p. 136.)

1601. DECEMBER 27 (SUNDAY). WHITEHALL.

A play by the Lord Chamberlain's Company. Payment £10, on the same warrant as that for the play of December 26. (Chambers, *Eliz. Stage*, iv, 167. See also *M. L. R.*, ii, 12.)

1601. DECEMBER 27 (SUNDAY). WHITEHALL.

A play by the Admiral's [Nottingham's] Company (Edward Allen). Payment £10, on warrant dated at Richmond, February 28, 1601–2. (Chambers, *Eliz. Stage*, iv, 167. See also *M. L. R.*, ii, 12.)

1601. DECEMBER 29 (TUESDAY). BLACKFRIARS.

A play before the Queen at the Lord Chamberlain's house, in Blackfriars.

On December 29 Chamberlain wrote to Carleton: "The Queen dined to-day privately at my Lord Chamberlain's. I have just come from the Blackfriars, where I saw her at the play with all her *candidae auditrices*." (*Cal. State Papers, Domestic*, 1601–1603, p. 136. See also Adams, *Shakespearean Playhouses*, p. 212, *n.*)

1601–2. JANUARY 1 (FRIDAY). WHITEHALL.

A play by the Lord Chamberlain's Company. Payment £10, on the same warrant as that for the play of December 26. (Chambers, *Eliz. Stage*, iv, 166. See also *M. L. R.*, ii, 12.)

1601–2. JANUARY 3 (SUNDAY). WHITEHALL.

A play by the Earl of Worcester's Company (William Kempe and Thomas Heywoode). Payment £10, on warrant dated at Richmond, February 28, 1601–2. (Chambers, *Eliz. Stage*, iv, 167. See also *M. L. R.*, ii, 12.)

1601–2. JANUARY 6 (WEDNESDAY). WHITEHALL.

A play by the Children of the Chapel (Nathanyell Gyles). Payment £10, on warrant dated at Richmond, March 7, 1601–2. (Chambers, *Eliz. Stage*, iv, 167. See also *M. L. R.*, ii, 12.)

1601–2. JANUARY 10 (SUNDAY). WHITEHALL.

A play by the Children of the Chapel. Payment £10, on the same warrant as that for the preceding play. (Chambers, *Eliz. Stage*, iv, 167. See also *M. L. R.*, ii, 12.)

1601–2. FEBRUARY 14 (SHROVE SUNDAY). WHITEHALL.

A play by the Lord Chamberlain's Company. Payment £10, on the same warrant as that for the play of December 26. (Chambers, *Eliz. Stage*, iv, 167. See also *M. L. R.*, ii, 12.)

1601–2. FEBRUARY 14 (SHROVE SUNDAY). WHITEHALL.

A play by the Children of the Chapel. Payment £10, on the same warrant as that for the play of January 6. (Chambers, *Eliz. Stage*, iv, 167. See also *M. L. R.*, ii, 12, where it is ascribed to the Earl of Worcester's Company.)

The Court was at Whitehall until February 19. (Chambers, iv, 114.)

THE SEASON 1602–1603

On December 23, 1602, Chamberlain wrote to Carleton from London:

These feastings have had theire effect to stay the Court here this Christmas, though most of the cariages were well onward on theire waye to Richmond . . . . There is no shew of any great doings at Court this Christmas. (*Letters*, ed. by Williams, pp. 170–171.)

Nevertheless, the Court "flourished more than ordinary," as he wrote to Winwood on January 17, after the festivities were over:

The world hath not ben altogether so dull and dead this Christmas as was suspected, but rather the Court hath flourisht more than ordinarie, whether it be that the new Controller [Sir Edward Wotton] hath put new life into it by his example (being allwayes freshly attired, and for the most part all in white *cap à pied*), or that the humors of themselves grow more gallant; for, besides much dauncing, beare baiting, and many playes, there hath ben great golden play, wherin Mr. Secretarie lost better than 800*l.* in one night. (*Ibid.*, p. 172.)

[1602]. NOVEMBER 2 (TUESDAY).

A masque at Court.

The verses which constitute the second entry in Manningham's *Diary* are entitled, "Songs to the Queene at the Maske at Court. Nov. 2."

1602. DECEMBER 26 (SATURDAY). WHITEHALL.

A play before the Queen "uppon St Stephens day at nighte" by the Lord Chamberlain's Company (John Hemynges). Payment £10, on warrant dated Whitehall, April 20, 1603. (Cunningham, *Revels*, p. xxxiv. See also Stopes, *Burbage*, p. 253; Chambers, *Eliz. Stage*, iv, 167, in which the warrant is dated at Westminster.)

1602. DECEMBER 27 (SUNDAY). WHITEHALL.

A play before the Queen "upon St Johns day at night" by the Lord Admiral's Company (Edwarde Allen). Payment £10, on warrant dated at Whitehall, April 22, 1603. (Cunningham, *Revels*, p. xxxiv; Chambers, *Eliz. Stage*, iv, 167, in which the warrant is dated at Westminster.)

The Admiral's Men presented three plays this season. It is probable that two of them were *As Merry as May Be*, and *Friar Bacon and Friar Bungay*. On November 9 Henslowe lent Edward Juby 40*s.* "to geue vnto John daye in earneste of a Boocke called *mery as may be* for the corte," and on November 17 he lent Thomas Downton £6 "to paye untoJohn daye & m^r smythe & hathwaye in fulle paymente for" the same play. (*Diary*, ed. by Greg, p. 171.)

On December 14 Henslowe also lent Downton 5*s.* to be paid to Middleton "for a prologe & a epeloge for the playe of *bacon* for the corte." (*Ibid.*, p. 172.)

A third play intended by the Admiral's Men for the Court is unnamed. On December 29 Henslowe lent Downton 5*s.* to be paid to Chettle "for a prologe & a epyloge for the corte." (*Ibid.*, p. 173.) Fleay (*Stage*, p. 124) and Murray (*English Dramatic Companies*, i, 138 and *n.*) identify the last-mentioned play with the *London Florentine*, apparently because in the *Diary* the payment to Chettle follows several entries which relate to that play.

1602–3. Date Uncertain.

A play at Court by the Earl of Worcester's Company?

On January 1, 1602–3, Henslowe lent John Thayer 10*s.* "to geue vnto m^{rs} calle for ij cvrenetes for hed tyers for the corte." (*Diary*, ed. by Greg. p. 186.)

1602–3. January 1 (Saturday). Whitehall.

A play by the Children of Paul's (Edward Piers). Payment £10, on warrant dated at Greenwich, May 31, 1602. (Chambers, *Eliz. Stage*, iv, 167. See also *M. L. R.*, ii, 12.)

1602–3. January 6 (Thursday). Whitehall.

A play by the Earl of Hertford's Company (Martyn Slater). Payment £10, on warrant dated April 20, 1602. (Chambers, *Eliz. Stage*, iv, 167. See also *M. L. R.*, ii, 167.)

1602–3. February 2 (Wednesday). Richmond.

A play before the Queen "upon Candlemas day at night" by the Lord Chamberlain's Company. Payment £10, on the same warrant as that for the play of December 26. (Cunningham, *Revels*, p. xxxiv. See also Chambers, *Eliz. Stage*, iv, 167; Stopes, *Burbage*, p. 253.)

On January 27 Chamberlain wrote to Carleton from London: "The Court removed hence to Richmond the 21th of this moneth in very fowle and wet weather." (*Letters*, ed. by Williams, p. 174.)

1602–3. MARCH 6 (SHROVE SUNDAY). RICHMOND.

A play before the Queen on "Shrouesonday at night" by the Lord Admiral's Company. Payment £10, on the same warrant as that for the play of December 27. (Cunningham, *Revels*, p. xxxiv; Chambers, *Eliz. Stage*, iv, 167.)

1602–3. DATE UNCERTAIN.

A play before the Queen on "———— at nighte laste before the date aforedsaide" [i. e. Shrove Sunday?] by the Admiral's Company. Payment £10, on the same warrant as that for the play of December 27. (Cunningham, *Revels*, p. xxxiv. See also Chambers, *Eliz. Stage*, iv, 167.)

MISCELLANEOUS COURT PERFORMANCES OF UNCERTAIN DATE

The *Araygnement of Paris A Pastorall. Presented before the Queenes Maiestie, by the Children of her Chappell.* London. 1584.

By George Peele. The court performance is dated by Ward (*History of Dramatic Literature*, i, 205) 1584.

The *Rare Triumphs of Loue and Fortune. Plaide before the Queenes most excellent Maiestie: wherein are many fine Conceites with great delight.* London. 1589.

Schelling (*Elizabethan Drama*, i, 122-3) suggests that the play may be identified with the *Play of Fortune* mentioned in the Revels Accounts of 1572. Compare, also, *The Triumph of Love and Bewte* written by William Cornyshe and presented before Henry VIII in 1515. (J. P. Collier, *History of English Dramatic Poetry*, 1879, i, 69).

Endimion, The Man in the Moone. Playd before the Queenes Maiestie at Greenewich on Candlemas day at night, by the Chyldren of Paules. London. 1591.

By John Lyly. Entered S. R. October 4, 1591. Bond (*Works*, ii, 230) and Feuillerat (*John Lyly*, p. 577) assign the court performance to 1585-6; Chambers (*Eliz. Stage*, iv, 415) prefers 1588.

The Tragedie of Tancred and Gismund. Compiled by the Gentlemen of the Inner Temple, and by them presented before her Maiestie. Newly reuiued and polished according to the decorum of these daies. By R. W. [Robert Wilmot.] London. 1591.

Internal evidence, according to Chambers (*Eliz. Stage*, iii, 514) points to a performance at Greenwich in 1567.

Midas. Plaied before the Queenes Maiestie upon Twelfe day at night. By the Children of Paules. London. 1592.

By John Lyly. Entered S. R. October 4, 1591. Feuillerat (*Lyly*, p. 578) suggests 1588–9 as the date of the court performance. Fleay (*Drama*, ii, 42), Bond (*Works*, ii, 230), and Chambers (*Eliz. Stage*, iii, 416) incline to 1589–90.

The Woman in the Moone. As it was presented before her Highnesse. By Iohn Lyllie maister of Artes. London. 1597.

Entered S. R. September 17, 1595. R. W. Bond (*Works*, ii, 230) assigns the court performance to 1593–5; Feuillerat (*John Lyly*, p. 580) to 1593–4.

Every Man Out of his Humour. Ben Jonson.

There is a court epilogue, addressed to Queen Elizabeth. The play was first acted in 1599, and the performance before the Queen doubtless took place soon after. For a discussion of the arrangement of the epilogues in the first quarto and the first folio, see Chambers, *Eliz. Stage*, iii, 361–2.

A Pleasant Comedie, called Summers last will and Testament. Written by Thomas Nash. London. 1600.

Internal evidence, according to R. B. McKerrow (*Works of Thomas Nashe*, iv, 416), points to a performance of this play before Archbishop Whitgift, in his palace at Croydon, in the autumn of 1592. And other internal evidence (see lines 124–38, 388–403, and 1840–62) shows seemingly beyond question that it was also presented before the Queen on a progress. Since, however, the Queen is not known to have been in Croydon in 1592, and since the play shows signs of having been revised, McKerrow suggests that while it was originally written for performance before Whitgift, "on a later occasion, perhaps on Aug. 14, 1600, when the Queen visited the Archbishop at Croydon, it was brought out again, somewhat revised, and two or three speeches in praise of the Queen added."

A Pleasant Comedie Shewing the contention betweene Liberalitie and Prodigalitie. As it was playd before her Maiestie. London. 1602.

The author is unknown. Fleay (*Drama*, ii, 288) is convinced that this play is not to be identified with the *Prodigality* of 1567/1567-8. Chambers, however (*Eliz. Stage*, iv, 26), thinks it not impossible that it was a revival, and suggests February 22, 1600-1, as a possible date of performance.

A play of Tarleton's before the Queen.

The play is mentioned by Edmund Bohun, in his *Character of Queen Elizabeth:*

At supper she would divert herself with her friends and attendants; and if they made her no answer, she would put them upon mirth and a pleasant discourse with great civility. She would then also admit Tarleton, a famous comedian, and a pleasant talker, and other such like men, to divert her with stories of the town, and the common jests or accidents; but so that they kept within the bounds of modesty and chastity. In the winter-time, after supper, she would sometime hear a song, or a lesson or two played upon the lute; but she would be much offended if there was any rudeness to any person, any reproach or licentious reflection used. Tarleton, who was then the best comedian in England, had made a pleasant play; and when it was acted before the Queen, he pointed at Sir Walter Rawleigh, and said, "See the Knave commands the Queen"; for which he was corrected by a frown from the Queen; yet he had the confidence to add, that he was of too much and too intolerable a power; and, going on with the same liberty he reflected on the over-great power and riches of the Earl of Leicester, which was so universally applauded by all that were present. that she thought fit for the present to bear these reflections with a seeming unconcernedness. But yet she was so offended, that she forbad Tarleton, and all her jesters, from coming near her table, being inwardly displeased with this impudent and unreasonable liberty. (Nichols, *Progresses Elizabeth*, ii.)

A masque at Court by Gray's Inn?

Bound up with Lord Burghley's papers in the Landsdowne MSS. is the following undated letter of Francis Bacon's:

Yt may please yor good L. I am sory the joynt maske from the fowr Innes of Cowrt faileth. Whearin I conceyue thear is no other grownd of that euent, but impossibility. Neuerthelesse bycause it falleth owt that at this tyme Graies Inne is well furnyshed, of galant yowng gentlemen, yor lordship may be pleased to know, that rather then this occasion shall passe withowt some demonstration of affection from the Inns of Cowrt, Thear are a dozen gentlemen of Graies Inne, that owt of the honor which they bear to yor l., and my l. Chamberlayne to whome at theyr last maske they were so much bownde, will be ready to furnysh a maske wyshing it were in their powers to perform it according to theyr mynd. And so for the p^rsent I humbly take my leaue resting

lordships
yor very humbly
and much bownde
Fr. Bacon

[Endorsed] "M^r Fr. Bacon." (Chambers, E. K., and W. W. Greg, "Dramatic Records from the Landsdowne MSS.," Malone Soc. *Collections*, I, 2, pp. 214–5. See also Collier, *History of English Dramatic Poetry*, i, 262; J. Spedding, *Works of Bacon*, ii, 370; iv, 394.)

Evidently the letter belongs to the Eliżabethan period. For, as Chambers points out, Bacon was knighted on July 23, 1603, and after that time would scarcely have been referred to as "Mr. Fr. Bacon."

THE REIGN OF JAMES I
1603-1625

THE REIGN OF JAMES I

THE SEASON 1603–1604

1603. SEPTEMBER 20–OCTOBER 6. WINCHESTER.

An "interlude."

Arabella Stuart, in a letter to the Earl of Shrewsbury, December 8, 1603, after describing the childish games played by the ladies of the Court when she was at Winchester, says: "There was an interlude, but not so ridiculous (ridiculous as it was) as my letter, which I now conclude." (*Notes and Queries*, 2nd Series, x, 461.)

1603. SEPTEMBER 20–OCTOBER 17. WINCHESTER.

A masque of the Queen's, in honor of the arrival of Prince Henry at Winchester. (Nichols, *Progresses James*, i, 291. See also Reyher, *Masques Anglais*, p. 519.)

1603–4. DATE UNCERTAIN. HAMPTON.

"*The Faire Maide of Bristow. As it was plaide at Hampton, before the King and Queenes most excellent Maiesties.* London. 1605.

It was entered on the Stationers' Register February 8, 1604–5. Fleay says: "*The Fair Maid of Bristol* was one of the 1603–4 plays presented by the King's Men at Hampton Court before the King and Queen." (*Stage*, p. 177.)

1603. DECEMBER 2 (FRIDAY). WILTON.

A play before the King "on the second of December last" by the King's Company (John Hemyngs). Payment £30, on warrant dated at Wilton, December 3, 1603. The unusually large sum was paid by way of the King's reward "for the paynes and expences of himselfe and the rest of his Companye in comynge from Mortelacke in the Countie of Surrie unto the Courte aforesaide." (Cunningham, *Revels*, p. xxxiv. See also Stopes, *Burbage*, p. 253; Chambers, *Eliz. Stage*, iv, 168.)

On account of the plague in London, the Court was established in the Earl of Pembroke's house at Wilton. This is the first officially recorded play seen by the King in England.

1603. DECEMBER 26 (MONDAY). HAMPTON COURT.

A play before the King "on St Stephens daye at night" by the King's Company (John Hemynges). Payment £10, on warrant dated at Hampton Court, January 18, 1603–4. (Cunningham, *Revels*, p. xxxv. See also Stopes, *Burbage*, p. 353; Chambers, *Eliz. Stage*, iv, 168.)

On November 27 Sir Dudley Carleton wrote to John Chamberlain: "The Court is like to Christmas at Windsor; and many plays and shews are bespoken to give entertainment to our Ambassadors." (*Miscellaneous State Papers*, i, 383.)

Christmas, however, was spent at Hampton Court. Possibly the plays were even more numerous than the official records for the season show. Lady Arabella Stuart, in a letter to the Earl of Shrewsbury on December 18, after mentioning three projected masques, adds, "It is said there shall be 30 playes." (*Notes and Queries*, 2nd Series, x, 461.)

On account of the plague in London the playhouses were closed, and the players' chief source of revenue was thus cut off. Court payments doubtless tided them over, but the King's Men were given extra assistance. On February 8 Burbage was paid "by waye of his Maties free gifte" the sum of £30 "for the maintenance and reliefe of himselfe and the reste of his Companye." (Cunningham, *Revels*, p. xxxv.)

1603. DECEMBER 27 (TUESDAY). HAMPTON COURT.

A play before the King on "St Johns daye at night" by the King's Company. Payment £10, on the same warrant as that for the play of December 26. (Cunningham, *Revels*, p. xxxv. See also Stopes, *Burbage*, p. 253; Chambers, *Eliz. Stage*, iv, 168.)

1603. DECEMBER 28 (WEDNESDAY). HAMPTON COURT.

A play before the King on "Innocents daye" at night by the King's Company. Payment £10, on the same warrant as that for the play of December 26. (Cunningham, *Revels*, p. xxxv. See also Stopes, *Burbage*, p. 253; Chambers, *Eliz. Stage*, iv, 168.)

1603. DECEMBER 30 (FRIDAY). HAMPTON COURT.

A play before the prince "on the xxxth of December" by the King's Company. Payment £6. 13s. 4d., on the same warrant as that for the play of December 26. (Cunningham, *Revels*, p. xxxv. See also Chambers, *Eliz. Stage*, iv, 168.)

1603–4. JANUARY 1 (SUNDAY). HAMPTON COURT.

A play before the King on "Newyeres daye at night" by the King's Company. Payment £10, on the same warrant as that for the play of December 26. (Cunningham, *Revels*, p. xxxv. See also Stopes, *Burbage*, p. 253; Chambers, *Eliz. Stage*, iv, 168.)

1603–4. JANUARY 1 (SUNDAY). HAMPTON COURT.

A play before the Prince on "the firste of January 1603" by the King's Company. Payment £6. 13s. 4d., on the same warrant as that for the play of December 26. (Cunningham, *Revels*, p. xxxv. See also Chambers, *Eliz. Stage*, iv, 168.)

One of these was a "play of Robin goode-fellow" presented on "New yeares night" with the "maske brought in by a magicien of China." (Sullivan, *Court Masques*, p. 192.) See below.

1603–4. JANUARY 1 (SUNDAY). HAMPTON COURT.

A Masque of the Knights of India and China. (Reyher, *Masques Anglais*, p. 519.)

1603–4. JANUARY 2 (MONDAY). HAMPTON COURT.

A play before the Prince on the second of January by the Queen's Company (John Duke). Payment £6. 13s. 4d., on a warrant dated at Whitehall, February 19, 1603–4. (Cunningham, *Revels*, pp. xxxv–xxxvi. See also Chambers, *Eliz. Stage*, iv, 168, in which the warrant is dated at Westminster.)

1603–4. JANUARY 4 (WEDNESDAY). HAMPTON COURT.

A play before the Prince on the fourth of January, by the Prince's Company (Edward Allen and Edward Jubie). Payment £6. 12*s*. 4*d*., on warrant dated at Whitehall, February 19, 1603–4. (Cunningham, *Revels*, p. xxxv. See also Chambers, *Eliz. Stage*, iv, 168, in which the warrant is dated at Westminster.)

1603–4. JANUARY 6 (FRIDAY). HAMPTON COURT.

A play before the Queen.

On January 15, 1603–4, Sir Dudley Carleton wrote to John Chamberlain: "The Twelfth-day the French ambassador was feasted publicly, and at night there was a play in the Queen's presence, with a masquerade of certain Scotchmen, who came in with a sword dance, not unlike a matachin, and performed it cleanly." (Law, *History of Hampton Court Palace*, ii, 15–16.)

1603–4. JANUARY 6 (FRIDAY). HAMPTON COURT.

A masque of English and Scottish lords.

This masque is mentioned by Sir Roger Wilbraham (*Journal*, ed. by H. S. Scott, p. 66) in a general description of the holiday festivities:

The first Christmas of worthy king James was at his court at Hampton, Aº 1603: Wher the French, Spanish, & Polonian Ambassadors were severallie solemplie feasted: manie plaies & daunces with swordes: one mask by English & Scottish lords: another by the Queen's Maiestie & eleven more ladies of her chamber presenting giftes as goddesses.

See also the note to the preceding entry.

1603–4. JANUARY 8 (SUNDAY). HAMPTON COURT.

The Vision of the 12. Goddesses, presented in a Maske the 8 of Ianuary, at Hampton Court: By the Queenes most excellent Maiestie, and her Ladies. London. 1604. By Samuel Daniel. See Reyher, *Masques Anglais*, p. 519.

According to a letter of Beaumont to the French king (Sullivan, p. 193), the masque was originally intended for Twelfth Night.

1603–4. JANUARY 13 (FRIDAY). HAMPTON COURT.

A play before the Prince on the thirteenth of January, by the Queen's Company. Payment £6. 13s. 4d., on the same warrant as that for the play of January 2. (Cunningham, *Revels*, pp. xxxv-xxxvi. See also Chambers, *Eliz. Stage*, iv, 168.)

1603–4. JANUARY 15 (SUNDAY). HAMPTON COURT.

A play before the Prince on the fifteenth of January, by the Prince's Company. Payment £6. 13s. 4d., on the same warrant as that for the play of January 4. (Cunningham, *Revels*, p. xxxv. See also Chambers, *Eliz. Stage*, iv, 168.)

1603–4. JANUARY 21 (SATURDAY). HAMPTON COURT.

A play before the King "on the xxjth of Januarie last at night" by the Prince's Company. Payment £10, on the same warrant as that for the play of January 4. (Cunningham, *Revels*, p. xxxv. See also Chambers, *Eliz. Stage*, iv, 168.)

1603–4. JANUARY 22 (SUNDAY). HAMPTON COURT.

A play before the Prince on the "twoe and twentieth of Januarie" by the Prince's Company. Payment £6. 13s. 4d., on the same warrant as that for the play of January 4. (Cunningham, *Revels*, p. xxxv. See also Chambers, *Eliz. Stage*, iv, 168.)

1603–4. FEBRUARY 2 (THURSDAY). HAMPTON COURT.

A play before the King "on Candlemas day at night" by the King's Company (John Hemyng). Payment £10, on warrant dated at Whitehall, ultimo die February, 1603–4. (Cunningham, *Revels*, p. xxxvi. See also Stopes, *Burbage*, p. 253; Chambers, *Eliz. Stage*, iv, 169, in which the warrant is dated at Westminster.)

On February 2 the Earl of Worcester wrote to the Earl of Shrewsbury: "This day the King dined abrode with the Florentine Imbassadore, who takethe now his leave very shortly. He was wth the King at the Play at nyght." (Nichols, *Progresses James*, i, 317.)

This was probably the last play of the season to be performed at Hampton Court. Ernest Law (*A History of Hampton Court Palace*, ii, 45) says: "Early in February, 1604, the Court left Hampton Court for Royston, whence it shortly after moved to Whitehall, and thence to the Tower, preparatory to the triumphal passage of the King and Queen through the City of London." See also Nichols, *op. cit.*, i, 318; Winwood, *Memorials*, ii, 17; *Letters of Philip Gawdy*, ed. by Jeayes, pp. 140-1.)

1603-4. FEBRUARY 19 (SHROVE SUNDAY). WHITEHALL.

A play before the King "on Shrouesonday at night" by the King's Company. Payment £10, on the same warrant as that for the play of February 2. (Cunningham, *Revels*, p. xxxvi. See also Stopes, *Burbage*, p. 253; Chambers, *Eliz. Stage*, iv, 169.)

1603-4. FEBRUARY 20 (SHROVE MONDAY). WHITEHALL.

A play before the King "on Shrouemondaye at nighte" by the Prince's Company (Edward Jubie). Payment £10, on warrant dated at Whitehall, April 17, 1604. (Cunningham, *Revels*, p. xxxvii. See also Chambers, *Eliz. Stage*, iv, 169, in which the warrant is dated at Westminster.)

1603-4. FEBRUARY 20 (SHROVE MONDAY). WHITEHALL.

A play before the King by the Children of Paul's (Edward Pearce). Payment £10, on warrant dated at Westminster April 17, 1604. (Chambers, *Eliz. Stage*, iv, 169. See also *M. L. R.*, iv, 154.)

On February 20, 1603-4, Philip Gawdy wrote to his brother: "Ther hath bene ij playes this shroftyde before the King and ther shall be an other to morrow." (*Letters of Philip Gawdy*, ed. by Jeayes, p. 141.)

1603-4. FEBRUARY 21 (SHROVE TUESDAY). WHITEHALL.

A play before the King "uppon Shrouetuesdaye last at night" by the Children of the Queen's Majesty's Revels (Edward Kirkham). Payment £10, on warrant dated Whitehall, April 20, 1604. (Cunningham, *Revels*, p. xxxvii. See also Chambers, *Eliz. Stage*, iv, 169, in which the warrant is dated at Westminster.)

THE SEASON 1604–1605

1604. NOVEMBER 1 (THURSDAY). WHITEHALL. THE BANQUETING HOUSE.

"By the Kings Ma^tis plaiers. Hallamas Day being the first of Nouembar A play in the Banketinge house att Whithall called *the Moor of Venis*" [Shakespeare's *Othello*]. (Cunningham, *Revels*, p. 203.)

£10 was paid, on a warrant dated at Whitehall, January 21, 1604–5, for a play before the King "on all Saintes day at nighte" by the King's Company (John Hemynges). (*Ibid.*, p. xxxvi. See also Stopes, *Burbage*, p. 253; Chambers, *Eliz. Stage*, iv, 171, in which the warrant is dated at Westminster.)

1604. NOVEMBER 4 (SUNDAY). WHITEHALL. THE GREAT HALL.

"By his Ma^tis plaiers. The Sunday ffollowinge A Play of *the Merry Wiues of Winsor*." (Cunningham, *Revels*, p. 203.)

£10 was paid, on the same warrant as that for the play of November 1, for a play before the King on "the Sonday at nighte followinge beinge the 4th of November 1604" by the King's Company. (Cunningham, *op. cit.*, p. xxxvi. See also Stopes, *Burbage*, p. 253; Chambers, *Eliz. Stage*, iv, 171.)

The play was acted in the Great Hall of the palace of Whitehall. (See Adams, *Shakespearean Playhouses*, pp. 385–88.)

1604. NOVEMBER 23 (FRIDAY). WHITEHALL.

A play before the Queen "the 23rd November 1604" by the Prince's Company (Edward Jubie). Payment £10, on warrant dated at Whitehall, December 10, 1604. (Cunningham, *Revels*, p. xxxvii. See also Chambers, *Eliz. Stage*, iv, 171, in which the warrant is dated at Westminster.)

1604. NOVEMBER 24 (SATURDAY). WHITEHALL.

A play before the Prince "the 24th of November" by the Prince's Company. Payment £6. 13*s.* 4*d.*, on the same warrant as that for the preceding play. (Cunningham, *Revels*, p. xxxvii. See also Chambers, *Eliz. Stage*, iv, 171.)

1604. DECEMBER 14 (FRIDAY). WHITEHALL.

A play before the Prince on December 14 by the Prince's Company (Edward Jubye). Payment £6. 13s. 4d., on warrant dated February 22, 1604–5. (Cunningham, *Revels*, p. xxxvi. See also Chambers, *Eliz. Stage*, iv, 172.)

1604. DECEMBER 19 (WEDNESDAY). WHITEHALL.

A play before the Prince on December 19 by the Prince's Company. Payment £6. 13s. 4d., on the same warrant as that for the preceding play. (Cunningham, *Revels*, p. xxxvi. See also Chambers *Eliz. Stage*, iv, 172.)

1604. DECEMBER 26 (WEDNESDAY). WHITEHALL. THE GREAT HALL.

"By his Ma^{tis} plaiers. On St Stiuens Night in the Hall A Play called *Mesur for Mesur*. Shaxberd." (Cunningham, *Revels*, p. 204.)

£10 was paid, on the same warrant as that for the play of November 1, for a play before the King on "St Stephens daie at nighte" by the King's Company. (*Ibid.*, p. xxxvi. See also Stopes, *Burbage*, p. 253; Chambers, *Eliz. Stage*, iv, 171.)

1604. DECEMBER 27 (THURSDAY). WHITEHALL. THE GREAT HALL.

A Masque for the Marriage of Sir Philip Herbert and Lady Susan Vere. (Reyher, *Masques Anglais*, pp. 519, 341.)

1604. DECEMBER 28 (FRIDAY). WHITEHALL.

"By his M^{tis} Plaiers. On Inosents Night *The Plaie of Errors*. Shaxberd." (Cunningham, *Revels*, p. 204.)

£10 was paid, on the same warrant as that for the play of November 1, for a play before the King on "Innocents day at nighte" by the King's Company. (*Ibid.*, p. xxxvi. See also Stopes, *Burbage*, p. 253; Chambers, *Eliz. Stage*, iv, 171.)

1604. DECEMBER 30 (SUNDAY). WHITEHALL.

"By the Queens Ma^{tis} plaiers. On Sunday ffollowinge A plaie *How to larne of a woman to wooe*. Hewood." (Cunningham, *Revels*, p. 204.)

£10 was paid, on a warrant dated February 19, 1604–5, for a play before the King "on Sunday night the 30th of December" by the Queen's Company (John Duke). (*Ibid.*, p. xxxvi. See also Chambers, *Eliz. Stage*, iv, 171.)

1604–5. JANUARY 1 (TUESDAY). WHITEHALL.

"The Boyes of the Chapell. On Newers Night A Playe cauled: *All Fouelles* By Georg Chapman." (Cunningham, *Revels*, p. 204.)

£10 was paid, on a warrant dated at Whitehall, February 24, 1604–5, for a play before the King on "Newyeres day at night 1604" by the Children of the Queen's Majesty's Revels (Samuell Danyell and Henry Evans). (*Ibid.*, p. xxxvi. See also Chambers, *Eliz. Stage*, iv, 171, in which the warrant is dated at Westminster.)

1604–5. JANUARY 2–5. SOUTHAMPTON'S HOUSE?

"By his Ma^{tis} plaiers. Betwin Newers Day and Twelfe day A Play of *Loues Labours Lost*." (Cunningham, *Revels*, p. 204.)

Some light is thrown on this entry from the Revels Book by the following letter, endorsed "1604" [1604–5], written by Sir William Cope to Lord Cranborne, the King's Secretary:

Sir,—I have sent and bene all thys morning huntyng for players Juglers & Such kinde of Creaturs, but fynde them harde to finde, wherfore Leavinge notes for them to seeke me, burbage ys come, & Sayes ther ys no new playe that the quene hath not seene, but they have Revyved an olde one, Cawled *Loves Labore lost*, which for wytt & mirthe he sayes will please her excedingly. And Thys ys apointed to be playd to Morowe night at my Lord of Sowthamptons, unless yow send a wrytt to Remove the Corpus Cum Causa to your howse in strande. Burbage ys my messenger Ready attendyng your pleasure.

Yours most humbly,
Walter Cope.

(Hatfield House MSS., quoted in *Shakespeare Allusion-Book*, ed. J. Munro, i, 139. See Adams, *A Life of William Shakespeare*, pp. 371–2; Chambers, *Eliz. Stage*. iv, 139–40.)

1604–5. JANUARY 3 (THURSDAY). WHITEHALL.

A play before the King "on the thirde day of Januarye at nighte nexte followinge" by the Children of the Queen's Majesty's Revels. Payment £10, on the same warrant as that for the play of January 1. (Cunningham, *Revels*, p. xxxvi. See also Chambers, *Eliz. Stage*, iv, 171.)

1604–5. JANUARY 6 (SUNDAY). WHITEHALL. THE BANQUETING HOUSE.

The Masque of Blackness, by Ben Jonson. (Reyher, *Masques Anglais*, p. 520; Winwood, *Memorials*, ii, 44.)

The title-page from the folio of 1616 reads: "The Queenes Masques. The first, of Blackness: Personated at the Court, at White-Hall, on the Twelu'th night, 1605."

1604–5. JANUARY 7 (MONDAY). WHITEHALL.

"By his Ma^tis plaiers. On the 7 of January was played the play of *Henry the fift*." (Cunningham, *Revels*, p. 204.)

£10 was paid, on the same warrant as that for the play of November 1, for a play by the King's Company on January 7. (*Ibid.*, p. xxxvi. See also Stopes, *Burbage*, p. 253; Chambers, *Eliz. Stage*, iv, 171.)

1604–5. JANUARY 8 (TUESDAY). WHITEHALL.

"By his Ma^tis plaiers. The 8 of January A play cauled *Euery on out of his Umer*" [Ben Jonson]. (Cunningham, *Revels*, p. 204.)

£10 was paid, on the same warrant as that for the play of November 1, for a play on January 8 by the King's Company. (*Ibid.*, p. xxxvi. See also Stopes, *Burbage*, p. 253; Chambers, *Eliz. Stage*, iv, 171.)

1604–5. JANUARY 15 (TUESDAY). WHITEHALL.

A play before the Prince on January 15 by the Prince's Company. Payment £6. 13s. 4d., on the same warrant as that for the play of December 14. (Cunningham, *Revels*, p. xxxvi. See also Chambers, *Eliz. Stage*, iv, 172.)

1604–5. JANUARY 22 (TUESDAY). WHITEHALL.

A play before the Prince on January 22 by the Prince's Company. Payment £6. 13s. 4d., on the same warrant as that for the play of December 14. (Cunningham, *Revels*, p. xxxvi. See also Chambers, *Eliz. Stage*, iv, 172.)

1604–5. FEBRUARY 2 (SATURDAY). WHITEHALL.

"By his Ma^tis plaiers. On Candelmas night. A playe *Euery one in his Umor*" [Ben Jonson]. (Cunningham, *Revels*, p. 204.)

£10 was paid, on a warrant dated February 24, 1604–5, for a play before the King "on Candlemas daye at night" by the King's Company (John Hemynge). (*Ibid.*, p. xxxvii. See also Stopes, *Burbage*, p. 253; Chambers, *Eliz. Stage*, iv, 172.)

1604–5. FEBRUARY 3 (SUNDAY).

"The Sunday ffollowing A playe provided and discharged." (Cunningham, *Revels*, p. 204.)

£10 was paid, on a warrant dated April 28, 1605, for a play before the King "at ye Courte the thirde of February 1604" by the King's Company (John Hemynges). (*Ibid.*, p. xxxvii. See also Stopes *Burbage*, p. 253. Cf. Chambers, *Eliz. Stage*, iv, 172.)

The entry in the Revels Book probably means that the play was countermanded. In such cases the actors were paid.

1604–5. FEBRUARY 5 (TUESDAY). WHITEHALL.

A play before the Prince by the Prince's Company. Payment £6. 13s. 4d., on the same warrant as that for the play of December 14. (Cunningham, *Revels*, p. xxxvi. See also Chambers, *Eliz. Stage*, iv, 172.)

1604–5. FEBRUARY 10 (SHROVE SUNDAY). WHITEHALL.

"By his Matie plaiers. On Shrousunday A play of the *Marchant of Venis*. Shaxberd." (Cunningham, *Revels*, p. 204.)

£10 was paid, on the same warrant as that for the play of February 2, for a play before the King "on Shrouesunday at night" by the King's Company. (*Ibid.*, p. xxxvii. See also Stopes, *Burbage*, p. 253; Chambers, *Eliz. Stage*, iv, 172.)

1604–5. FEBRUARY 11 (SHROVE MONDAY). WHITEHALL.

"By his Ma^tis plaiers. On Shroumonday A Tragidye of *The Spanish Maz*." (Cunningham, *Revels*, p. 205.)

£10 was paid, on the same warrant as that for the play of February 2, for a play before the King on "Shrouemonday at night" by the King's Company. (*Ibid.*, p. xxxvii. See also Stopes, *Burbage*, p. 253; Chambers, *Eliz. Stage*, iv, 172.)

1604–5. FEBRUARY 12 (SHROVE TUESDAY). WHITEHALL.

"By his Ma^tis plaiers. On Shroutusday A play cauled *The Martchant of Venis* againe commanded by the Kings Matie. Shaxberd." (Cunningham, *Revels*, p. 205.)

£10 was paid, on the same warrant as that for the play of February 2, for a play before the King on "Shrouetuesday at nighte 1604" by the King's Company. (*Ibid.*, p. xxxvii. See also Stopes, *Burbage*, p. 253; Chambers, *Eliz. Stage*, iv, 172.)

1604–5. FEBRUARY 19 (TUESDAY). WHITEHALL.

A play before the Prince on February 19 by the Prince's Company. Payment £6. 13s. 4d., on the same warrant as that for the play of December 14. (Cunningham, *Revels*, p. xxxvi. See also Chambers, *Eliz. Stage*, iv, 172.)

The Court removed to Greenwich between February 28 and March 6. (Chambers, iv, 119.)

OXFORD, AUGUST 27–30, 1605

King James, accompanied by the Queen, Prince Henry, and many members of the Court, paid his first visit to Oxford during the summer progress of 1605. Elaborate preparation was made by the University for the reception and entertainment of the royal guests. "Heare is no newes but praeparation for the Kinges cominge, who will be heare on Teusday come forthenighte, Playes, Verses, &c," wrote Robert Burton to his brother on August 11.

According to the contemporary account by Philip Stringer, aid from without was sought:

For the better contriving and finishing of the stages, seates, and scaffolds in St. Marie's and Christ Church, they entertained two of his Majestie's Master Carpenters, and they had the advice of the Comptroller of his Works. They also hired one Mr. Jones, a great Traveller, who undertook to further them much, and furnish them with rare devices, but performed very little, to that which was expected. He had for his pains, as I heard it constantly reported, £50. (Nichols, *Progresses James*, i, 558.)

"Mr. Jones" was, of course, Inigo Jones, the great court architect. The stage in Christ Church, the building of which presumably he supervised, is thus described:

The stage was built close to the upper end of the Hall, as it seemed at the first sight. But indeed it was but a false wall fair painted and adorned with stately pillars, which pillars would turn about, by reason whereof, with the help of other painted clothes, their stage did vary three times in the acting of one Tragedy [*Ajax Flagellifer*]. Behinde the foresaid false wall there was reserved five or six paces of the upper end of the Hall, which served them to good uses for their howses and the receipt of the actors, etc. (*Ibid.*, p. 538.)

When, on August 22, the Lord Chamberlain and other noblemen arrived to inspect what had been done, they were not altogether pleased:

They (but especially Lord Suffolk) utterly disliked the stage at Christ Church, and above all, the place appointed for the chair of Estate, because it was no higher, and the King so placed that the auditory could see but his cheek only; this dislike of the Earle of Suffolk much troubled the Vice-chancellor and all the workmen, yet they stood in defence of the thing done, and maintained that by the art perspective the King should behold all better then if he sat higher. Their Chancellor also, after his coming, tooke part with the University, and on the Sunday morning the matter was debated in the Councill-chamber.

The upshot of it was, however, that "the place was removed, and sett in the midst of the Hall, but too far from the stage, viz. 28 foote, so that there were many long Speeches delivered which neither the King nor any near him could well hear or understand."

Preparations for the plays were completed by the hiring of costumes and properties from London. For an inventory of these articles, which were supplied by Edward Kirkham and Thomas Kendall, see "James I at Oxford in 1605. Property lists from the University Archives," ed. by F. S. Boas and W. W. Greg, Malone Society's *Collections*, Part III.

1605. AUGUST 27 (TUESDAY). CHRIST CHURCH HALL.

Alba, a pastoral, before the King and Queen.

The royal party arrived in Oxford on August 27, and on the evening of that day the first play was presented. Stringer thus describes the performance:

The comedy began between nine and ten, and ended at one, the name of it was *Alba*, whereof I never saw reason; it was a Pastoral much like one I have seen in King's Colledge in Cambridge. In the acting thereof they brought in five or six men almost naked, which were much disliked by the Queen and Ladies, and also many rusticall songs and dances, which made it very tedious, insomuch that if the Chancellors of both Universities had not intreated his Majesty earnestly, he would have gone before half the Comedy had been ended. (Nichols, *Progresses James*, i, 547-8.)

The play is not extant. But characters from classical mythology seem to have figured in it (see Boas and Greg, *op. cit.*, pp. 249-50), and on account of the fact that Daniel's play is described by Chamberlain as an "English Pastorall," it may be supposed to have been in Latin.

1605. August 28 (Wednesday). Christ Church Hall.

Ajax Flagellifer, before the King.

Stringer writes:

The same day, after supper, about nine of the clock, they began to act the Tragedy of *Ajax Flagellifer*, wherein the stage varied three times; they had all goodly antique apparell, but for all that, it was not acted so well by many degrees as I have seen it in Cambridge. The King was very weary before he came thither, but much more wearied by it, and spoke many words of dislike. (Nichols, *Progresses James*, i, 550.)

Stringer, who was a Cambridge man, had always a keen eye for the shortcomings of Oxford. But it is evident that the play was not a success, for Chamberlain wrote to Sir Ralph Winwood that "Magdalen's Tragedy of Ajax" "was very tedious, and wearied all the company." (*Ibid.*, p. 561.)

1605. August 29 (Thursday). Christ Church Hall.

Vertumnus, sive Annus Recurrens, acted before the King.

That night, after supper, about nine, began their Comedy called *Vertumnus*, very well and learnedly penned by Dr. Gwynn. It was acted much better than either of the other, and chiefly by St. John's men, yet the King was so over-wearied at St. Marie's, that after a while he distasted it, and fell asleep; when he awaked, he would have bin gone, saying, "I marvell what they think me to be," with such other like speeches showing his dislike thereof, yet he did tarry till they had ended it, which was after one of the clock. The Queen was not there that night. (Nichols, *Progresses James*, i, 552–53.)

1605. August 30 (Friday). Christ Church Hall.

The Queenes Arcadia. A Pastorall Trage-comedie presented to her Maiestie and her Ladies, by the Vniuersity of Oxford in Christs Church, In August last. 1605. London. 1606.

Stringer gives the following account:

There was an English play acted in the same place before the Queen and the young Prince, with all the ladies and Gallants attending the Court. It was penned by Mr. Daniel, and drawn out of *Fidus Pastor*, which was sometimes acted by King's College

Men in Cambridge. I was not there present, but by report it was well acted and greatly applauded. It was named *Arcadia Reformed*. (Nichols, *Progresses James*, i, 553.)

The last of the four plays seems to have been by far the best-liked. Chamberlain wrote that on the day of departure "an English Pastorall of Samuel Daniel's, presented before the Queen, made amends for all, being indeed very excellent, and some parts exactly acted." (*Ibid.*, pp. 561–2.)

THE SEASON 1605–1606

1605/1605–6. CHRISTMAS AND AFTER.

Ten plays before the King "in the tyme of Christmas laste and since" by the King's Company (John Hemyngs). Payment £10 each, on warrant dated March 24, 1605–6. (Cunningham, *Revels*, p. xxxviii. Mrs. Stopes in her abstract of this warrant, *Burbage*, p. 254, mentions a "schedule annexed," which has of course been lost. See also Chambers, *Eliz. Stage*, iv, 173.)

1605/1605–6. [CHRISTMAS OR AFTER.]

Two plays before the Prince and the Duke of York by the Children of Paul's (Edward Kerkham). Payment £16. 13s. 4d., on warrant dated March 31, 1606. (Cunningham, *Revels*, p. xxxviii. See also Chambers, *Eliz. Stage*, iv, 173.)

Fleay (*Stage*, p. 177; *Drama*, ii, 92), followed by Murray (*English Dramatic Companies*, i, 353) identifies these plays as *A Trick to Catch the Old One* and *The Phoenix*. Both these plays, according to the title-pages, were presented "before His Maiestie." The payment above seems to indicate the presence of the King at one performance. See the entry for January 1, 1606–7, and the title-page of the *Phoenix*, quoted under "Miscellaneous Court Performances of Uncertain Date."

1605. DECEMBER 1 (SUNDAY).

A play before the Prince by the Prince's Company (Edward Jubie). Payment £6. 13s. 4d., on warrant dated April 30, 1606.

(Chambers, *Eliz. Stage*, iv, 173. See also Cunningham, *Revels*, p. xxxviii, in which dates are not given for the six plays included in the warrant.)

1605. DECEMBER 27 (FRIDAY).

A play before the King "upon St Johns day at night" by the Queen's Company (John Duke). Payment £8. 6s. 8d., on warrant dated April 30, 1606. (Cunningham, *Revels*, p. xxxviii. See also Chambers, *Eliz. Stage*, iv, 173.)

1605. DECEMBER 30 (MONDAY).

A play before the Prince by the Prince's Company. Payment £6. 13s. 4d., on the same warrant as that for the play of December 1. (Chambers, *Eliz. Stage*, iv, 173. See also Cunningham, *Revels*, p. xxxviii.)

1605–6. JANUARY 1 (WEDNESDAY).

A play before the King by the Prince's Company. Payment £10, on the same warrant as that for the play of December 1. (Chambers, *Eliz. Stage*, iv, 173. See also Cunningham, *Revels*, p. xxxviii.)

1605–6. JANUARY 4 (SATURDAY).

A play before the Prince by the Prince's Company. Payment £6. 13s. 4d., on the same warrant as that for the play of December 1. (Chambers, *Eliz. Stage*, iv, 173. See also Cunningham, *Revels*, p. xxxviii.)

1605–6. JANUARY 5 (SUNDAY). WHITEHALL. THE BANQUETING HOUSE.

Hymenaei: or the Solemnities of Masque, and Barriers, Magnificently performed on the eleventh, and twelfth Nights, from Christmas; At Court: To the auspicious celebrating of the Marriage-vnion, betweene Robert, Earle of Essex, and the Lady Frances, second Daughter to the most noble Earle of Suffolke. By Ben: Ionson. London. 1606.

The masque was given on January 5, and the Barriers on Twelfth Night. See the letter of John Pory to Sir Robert Cotton, printed by Nichols, *Progresses James*, ii, 33. With regard to the place of performance, Reyher (*Masques Anglais*, p. 340) says: "The *Masque of Blackness* and without doubt *Hymenaei* were shown in the Banqueting House of Elizabeth."

1605–6. March 3 (Shrove Monday).

A play before the King by the Prince's Company. Payment £10, on the same warrant as that for the play of December 1. (Chambers, *Eliz. Stage*, iv, 173. See also Cunningham, *Revels*, p. xxxviii.)

1605–6. March 4 (Shrove Tuesday).

A play before the King by the Prince's Company. Payment £10, on the same warrant as that for the play of December 1. (Chambers, *Eliz. Stage*, iv, 173. See also Cunningham, *Revels*, p. xxxviii.)

THE VISIT OF THE KING OF DENMARK
SUMMER, 1606

1606. July 17–August 11. Greenwich and Hampton Court.

Three plays before the King and the King of Denmark, "twoe of them at Grenewich and one at Hampton Courte," by the King's Company (John Hemynges). Payment £10 each, on warrant dated October 18, 1606. (Cunningham, *Revels*, p. xxxviii. See also Stopes, *Burbage*, p. 254; Chambers, *Eliz. Stage*, iv, 173.)

The King of Denmark, brother of Queen Anne, arrived at Gravesend on July 17, and left on August 11. See Nichols, *Progresses James*, ii, 54, 83.

The Hampton Court performance is dated August 7 by Chambers (*op. cit.*, iv, 173).

1606. July 24–28. Theobalds.

Solomon and the Queen of Sheba, before the Kings of England and Denmark.

This tipsy performance, which seems to have been a masque, is described in satirical fashion by Sir John Harington:

One day, a great feast was held, and, after dinner, the representation of Solomon his Temple and the coming of the Queen of Sheba was made, or (as I may better say) was meant to have been made, before their Majesties, by device of the Earl of Salisbury and others.—But alas! as all earthly things do fail to poor mortals in enjoyment, so did prove our presentment hereof. The lady who did play the Queen's part, did carry most precious gifts to both their Majesties; but, forgetting the steppes arising to the canopy, overset her caskets into his Danish Majesties lap, and fell at his feet, tho I rather think it was in his face. Much was the hurry and confusion; cloths and napkins were at hand to make all clean. His Majesty then got up, and woud dance with the Queen of Sheba; but he fell down and humbled himself before her, and was carried to an inner chamber and laid on a bed of state; which was not a little defiled with the presents of the Queen bestowed on his garments; such as wine, cream, jelly, beverage, cakes, spices, and other good matters. The entertainment and show went forward, and most of the presenters went backward, or fell down, wine did so occupy their upper chambers. Now did appear in rich dress, Hope, Faith, and Charity. Hope did assay to speak, but wine rendered her endeavours so feeble that she withdrew, and hoped the King would excuse her brevity: Faith was then all alone, for I am certain that she was not joyned with good works, and left the Court in a staggering condition: Charity came to the King's feet, and seemed to cover the multitude of sins her sisters had committed; in some sort she made obeysance and brought gifts, but said she would return home again, as there was no gift which heaven had not already given his Majesty. She then returned to Hope and Faith, who were both sick and spewing in the lower hall. Next comes Victory, in bright armour, and presented a rich sword to the King, who did not accept it, but put it by with his hand; and by a strange medley of versification, did endeavour to make suit to the King. But Victory did not triumph long; for, after much lamentable utterance, she was led away like a silly captive, and laid to sleep on the outer steps of the antichamber. Now did Peace make entry, and strive to get foremost to the King; but I grieve to tell how great wrath she did discover unto those of her attendants; and much contrary to her semblance, most rudely made war with her olive branch, and laid on the pates of those who did oppose her coming. (*Nugae Antiquae*, ed. by Thomas Park, i, 349-51.)

1606. July 30 (Wednesday). Greenwich.

"On the 30th of July the Youthes of Paules, commonly called the Children of Paules, plaide before the two Kings [of England and Denmark] a Play called *Abuses*, containing both a Comedie and a Tragedie, at which the Kinges seemed to take delight and be much pleased." (Nichols, *Progresses James*, iv, 1073. For the place of performance, see Chambers, *Eliz. Stage*, iv, 121.)

THE SEASON 1606–1607

1606. December 26 (Friday). Whitehall.

M. *William Shak-speare: His True Chronicle Historie of the life and death of King Lear and his three Daughters. With the vnfortunate life of Edgar, sonne and heire to the Earle of Gloster, and his sullen and assumed humor of Tom of Bedlam. As it was played before the Kings Maiestie at Whitehall upon S. Stephans night in Christmas Hollidayes. By his Maiesties seruants playing vsually at the Gloabe on the Banckeside.* London. 1608.

This play was entered on the Stationers' Register November 26, 1607, as "A Book called Master William Shakespeare his 'historye of King Lear' as yt was played before the kinges maiestie at Whitehall vpon Sainct Stephens night at Christmas Last by his maiesties seruantes playinge vsually at the 'Globe' on the Banksyde." (Arber, *Transcript*, iii, 161.)

£10 was paid, on a warrant dated March 30, 1607, for a play before the King on December 26, 1606, by the King's Company (John Hemynges). (Cunningham, *Revels*, p. xxxix. See also Stopes, *Burbage*, p. 254; Chambers, *Eliz. Stage*, iv, 173.)

1606. December 28 (Sunday). Whitehall.

A play before the King by the Prince's Company (Edwarde Jubye). Payment £10, on warrant dated February 28, 1606–7. (Chambers, *Eliz. Stage*, iv, 174. See also Cunningham, *Revels*, p. xxxviii, in which the six plays paid for on the warrant are undated.)

1606. DECEMBER 29 (MONDAY). WHITEHALL.

A play before the King on December 29, 1606, by the King's Company. Payment £10, on the same warrant as that for the play of December 26. (Cunningham, *Revels*, p. xxxix. See also Stopes, *Burbage*, p. 254; Chambers, *Eliz. Stage*, iv, 173.)

1606–7. JANUARY 4 (SUNDAY). WHITEHALL.

A play before the King on January 4 by the King's Company. Payment £10, on the same warrant as that for the play of December 26. (Cunningham, *Revels*, p. xxxix. See also Stopes, *Burbage*, p. 254; Chambers, *Eliz. Stage*, iv, 173.)

1606–7. JANUARY 6 (TUESDAY). WHITEHALL.

A play before the King on January 6 by the King's Company. Payment £10, on the same warrant as that for the play of December 26. (Cunningham, *Revels*, p. xxxix. See also Stopes, *Burbage*, p. 254; Chambers, *Eliz. Stage*, iv, 173.)

1606–7. JANUARY 6 (TUESDAY). WHITEHALL. THE GREAT HALL.

The Discription of a Maske, Presented before the Kinges Maiestie at White-Hall, on Twelfth Night last, in honour of the Lord Hayes, and his Bride, Daughter and Heire to the Honourable the Lord Dennye, their Marriage hauing been the same Day at Court solemnized. To this by occasion other small Poemes are adioyned. Inuented and set forth by Thomas Campion Doctor of Phisicke. London. 1607.

The old Banqueting House had been pulled down, and the new one was in process of construction. This accounts for the performance of the masque in the Great Hall. See Reyher, *Masques Anglais*, p. 341.

1606–7. JANUARY 8 (THURSDAY).

A play before the King on January 8, by the King's Company. Payment £10, on the same warrant as that for the play of December 26. (Cunningham, *Revels*, p. xxxix. See also Stopes, *Burbage*, p. 254; Chambers, *Eliz. Stage*, iv, 173.)

1606–7. JANUARY 13 (TUESDAY).

A play before the King by the Prince's Company. Payment £10, on the same warrant as that for the play of December 28. (Chambers, *Eliz. Stage*, iv, 174. See also Cunningham, *Revels*, p. xxxviii.)

1606–7. JANUARY 24 (SATURDAY).

A play before the King by the Prince's Company. Payment £10, on the same warrant as that for the play of December 28. (Chambers, *Eliz. Stage*, iv, 174. See also Cunningham, *Revels*, p. xxxviii.)

1606–7. JANUARY 30 (FRIDAY).

A play before the King by the Prince's Company. Payment £10, on the same warrant as that for the play of December 28. (Chambers, *Eliz. Stage*, iv, 174. See also Cunningham, *Revels*, p. xxxviii.)

1606–7. FEBRUARY 1 (SUNDAY).

A play before the King by the Prince's Company. Payment £10, on the same warrant as that for the play of December 28. (Chambers, *Eliz. Stage*, iv, 174. See also Cunningham, *Revels*, p. xxxviii.)

1606–7. FEBRUARY 2 (MONDAY).

The Divils Charter: A Tragaedie Conteining the Life and Death of Pope Alexander the sixt. As it was plaide before the Kings Maiestie, vpon Candlemasse night last: by his Maiesties Seruants. But more exactly reuewed, corrected, and augmented since by the Author, for the more pleasure and profit of the Reader. London. 1607.

By Barnabe Barnes. Entered S. R. October 16, 1607.

£10 was paid, on the same warrant as that for the play of December 26, for a play on February 2 by the King's Company. (Cunningham, *Revels*, p. xxxix. See also Stopes, *Burbage*, p. 254; Chambers, *Eliz. Stage*, iv, 173.)

1606–7. FEBRUARY 5 (THURSDAY).

A play before the King on February 5 by the King's Company. Payment £10, on the same warrant as that for the play of December 26. (Cunningham, *Revels*, p. xxxix. See also Stopes, *Burbage*, p. 254; Chambers, *Eliz. Stage*, iv, 173.)

1606–7. FEBRUARY 11 (WEDNESDAY).

A play before the King by the Prince's Company. Payment £10, on the same warrant as that for the play of December 28. (Chambers, *Eliz. Stage*, iv, 174. See also Cunningham, *Revels*, p. xxxviii.)

1606–7. FEBRUARY 15 (SUNDAY).

A play before the King on February 15 by the King's Company. Payment £10, on the same warrant as that for the play of December 26. (Cunningham, *Revels*, p. xxxix. See also Stopes, *Burbage*, p. 254; Chambers, *Eliz. Stage*, iv, 173.)

1606–7. FEBRUARY 27 (FRIDAY).

A play before the King on February 27 by the King's Company. Payment £10, on the same warrant as that for the play of December 26. (Cunningham, *Revels*, p. xxxix. See also Stopes, *Burbage*, p. 254; Chambers, *Eliz. Stage*, iv, 173.)

1607. MAY 25 (MONDAY).

A tragedy of *Aeneas and Dido*, acted before the King, Queen, and the Prince de Joinville.

M. de la Boderie, French Ambassador resident in London, writing on June 8, 1607, thus describes certain entertainments given in honor of the Prince de Joinville, Charles de Lorraine, during his visit to England:

La reine, un de ces soirs, le vint prendre au pied de son logis, qui repondoit sur la riviere, et le mena sur icelle avec trois bateaux chargés de musique, où ils demeurèrent quatre ou cinq heures. Le lendemain se fit le tournoi préparé pour l'amour de lui: il s'y porta fort bien, mais non tant toutefois, qu'il ne se reconnût de la faculte de son cheval, qu'on croit lui avoir été donné tel par les Anglais pour diminuer de sa gloire. Le soir le Comte d'Arundel donna un grand festin ou il se trouva avec le Roi, la Reine et force Dames; et à la fin d'ici-lui se présenta une *Tragédie d'Énée et de Didon*, qui les tint jusques á deux heures 'apres minuit. (*Ambassades*, ii, 263–4. The passage is pointed out by T. S. Graves, *M. L. Review*, ix [1914], 525.)

The performance is dated May 25 by Chambers (*Eliz. Stage*, iv, 122).

THE SEASON 1607–1608

On January 5, 1607–8, John Chamberlain wrote to Sir Dudley Carleton:

The Masque goes forward at Court for Twelfth day, tho' I doubt the New Room will be scant ready. All the Holidays there were Plays; but with so little concourse of strangers, that they say they wanted company. The King was very earnest to have one on Christmas-night; tho', as I take it, he and the Prince received that day; but the Lords told him it was not the fashion. Which answer pleased him not a whit; but said, "What do you tell me of the fashion? I will make it a fashion." (Nichols, *Progresses James*, ii, 162.)

1607. NOVEMBER 19 (THURSDAY). WHITEHALL.

A play before the King and the Prince by the Prince's Company (Edward Juby). Payment £10, on warrant dated May 8, 1608. (Chambers, *Eliz. Stage*, iv, 174; Cunningham, *Revels*, p. xxxix. In the warrant as printed by Cunningham the four plays are said to have been presented at Whitehall. Specific dates are not given.)

1607. DECEMBER 26 (SATURDAY). WHITEHALL.

A play before the King "on Sᵗ Stephens night" by the King's Company (John Hemynges). Payment £10, on warrant dated February 8, 1607–8. (Cunningham, *Revels*, p. xxxviii. See also Stopes, *Burbage*, p. 254; Chambers, *Eliz. Stage*, iv, 174.)

The thirteen plays covered by this warrant were presented "at the Court at Whitehall."

1607. DECEMBER 27 (SUNDAY). WHITEHALL.

A play before the King on "Sᵗ Johns night" by the King's Company. Payment £10, on the same warrant as that for the preceding play. (Cunningham, *Revels*, p. xxxviii. See also Stopes, *Burbage*, p. 254; Chambers, *Eliz. Stage*, iv, 174.)

1607. DECEMBER 28 (MONDAY). WHITEHALL.

A play before the King on "Childermas night" by the King's Company. Payment £10, on the same warrant as that for the play of December 26. (Cunningham, *Revels*, p. xxxviii. See also Stopes, *Burbage*, p. 254; Chambers, *Eliz. Stage*, iv, 174.)

1607. DECEMBER 30 (WEDNESDAY). WHITEHALL.

A play before the King and the Prince by the Prince's Company. Payment £10, on the same warrant as that for the play of November 19. (Chambers, *Eliz. Stage*, iv, 174; Cunningham, *Revels*, p. xxxix.)

1607–8. JANUARY 2 (SATURDAY). WHITEHALL.

A play before the King on "the second of January" by the King's Company. Payment £10, on the same warrant as that for the play of December 26. (Cunningham, *Revels*, p. xxxviii. Mrs. Stopes, *Burbage*, p. 254, gives "2nd January at night 2 plaies," and omits the Twelfth Night plays. See also Chambers, *Eliz. Stage*, iv, 174.)

1607–8. JANUARY 3 (SUNDAY). WHITEHALL.

A play before the King and Prince by the Prince's Company. Payment £10, on the same warrant as that for the play of November 19. (Chamber, *Eliz. Stage*, iv, 174; Cunningham, *Revels*, p. xxxix.)

1607–8. JANUARY 4 (MONDAY). WHITEHALL.

A play before the King and Prince by the Prince's Company. Payment £10, on the same warrant as that for the play of November 19. (Chambers, *Eliz. Stage*, iv, 174; Cunningham, *Revels*, p. xxxix.)

1607–8. JANUARY 6 (WEDNESDAY). WHITEHALL.

"Twelfnight two plaies" before the King by the King's Company. Payment £10 each, on the same warrant as that for the play of December 26. (Cunningham, *Revels*, p. xxxviii; Chambers, *Eliz. Stage*, iv, 174.)

The *Masque of Beauty* was intended for Twelfth Night, but was postponed, as Chamberlain wrote to Carleton, "by reason all things" were "not ready."

1607–8. JANUARY 7 (THURSDAY). WHITEHALL.

A play before the King on "the seaventh of January" by the King's Company. Payment £10, on the same warrant as that for the play of December 26. (Cunningham, *Revels*, p. xxxix. See also Stopes, *Burbage*, p. 254; Chambers, *Eliz. Stage*, iv, 174.)

1607–8. JANUARY 9 (SATURDAY). WHITEHALL.

A play before the King on "the ninth of January" by the King's Company. Payment £10, on the same warrant as that for the play of December 26. (Cunningham, *Revels*, p. xxxix. See also Stopes, *Burbage*, p. 254; Chambers, *Eliz. Stage*, iv, 174.)

1607–8. JANUARY 10 (SUNDAY). WHITEHALL. THE BANQUETING HOUSE.

The Masque of Beauty, by Ben Jonson.

The title-page from the folio of 1616 reads: "The Second Masque. Which was of Beautie; Was presented in the same Court, at White-Hall, on the Sunday night after the Twelfth Night. 1608."

This masque was given in the new Banqueting House at Whitehall, which had just been completed, and which, according to Stow, was "very strong and stately, being every way larger than the first." See Reyher, *Masques Anglais*, pp. 340, 520.

1607–8. JANUARY 17 (SUNDAY). WHITEHALL.

"The xvijth of January two plaies" before the King by the King's Company. Payment £10 each, on the same warrant as that for the play of December 26. (Cunningham, *Revels*, p. xxxix. See also Stopes, *Burbage*, p. 254; Chambers, *Eliz. Stage*, iv, 174.)

1607–8. JANUARY 26 (TUESDAY). WHITEHALL.

A play before the King "the xxvjth of January" by the King's Company. Payment £10, on the same warrant as that for the play of December 26. (Cunningham, *Revels*, p. xxxix. See also Stopes, *Burbage*, p. 254; Chambers, *Eliz. Stage*, iv, 174.)

1607–8. FEBRUARY 2 (TUESDAY). WHITEHALL.

A play before the King on "Candlemas night" by the King's Company. Payment £10, on the same warrant as that for the play of December 26. (Cunningham, *Revels*, p. xxxix. See also Stopes, *Burbage*, p. 254; Chambers, *Eliz. Stage*, iv, 174.)

1607–8. FEBRUARY 7 (SHROVE SUNDAY). WHITEHALL.

A play before the King on "Shrovesunday at night" by the King's Company. Payment £10, on the same warrant as that for the play of December 26. (Cunningham, *Revels*, p. xxxix. See also Stopes, *Burbage*, p. 254; Chambers, *Eliz. Stage*, iv, 174.)

1607–8. FEBRUARY 9 (SHROVE TUESDAY). WHITEHALL.

The Hue and Cry after Cupid, by Ben Jonson.

The title-page from the folio of 1616 reads: "The Description of the Masque. With the Nuptiall songs. At the Lord Vicount Hadingtons marriage at Court. On the Shroue-tuesday at night. 1608." See Reyher, *Masques Anglais*, p. 520.

THE SEASON 1608–1609

1608/1608–9. DATES UNCERTAIN.

Five plays before the King and Prince by the Queen's Company (Thomas Greene). Payment £10 each, on warrant dated April 5, 1609. (Chambers, *Eliz. Stage*, iv, 175.)

1608/1608–9. DATES UNCERTAIN.

Three plays before the King and the Prince "on severall nights" by the Prince's Company (Edward Jubye). Payment £10 each, on warrant dated April 5, 1609. (Cunningham, *Revels*, p. xxxix. See also Chambers, *Eliz. Stage*, iv, 175.)

1608/1608–9. CHRISTMAS. WHITEHALL.

Two plays before the King by the Children of the Blackfriars (Roberte Keyser). Payment £10 each, on warrant dated at Westminster, March 10, 1608–9. (Chambers, *Eliz. Stage*, iv, 175. See also *M. L. R.*, iv, 154.)

Chamberlain did not find the Christmas entertainment to his taste. On January 3 he wrote to Carleton:

We have had a dull and heavy Christmas hitherto, like the weather; no manner of delight nor lightsome news, only there have been plays at Court, and the Spanish ambassadors were feasted there the last of the holidays. (*Court and Times of James I*, i, 85.)

Christmas was probably kept at Whitehall. On December 23 Chamberlain wrote: "The King came to town on Tuesday." (*Ibid.*, i, 84.)

1608/1608-9. Christmas. Whitehall.

Twelve plays before the King, the Queen, the Prince, and the Duke of York "at severall tymes in Christmas 1608" by the King's Company (John Hemynges). Payment £10 each, on warrant dated April 5, 1609. (Cunningham, *Revels*, p. xxxix. See also Stopes, *Burbage*, p. 254; Chambers, *Eliz. Stage*, iv, 175.)

1608-9. January 1 (Thursday). Whitehall.

A Trick to Catch the Old One. As it hath beene often in Action, both at Paules, and the Black-Fryers. Presented before his Maiestie on New yeares night last. Composed by T. M. [Thomas Middleton.] London. 1608.

Entered S. R. October 7, 1607. Chambers (*Eliz. Stage*, iii, 439) is of the opinion that the quarto belongs to 1608-9, and the court performance likewise to that year.

1608-9. January 4 (Wednesday). Whitehall. The Cockpit.

A play before the Prince "in the Cockpitt at Whitehall" by the Children of the Blackfriars (Robert Keyser). Payment £10, on warrant dated March 10, 1608-9. (Chambers, M. L. R., iv, 154; *Eliz. Stage*, iv, 175. The payment indicates that the King was also present.)

1608-9. January 6 (Friday).

The Masque of Queens, by Ben Jonson, was intended for Twelfth night, but postponed. See the entry for February 2.

On January 9 [O. S. December 30] the Venetian Ambassador, Marc' Antonio Correr, wrote to the Doge and Senate:

From Sunday last on which day they kept Christmas, till now the Court has been entirely taken up with balls and comedies. The Queen is deeply engaged in preparing a Masque of Ladies to wind up with. It will be given to-day week. She is sparing no expense to make it as fine as possible. (*Cal. State Papers, Venetian,* xi, 212.)

The Masque was postponed on account of the squabbling of certain ambassadors. See Sullivan, *Court Masques of James I,* p. 49 ff.

1608–9. FEBRUARY 2 (THURSDAY). WHITEHALL. THE BANQUETING HOUSE.

The Masque of Queenes Celebrated From the House of Fame: By the most absolute in all State, And Titles. Anne Queene of Great Britaine, &c. With her Honourable Ladies. At White Hall, Febr. 2. 1609. Written by Ben: Ionson. London. 1609.

See Reyher, *Masques Anglais,* p. 520; Sullivan, *Court Masques,* p. 54.

THE SEASON 1609–1610

On April 26, 1609, John Heminges was paid the sum of £40 on behalf of himself and the rest of his Company "by way of his ma^tes rewarde for their private practise in the time of infeccon that thereby they mighte be inhabled to performe their service before his Matie in Christmas hollidaies 1609." (Chambers, *Eliz. Stage,* iv, 175. See also Cunningham, *Revels,* p. xxxix.)

1609/1609–10. BEFORE CHRISTMAS, CHRISTMAS, AND AFTER.

Thirteen plays before the King, Queen, Prince, Duke of York, and Lady Elizabeth, "before xpenmas and in the tyme of the holidayes and afterwardes" by the King's Company (John Heminges). Payment £10 each, on warrant dated at Westminster,

March 2, 1609–10. (Chambers, *Eliz. Stage*, iv, 175. See also M. L. R., iv, 154; Stopes, *Burbage*, p. 254.)

1609/1609–10. CHRISTMAS.

Five plays before the King and Prince Henry by the Children of the Whitefriars (Roberte Keysar). Payment £10 each, on warrant dated at Westminster, May 10, 1610. (Chambers, *Eliz. Stage*, iv, 175. See also M. L. R., iv, 154.)

One of these plays was doubtless Nathaniel Field's *Woman is a Weathercock*, entered S. R. November 23, and printed in 1612 as "A New Comedy, As it was acted before the King in Whitehall. And diuers times Priuately at the White-Friers by the Children of her Maiesties Reuels."

The company was not called "Children of the Queen's Revels" until January 4, 1610, but this fact is probably not sufficient to warrant the dating of the performance subsequent to January 4, since the title-page merely names the Children as they were called at the time of the publication of the play.

1609. DECEMBER 26 (TUESDAY).

A play before the King by Prince Henry's Company (Edwarde Jubye). Payment £10 each, on warrant dated at Westminster, March 10, 1609–10. (Chambers, *Eliz. Stage*, iv, 176. See also M. L. R., iv, 154.)

1609. DECEMBER 27 (WEDNESDAY).

A play before the King by the Queen's Company (Thomas Greene). Payment £10, on warrant dated at Westminster, March 31, 1610. (Chambers, *Eliz. Stage*, iv, 176. See also M. L. R., iv, 154.)

1609. DECEMBER 28 (THURSDAY).

A play before the King by Prince Henry's Company. Payment £10, on the same warrant as that for the play of December 26. (Chambers, *Eliz. Stage*, iv, 176. See also M. L. R., iv, 154.)

1609–10. JANUARY 7 (SUNDAY). ST. JAMES'S.

A play before the King [and the Prince] by Prince Henry's Company. Payment £10, on the same warrant as that for the play of December 26. (Chambers, *Eliz. Stage*, iv, 176. See also *M. L. R.*, iv, 154.)

Birch (*Life of Prince Henry*, p. 185) gives the following account of the occasion on which this play was presented:

These feats of arms, with their triumphant shews, began before ten at night [on Twelfth Day], and continued till three the next morning, being Sunday. On that day his Highness, with his assistants all in a livery, and the defendants richly drest, rode in great pomp to conduct the King to St. James's, whither the Prince had invited him and all the court to supper, the Queen only being absent. The supper was not ended till after ten at night; from whence they went to the play; after which they returned to a set banquet in the gallery, where they had supper, at a table 120 feet in length; and the whole entertainment did not end till three in the morning.

1609–10. JANUARY 18 (THURSDAY).

A play before the King by Prince Henry's Company. Payment £10, on the same warrant as that for the play of December 26. (Chambers, *Eliz. Stage*, iv, 176. See also *M. L. R.*, iv, 154.)

1609–10. FEBRUARY 9 (FRIDAY).

A play before the Prince, the Duke of York, and the Lady Elizabeth "upon the 9th of February 1609" by the Duke of York's Company (William Rowley). Payment £6. 13s. 4d., on warrant dated January 20, 1612–3. (Cunningham, *Revels*, p. xlii. See also Chambers, *Eliz. Stage*, iv, 176.)

SUMMER, 1610

1610. JUNE 5 (TUESDAY). WHITEHALL.

Tethys Festiual: or the Queenes Wake. Celebrated at Whitehall, the fifth day of June 1610. Deuised by Samuel Daniel, one of the Groomes of her Maiesties most Honourable priuie Chamber. London. 1610.

See Reyher, *Masques Anglais*, p. 521.

THE SEASON 1610–1611

1610/1610–11. DATES UNCERTAIN.

Fifteen plays before the King, the Queen, and the Prince, by the King's Company (John Hemynges). Payment £10 each, on warrant dated February 12, 1610–1. (Cunningham, *Revels*, p. xl. See also Stopes, *Burbage*, p. 254; Chambers, *Eliz. Stage*, iv, 176.)

On January 29 Chamberlain wrote to Carleton that there had been "every night a play." (*Court and Times of James I*, i, 133.)

1610. DECEMBER 10 (MONDAY).

Three several plays before the Prince "uppon the xth of Decemb:" by the Queen's Company (Thomas Greene). Payment £6. 13s. 4d. each, on warrant dated March 18, 1610–1. (Chambers, *Eliz. Stage*, iv, 176. See also Cunningham, *Revels*, p. xl. The date is supplied by Chambers from the Rawlinson MS.)

1610. DECEMBER 12 (WEDNESDAY).

A play before the Prince, the Duke of York, and the Lady Elizabeth, by the Duke of York's Company (William Rowley). Payment £6. 13s. 4d., on warrant dated at Westminster, January 20, 1612–3. (Chambers, *Eliz. Stage*, iv, 177. See also Cunningham, *Revels*, p. xlii.)

Possibly this play, and the play of December 20, were two of the four which were given, as it appears from an item in one of the rolls of Prince Henry's expenses, in the month of December in the Cockpit. The item reads:

For makinge readie the Cocke pitt fower seuerall tymes for playes by the space of fower dayes in the month of December 1610. ij. x. viij. (Cunningham, *Revels*, p. xiii.)

1610. DECEMBER 19 (WEDNESDAY).

A play before the King by the Prince's Company (Edwarde Jubye). Payment £10, on warrant dated March 20, 1610–1. (Chambers, *Eliz. Stage*, iv, 177. See also Cunningham, Revels, p. xl, in which the four plays included in the warrant are not dated.)

1610. DECEMBER 20 (THURSDAY).

A play before the Duke of York and the Lady Elizabeth by the Duke of York's Company. Payment £6. 13s. 4d., on the same warrant as that for the play of December 12. (Chambers, *Eliz. Stage*, iv, 177. See also Cunningham, *Revels*, p. xlii.)

1610. DECEMBER 27 (THURSDAY).

A play on "St Johns daye at night 1610 before the Kinges Matie" by the Queen's Company. Payment £10, on the same warrant as that for the play of December 10. (Chambers, *Eliz. Stage*, iv, 176. The date is supplied from the Rawlinson MS. See also Cunningham, *Revels*, p. xl.)

1610. DECEMBER 28 (FRIDAY).

A play before the King by the Prince's Company. Payment £10, on the same warrant as that for the play of December 19. (Chambers, *Eliz. Stage*, iv, 177. See also Cunningham, *Revels*, p. xl.)

1610–1. JANUARY 1 (TUESDAY). WHITEHALL. THE BANQUETING HOUSE.

Oberon, the Fairy Prince, by Ben Jonson.

The title-page, from the 1616 folio, reads: "Oberon, The Faery Prince. A Masque of Prince Henries."

"Uppon New-yeeres night," wrote Edmund Howes, "the Prince of Wales being accompanyed with twelve others . . . performed a very stately Maske, in which was an excellent scene, ingenious speeches, rare songs, and great varieties of most delicate musique, in the beautifull roome at Whitehall; which roome is generally called the Banquetting-house, and the King new builded it about foure yeares past." (Stow's *Annals*, continued by Edmund Howes, 1631, p. 999.) See Reyher, *Masques Anglais*, p. 521.

1610–1. JANUARY 6 (SUNDAY).

The Queen's Masque (*Love Freed from Ignorance and Folly*) was intended for Twelfth Night, but was postponed.

On January 14 [O. S. 4], Marc' Antonio Correr, the Venetian Ambassador in England, wrote from London to the Doge and Senate:

On Tuesday [January 1] the Prince gave his Masque, which was very beautiful throughout, very decorative, but most remarkable for the grace of the Prince's every movement. . . . The Queen, next whom I sat, said that on Sunday next she intended to give her Masque, and she hoped the King would invite me to it. (*Cal. State Papers, Venetian*, xii, 106.)

The performance took place on February 2 or 3, probably on the latter date.

1610–1. JANUARY 14 (MONDAY).

A play before the King by the Prince's Company. Payment £10, on the same warrant as that for the play of December 19. (Chambers, *Eliz. Stage*, iv, 177. See also Cunningham, *Revels*, p. xl.)

1610–1. JANUARY 15 (TUESDAY).

A play before the Duke of York, and the Lady Elizabeth, by the Duke of York's Company. Payment £6. 13s. 4d., on the same warrant as that for the play of December 12. (Chambers, *Eliz. Stage*, iv, 177. See also Cunningham, *Revels*, p. xlii.)

1610–1. JANUARY 16 (WEDNESDAY).

A play before the King, by the Prince's Company. Payment £10, on the same warrant as that for the play of December 19. (Chambers, *Eliz. Stage*, iv, 177. See also Cunningham, *Revels*, p. xl.)

1610–1. FEBRUARY 3 (SUNDAY).

Love Freed from Ignorance and Folly, by Ben Jonson. (See Reyher, *Masques Anglais*, p. 521.)

The title-page, from the folio of 1616, reads: "A Masque of her Maiesties. Love freed from Ignorance and Folly." It was doubtless intended for February 2, and postponed. On February 11 [O .S .1], the Venetian Ambassador wrote: "The Queen's Masque . . . takes place the day after to-morrow." (*Cal. State Papers, Venetian*, xii, 115.)

THE SEASON 1611–1612

Three of the season's plays, one in December and two in January and February, were performed in the Cockpit, as it appears from the following items from one of the rolls of Prince Henry's expenses:

For makeinge readie the Cockepitt for a playe by the space of twoe dayes in the month of December 1611 xxx iiij. (Cunningham, *Revels*, p. xiv.)

For makeinge readie the Cockepitt for playes twoe severall tymes by the space of ffower dayes in the monthes of January and February 1611 lxx viij. (*Ibid.*, p. xiv.)

Probably the plays were among those given before the younger members of the royal family.

1611–1612. DATE UNCERTAIN.

A play before the Prince and the Duke of York by the King's Company.

On the warrant of June 1, 1612, Hemings was paid for twelve plays at the rate of twenty nobles each. Only eleven, however, are given dates. See Cunningham, *Revels*, p. xli; Stopes, *Burbage*, p. 255; Chambers, *Eliz. Stage*, iv, 179. Possibly this was *The Twins' Tragedy*. See the entry for January 1.

1611. OCTOBER 31 (THURSDAY).

A play before the King "upon the laste of October" by the King's Company (John Heminges). Payment £10, on warrant dated June 1, 1612. (Cunningham, *Revels*, p. xl. See also Stopes, *Burbage*, p. 255; Chambers, *Eliz. Stage*, iv, 177.)

1611. NOVEMBER 1 (FRIDAY). WHITEHALL.

"By the Kings Players: Hallomas nyght was presented att Whithall before ye Kings Matie a play called *the Tempest*." (Cunningham, *Revels*, p. 210.)

£10 was paid, on the same warrant as that for the preceding play, for a play before the King "upon the first of November" by the King's Company. (*Ibid.*, pp. xl–xli. See also Stopes, *Burbage*, p. 255; Chambers, *Eliz. Stage*, iv, 177.)

1611. NOVEMBER 5 (TUESDAY).

"The Kings players: The 5th of Nouember; A play called *ye winters nightes Tayle*." (Cunningham, *Revels*, p. 210.)

£10 was paid, on the same warrant as that for the play of October 31, for a play before the King "on the 5th of Nov^r" by the King's Company. (*Ibid.*, pp. xl–xli. See also Stopes, *Burbage*, p. 255; Chambers, *Eliz. Stage*, iv, 177.)

1611. NOVEMBER 9 (SATURDAY).

A play before the Prince and the Duke of York "upon the 9th of Novr last" by the King's Company (John Hemynges). Payment £6. 13s. 4d., on warrant dated June 1, 1612. (Cunningham, *Revels*, p. xli. See also Stopes, *Burbage*, p. 255; Chambers, *Eliz. Stage*, iv, 178.)

1611. NOVEMBER 19 (TUESDAY).

A play before the Prince and the Duke of York "upon the 19th of the same" by the King's Company. Payment £6. 13s. 4d., on the same warrant as that for the preceding play. (Cunningham, *Revels*, p. xli. See also Stopes, *Burbage*, p. 255; Chambers, *Eliz. Stage*, iv, 178.)

1611. DECEMBER 16 (MONDAY).

A play before the Prince and the Duke of York "upon the 16th of December" by the King's Company. Payment £6. 13s. 4d., on the same warrant as that for the play of November 9. (Cunningham, *Revels*, p. xli. See also Stopes, *Burbage*, p. 255; Chambers, *Eliz. Stage*, iv, 178.)

1611. DECEMBER 26 (THURSDAY).

"The Kings players: On St Stiuenes night A play called *A King [and] no King*" [Beaumont and Fletcher]. (Cunningham, *Revels*, p. 211.)

£10 was paid, on the same warrant as that for the play of October 31, for a play before the King "on the 26th Dec^r" by the King's Company. (*Ibid.*, pp. xl–xli. See also Stopes, *Burbage*, p. 255; Chambers, *Eliz. Stage*, iv, 177.)

1611. DECEMBER 27 (FRIDAY).

"The Queens players: St John night A play called *the City Gallant*" [Jo. Cooke]. (Cunningham, *Revels*, p. 211.)

£10 was paid, on a warrant dated June 18, 1612, for a play before the King and the Queen "upon the 27th of December last" by the Queen's Company (Thomas Greene). (*Ibid.*, p. xli. See also Chambers, *Eliz. Stage*, iv, 178.)

1611. DECEMBER 28 (SATURDAY).

A play before the King by the Prince's Company (Edward Juby). Payment £10, on warrant dated June 18, 1612. (Cunningham, *Revels*, p. xli. See also Chambers, *Eliz. Stage*, iv, 178.)

1611. DECEMBER 29 (SUNDAY).

"The Princes players. The Sunday followinge A play called *the Almanak.*" (Cunningham, *Revels*, p. 211.)

£10 was paid, on the same warrant as that for the preceding play, for a play before the King on December 29, by the Prince's Company. (*Ibid.*, p. xli. See also Chambers, *Eliz. Stage*, iv, 178.)

1611. DECEMBER 31 (TUESDAY).

A play before the Prince and the Duke of York "upon the last of the same" by the King's Company. Payment £6. 13s. 4d., on the same warrant as that for the play of November 9. (Cunningham, *Revels*, p. xli. See also Stopes, *Burbage*, p. 255; Chambers, *Eliz. Stage*, iv, 178.)

1611–2. JANUARY 1 (WEDNESDAY).

"The Kings players. On Neweres night A play called *the Twinnes Tragedie*" [Richard Niccols]. (Cunningham, *Revels*, p. 211.)

No warrant for payment has been found.

1611–2. JANUARY 5 (SUNDAY).

"The Childern of Whitfriars. The Sunday followinge A play called *Cupids Reueng*" [John Fletcher]. (Cunningham, *Revels*, p. 211.)

No warrant for payment has been found.

1611–2. JANUARY 5 (SUNDAY).

A play before the King "on the 5th of January" by the King's Company. Payment £10, on the same warrant as that for the play of October 31. (Cunningham, *Revels*, pp. xl–xli. See also Stopes, *Burbage*, p. 255; Chambers, *Eliz. Stage*, iv, 177.)

1611–2. JANUARY 6 (MONDAY).

Love Restored, by Ben Jonson.

The title-page, from the folio of 1616, reads: "Love restored, In a Masque at Court." For a discussion of the date of the performance, see R. Brotanek, *Englische Maskenspiele*, pp. 346–48. See also Reyher, *Masques Anglais*, p. 521.

1611–2. JANUARY 7 (TUESDAY).

A play before the Prince and the Duke of York "upon the 7th of January" by the King's Company. Payment £6. 13s. 4d., on the same warrant as that for the play of November 9. (Cunningham, *Revels*, p. xli. See also Stopes, *Burbage*, p. 255; Chambers, *Eliz. Stage*, iv, 178.)

1611–2. JANUARY 12 (SUNDAY).

A play before the Duke of York and the Lady Elizabeth "upon the 12th January 1611" by the Duke of York's Company (William Rowley). Payment £6. 13s. 4d., on a warrant dated at Westminster, June 20, 1612. (Cunningham, *Revels*, p. xlii. See also Chambers, *Eliz. Stage*, iv, 179.)

1611–2. JANUARY 12 (SUNDAY). GREENWICH.

"By the Queens players and the Kings Men. The Sunday followinge att Grinwidg before the Queen and the Prince was played *the Siluer Aiedg*" [Thomas Heywood]. (Cunningham, *Revels*, p. 211.)

1611–2. JANUARY 13 (MONDAY). GREENWICH.

"And yͤ next night following *Lucrecia*" [Heywood's *Rape of Lucrece*]. [By the Queen's players and the King's Men.] (Cunningham, *Revels*, p. 211.)

See the preceding entry. For an explanation of the union of the companies of the King and the Queen, see the article entitled "Shakespeare, Heywood, and the Classics," by Professor J. Q. Adams, in *Modern Language Notes*, June, 1919.

1611–2. JANUARY 15 (WEDNESDAY).

A play before the Prince and the Duke of York "upon the 15th of the same" by the King's Company. Payment £6. 13*s.* 4*d.*, on the same warrant as that for the play of November 9. (Cunningham, *Revels*, p. xli. See also Stopes, *Burbage*, p. 255, in which the play is dated January 13; Chambers, *Eliz. Stage*, iv, 178.)

1611–2. JANUARY 16 (THURSDAY).

A play before the Prince and the Lady Elizabeth on the "16th of January laste" by the Queen's Company (Thomas Greene). Payment £6. 13*s.* 4*d.*, on a warrant of June 18, 1612. (Cunningham, *Revels*, p. xli. See also Chambers, *Eliz. Stage*, iv, 178, in which the date is given as January 21.)

1611–2. JANUARY 19 (SUNDAY).

A play before the Prince and the Lady Elizabeth by the Lady Elizabeth's Company (Alexander Foster). Payment £6. 13*s.* 4*d.*, on warrant dated April 1, 1612. (Chambers, *Eliz. Stage*, iv, 179. See also Cunningham, *Revels*, p. xl, in which the two plays included in the warrant are not dated.)

1611–2. JANUARY 21 (TUESDAY).

See the entry for January 16.

1611–2. JANUARY 23 (THURSDAY).

A play before the Prince and the Lady Elizabeth "upon the 23rd of the same" by the Queen's Company. Payment £6. 13*s.* 4*d.*, on the same warrant as that for the preceding play. (Cunningham, *Revels*, p. xli. See also Chambers, *Eliz. Stage*, iv, 178.)

1611–2. JANUARY 28 (TUESDAY).

A play before the Prince, the Duke of York, and the Lady Elizabeth "upon the 28th of January" by the Duke of York's

Company. Payment £6. 13s. 4d., on the same warrant as that for the play of January 12. (Cunningham, *Revels*, p. xlii. See also Chambers, *Eliz. Stage*, iv, 179.)

1611–2. FEBRUARY 2 (SUNDAY).

"By the Queens players. Candelmas night A play called *Tu Coque*" [*Greene's Tu Quoque, or the City Gallant*, by Jo. Cooke]. (Cunningham, *Revels*, p. 211.)

£10 was paid, on the same warrant as that for the play of December 27, for a play before the King and Queen "upon the 2nd of February following" by the Queen's Company. (*Ibid.*, p. xli. See also Chambers, *Eliz. Stage*, iv, 178.)

1611–2. FEBRUARY 5 (WEDNESDAY).

A play before the Prince on February 5 by the Prince's Company (Edward Juby). Payment £6. 13s. 4d., on a warrant dated June 18, 1612. (Cunningham, *Revels*, p. xlii. See also Chambers, *Eliz. Stage*, iv, 178.)

1611–2. FEBRUARY 9 (SUNDAY).

A play before the Prince, the Lady Elizabeth, and the Duke of York "on the 9th of February last" by the King's Company (John Hemynges). Payment £6. 13s. 4d., on warrant dated June 1, 1612. (Cunningham, *Revels*, p. xli. See also Stopes, *Burbage*, p. 255; Chambers, *Eliz. Stage*, iv, 178.)

1611–2. FEBRUARY 13 (THURSDAY).

A play before the Prince, the Duke of York, and the Lady Elizabeth "upon the 13th of February" by the Duke of York's Company. Payment £6. 13s. 4d., on the same warrant as that for the play of January 12. (Cunningham, *Revels*, p. xlii. See also Chambers, *Eliz. Stage*, iv, 179.)

1611–2. FEBRUARY 18 (TUESDAY).

A play before the Prince, the Duke of York, and the Lady Elizabeth "upon the 18th of the same moneth" by the Duke of York's Company. Payment £6. 13s. 4d., on the same warrant as that for the play of January 12. (Cunningham, *Revels*, p. xlii. See also Chambers, *Eliz. Stage*, iv, 179, in which the date is given as February 24. See the entry under that date.)

1611–2. FEBRUARY 19 (WEDNESDAY).

A play before the Prince and the Duke of York "upon the 19th of February" by the King's Company. Payment £6. 13*s*. 4*d*., on the same warrant as that for the play of November 9. (Cunningham, *Revels*, p. xli. See also Stopes, Burbage, p. 255; Chambers, *Eliz. Stage*, iv, 178.)

1611–2. FEBRUARY 20 (THURSDAY).

A play before the Prince and the Duke of York "upon the 20th of the same" by the King's Company. Payment £6. 13*s*. 4*d*., on the same warrant as that for the play of November 9. (Cunningham, *Revels*, p. xli. See also Stopes, *Burbage*, p. 255; Chambers, *Eliz. Stage*, iv, 178.)

1611–2. FEBRUARY 20 (THURSDAY).

A play before Prince Henry on "the 20th of the same" by the King's Company. Payment £6. 13*s*. 4*d*., on the same warrant as that for February 9. (Cunningham, *Revels*, p. xli. See also Stopes, *Burbage*, p. 255; Chambers, *Eliz. Stage*, iv, 178.)

1611–2. FEBRUARY 23 (SHROVE SUNDAY).

"By the Kings players. Shroue Sunday: A play called *The Noblman*" [Cyril Tourneur]. (Cunningham, *Revels*, p. 211.)

£10 was paid, on the same warrant as that for the play of October 31, for a play before the King "upon Shrovesunday at night being the 23rd of February," by the King's Company. (*Ibid.*, pp. xl–xli. See also Stopes, *Burbage*, p. 255; Chambers, *Eliz. Stage*, iv, 177.)

1611–2. FEBRUARY 24 (SHROVE MONDAY).

"By the Duck of Yorks players. Shroue Munday: A play called *Himens Haliday*" [William Rowley]. (Cunningham, *Revels*, p. 211.)

If the date as given by Chambers is the correct one, the play was paid for on a warrant of June 20. See the entry for February 18.

1611–2. FEBRUARY 25 (SHROVE TUESDAY).

"By the Ladye Elizabeths players. Shroue Teuesday A play called *the proud Mayds Tragedie.*" (Cunningham, *Revels*, p. 211.)

£10 was paid, on a warrant dated April 1, 1612, for a play before the King "on Shrovetewsday laste at night called *the prowde Mayde*" by the Lady Elizabeth's Company (Alexander Foster). (*Ibid.*, p. xl. See also Chambers, *Eliz. Stage*, iv, 179.)

1611–2. FEBRUARY 28 (FRIDAY).

A play before the Prince and the Duke of York "upon the 28th of February" by the King's Company. Payment £6. 13s. 4d., on the same warrant as that for the play of November 9. (Cunningham, *Revels*, p. xli. See also Stopes, *Burbage*, p. 255; Chambers, *Eliz. Stage*, iv, 178; Cf. *ibid.*, p. 126.)

1611–2. FEBRUARY 29 (SATURDAY).

A play before the Prince on the "29th of February laste" by the Prince's Company. Payment £6. 13s. 4d., on the same warrant as that for the play of February 5. (Cunningham, *Revels*, p. xlii. See also Chambers, *Eliz. Stage*, iv, 178.)

1611–2. MARCH 11 (WEDNESDAY).

A play before the Prince and the Lady Elizabeth by the Lady Elizabeth's Company. Payment £6. 13s. 4d., on the same warrant as that for the play of January 19. (Chambers, *Eliz. Stage*, iv, 179. See also Cunningham, *Revels*, p. xl.)

1612. MARCH 28 (SATURDAY).

A play before the Lady Elizabeth on "the 28th of Marche" by the King's Company. Payment £6. 13s. 4d., on the same warrant as that for the play of February 9. (Cunningham, *Revels*, p. xli. See also Stopes, *Burbage*, p. 255; Chambers, *Eliz. Stage*, iv, 178.)

1612. APRIL 3 (FRIDAY).

A play before the Prince and the Duke of York "upon the 3rd of April" by the King's Company. Payment £6. 13s. 4d., on the same warrant as that for the play of November 9. (Cunningham, *Revels*, p. xli. See also Stopes, *Burbage*, p. 255; Chambers, *Eliz. Stage*, iv, 178.)

1612. APRIL 11 (SATURDAY).

A play before the Lady Elizabeth by the Prince Palatine's Company (Edward Jubye). Payment £6. 13s. 4d., on warrant dated March 31, 1613. (Chambers, *Eliz. Stage*, iv, 179. The date is supplied from the Rawlinson MS. See also Cunningham, *Revels*, p. xlii.)

1612. APRIL 16 (THURSDAY).

A play before the Prince and the Duke of York "upon the 16th of the same" by the King's Company. Payment £6. 13s. 4d., on the same warrant as that for the play of November 9. (Cunningham, *Revels*, p. xli. See also Stopes, *Burbage*, p. 255; Chambers, *Eliz. Stage*, iv, 178.)

1612. APRIL 26 (SUNDAY).

A play before the Prince, the Duke of York, and the Lady Elizabeth "on the 26th of April" by the King's Company. Payment £6. 13s. 4d., on the same warrant as that for the play of February 9. (Cunningham, *Revels*, p. xli. See also Stopes, *Burbage*, p. 255; Chambers, *Eliz. Stage*, iv, 178.)

THE SEASON 1612–1613

For the warrant printed by Cunningham (*Revels*, p. xlii) as of the date May 19, 1613, see the entry for 1614/1614-5, Dates Uncertain.

1612/1612-3. DATES UNCERTAIN.

"Six severall playes" before the King by the King's Company (John Hemings), "viz: one play called *A badd beginninge makes a good endinge*, One other called *ye Capteyne* [Beaumont and Fletcher], one other *the Alcumist* [Ben Jonson]. One other *Cardenno*, One other the Hotspur [*I Henry IV*?], And one other called *Benedicte and Betteris* [*Much Ado about Nothing*]." Payment £10 each, on warrant dated May 20, 1613. (Chambers, *Eliz. Stage*, iv, 180. See also Cunningham, "Plays at Court, Anno 1613," in *Shakespeare Society's Papers*, ii, 125; *Revels*, p. xliii; Stopes, *Burbage*, p. 255.)

1612/1612–3. DATES UNCERTAIN.

"Fowerteene severall playes" before Prince Charles, Lady Elizabeth, and the Prince Palatine by the King's Company (Hemmynges), "viz: one playe called *ffilaster* [Beaumont and Fletcher], One other called *the knott of ffooles*, One other *Much adoe aboute nothinge*, *The Mayeds Tragedy* [Beaumont and Fletcher], *The merye dyvell of Edmonton*, *The Tempest*, *A Kinge and no Kinge* [Beaumont and Fletcher], *The Twins Tragedie* [Richard Niccols], *The Winters Tale*, *Sir John ffalstaffe* [Shakespeare's *Merry Wives of Windsor*], *The Moore of Venice* [Shakespeare's *Othello*], *The Nobleman* [Cyril Tourneur], *Caesars Tragedye* [Shakespeare's *Julius Caesar*?], And on other called *Love lyes a bleedinge* [*Philaster*]". Payment £93. 6s. 8d., on warrant dated at Whitehall, May 20, 1613. (Chambers, *Eliz. Stage*, iv, 180. See also Cunningham, "Plays at Court, Anno 1613," in *Shakespeare Society's Papers*, ii, 124; *Revels*, xliii; Stopes, *Burbage*, p. 255, in which the warrant appears, without titles, and the payment is given as £94. 6s. 8d.)

1612. DATE UNCERTAIN.

"A Commedye called *the Coxcombe*" [Beaumont and Fletcher], acted before Prince Charles, the Princess Elizabeth, and the Elector Palatine by the Children of the Queen's Majesty's Revels (Phillip Rosseter). Payment £6. 13s. 4d., on warrant dated November 24, 1612. (Chambers, *Eliz. Stage*, iv, 181. See also Cunningham, in the *Shakespeare Society's Papers*, ii, 125; *Revels*, p. xlii.)

1612. OCTOBER 20 (TUESDAY). WHITEHALL. THE COCK-PIT.

A play before the Lady Elizabeth and the Elector Palatine in the Cockpit, by Lady Elizabeth's Company.

On October 22, 1612, John Chamberlain wrote to Sir Dudley Carleton: "On Tuesday she [Lady Elizabeth] sent to invite him [the Elector Palatine], as he sat at supper, to a play of her own servants in the Cockpit." (*Court and Times of James I*, i, 198.) Chambers (*Eliz. Stage*, iv, 181) suggests that this was probably the play for which £5 was paid "to her gracs plaiers for acting a Comedie in the Cocke pitt wch her highnes lost to Mr Edward Sackvile on a wager."

1612. NOVEMBER 1 (SUNDAY).

"Revelling and Plays" appointed for that night were put off on account of the illness of Prince Henry. (Winwood, *Memorials of Affairs of State*, iii, 406. See also Chamberlain to Carleton, *Court and Times of James I*, i, 201, in which the date is given as October 31.)

1612. NOVEMBER 2 (MONDAY).

A play before the Lady Elizabeth and the Elector Palatine. Possibly this was *The Coxcomb*. See the entry for 1612, Date Uncertain.

On November 3, 1612, Chamberlain wrote to Sir Ralph Winwood: "Yester Night her Grace invited him to a solemn Supper and a Play." (Winwood, *op. cit.*, iii, 406. See also Chamberlain to Carleton, *Court and Times of James I*, i, 201, in which the date is given as November 3.)

1612–3. JANUARY 1 (FRIDAY).

A play "called *Cupides Revenge*" acted before the King on January 1, "1613", by the Children of the Chapel (Phillip Rosseter). Payment £10, on warrant dated May 31. (Chambers, *Eliz. Stage*, iv, 181. See also Cunningham, in *Shakespeare Society's Papers*, ii, 126.)

1612–3. JANUARY 9 (SATURDAY).

"One called *Cupidds revenge*," acted before Prince Charles, Lady Elizabeth, and the Elector Palatine by the Children of the Queen's Majesty's Revels [Philip Rosseter]. Payment £6. 13s. 4d., on warrant dated May 31, 1613. (Chambers, *Eliz. Stage*, iv, 181. See also Cunningham, in *Shakespeare Society's Papers*, ii, 126; *Revels*, p. xlii.)

1612–3. FEBRUARY 14 (SUNDAY). WHITEHALL. THE BANQUETING HOUSE.

The Lords' Masque, by Thomas Campion.

According to the title-page (see the entry for April 27), the masque was presented in the Banqueting House on the marriage-night of the Lady Elizabeth and the Elector Palatine. See Reyher, *Masques Anglais*, p. 522.

1612–3. FEBRUARY 15 (SHROVE MONDAY). WHITEHALL. THE GREAT HALL.

The memorable Masque of the two honourable Houses or Innes of Court; the Middle Temple, and Lyncolnes Inne. As it was performed before the King, at White-hall on Shroue-Munday at night; being the 15. of Febr. 1613. At the princely Celebration of the most royall Nuptialls of the Palsgraue, and his thrice gratious Princesse Elizabeth, &c. With a description of their whole show, in the manner of their march on horse backe to the Court, from the Master of the Rolls his house: with all their right Noble consorts, and most showfull attendants. Inuented, and fashioned, with the ground, and speciall structure of the whole worke: By our Kingdomes most Artfull and Ingenious Architect Innigo Iones. Supplied, Applied, Digested, and written, By Geo. Chapman. London. [n.d.]

Chamberlain, in a letter of February 18 to Sir Dudley Carleton, notes the place of performance: "On Monday night was the Middle Temple and Lincoln's Inn Mask presented in the Hall at Court; whereas the Lords' was in the Banqueting-room." (Nichols, *Progresses James*, ii, 588.)

1612–3. FEBRUARY 16 (SHROVE TUESDAY).

The Masque of the Inner Temple and Gray's Inn was prepared for Shrove Tuesday, but postponed on account of the weariness of the King.

On February 18 Chamberlain wrote to Sir Dudley Carleton:

On Tuesday it came to Gray's Inn and the Inner Temple's turn to come with their Mask, whereof Sir Francis Bacon was the chief contriver; and because the former [masque of Shrove Monday] came on horseback and open chariots, they made choice to come by water . . . . But by what ill planet it fell out I know not; they came home as they went without doing anything; the reason whereof I cannot yet learn thoroughly, but only that the Hall was so full that it was not possible to avoid it, or make room for them; besides that most of the Ladies were in the Galleries to see them land, and could not get in. But the worst of all was, that the King was so wearied and sleepy with sitting up almost two whole nights before, that he had no edge to it. Whereupon Sir Francis Bacon ventured to entreat his Majesty, that by this disgrace he would not as it were bury them quick; and I hear the King should answer, that then they must bury him quick, for he could last no longer; but withal gave them very good words, and appointed them to come again on Saturday. (Nichols, *Progresses James*, ii, 589.)

The masque was successfully presented on the following Saturday.

1612–3. FEBRUARY 20 (SATURDAY). WHITEHALL. THE BANQUETING HOUSE.

The Masque of the Inner Temple and Grayes Inne: Grayes Inne and the Inner Temple, presented before his Maiestie, the Queenes Maiestie, the Prince, Count Palatine and the Lady Elizabeth their Highnesses, in the Banquetting house at White-hall on Saturday the twentieth day of Februarie, 1612. London. [n.d.]

By Francis Beaumont. See Reyher, *Masques Anglais*, p. 522.

1612–3. FEBRUARY 25 (THURSDAY).

"One playe called *Cockle-de-moye*" [John Marston's *The Dutch Courtesan*] before Prince Charles, the Elector Palatine, and the Lady Elizabeth by the Lady Elizabeth's Company (Joseph Taylor). Payment £6. 13s. 4d., on warrant dated June 28, 1613. (Chambers, *Eliz. Stage*, iv, 180. See also Cunningham, in *Shakespeare Society's Papers*, ii, 124, in which the play is dated February 20; *Revels*, p. xliii.)

1612–3. FEBRUARY 27 (SATURDAY).

"The other called *the Widdowes Teares*" [George Chapman] before Prince Charles, Lady Elizabeth, and the Elector Palatine by the Children of the Queen's Majesty's Revels. Payment £6. 13*s*. 4*d*., on the same warrant as that for the play of January 9. (Chambers, *Eliz. Stage*, iv, 181. See also Cunningham, in *Shakespeare Society's Papers*, ii, 126, in which the date of the play is given as February 20; *Revels*, p. xlii.)

1612–3. MARCH 1 (MONDAY).

"One other called *Raymond Duke of Lyons*," before Prince Charles, the Elector Palatine, and the Lady Elizabeth by the Lady Elizabeth's Company. Payment £6. 13*s*. 4*d*., on the same warrant as that for *Cockle de moy*. (Chambers, *Eliz. Stage*, iv, 180. See also Cunningham, in *Shakespeare Society's Papers*, ii, 123–4; *Revels*, pp. xlii–xliii.)

1612–3. MARCH 2 (TUESDAY).

"One called *the first parte of the Knaues*" before Prince Charles, the Elector Palatine, and the Lady Elizabeth by the Prince's Company (William Rowley). Payment £6. 13*s*. 4*d*., on warrant dated June 7, 1613. (Chambers, *Eliz. Stage*, iv, 180. See also Cunningham, in *Shakespeare Society's Papers*, ii, 123–4; *Revels*, pp. xlii–xliii.)

1612–3. MARCH 3 (WEDNESDAY). CAMBRIDGE. TRINITY COLLEGE.

Adelphe, a Latin comedy, before Prince Charles and the Elector Palatine.

The following account of the occasion is taken from an article entitled "Latin Plays Acted before the University of Cambridge", in the *Retrospective Review*, xii (1825), 31:

Upon the first night, the comedy of *Adelphe* was performed; it still exists in manuscript in Trinity College Library, without the author's name, bearing upon it the date of 1622, which will authorise the assertion that it was again acted in that year. It commenced at seven o'clock *aut circiter*, and continued until one in the morning; we have, therefore, no reason to be surprised when the unpublished record consulted tells us that the Count Palatine slept the greater part of it. Prince Charles was very attentive, and "notwithstanding it was so long, seemed to listen with very good patience and great contentment." However, both of them upon their return to Newmarket, complained of its immoderate length and stupidity.

Compare the letter of Chamberlain to Carleton, *Court and Times of James I*, i, 233. See the following entry.

1612–3. MARCH 4 (THURSDAY). CAMBRIDGE. TRINITY COLLEGE.

Scyros, a Latin pastoral by Samuel Brooke, before Prince Charles and the Elector Palatine.

The author of the article in the *Retrospective Review* continues:

The next night the Pastoral of *Scyros* was represented; this exists in manuscript in the same library [Trinity]; there is also a copy in the University Library which gives the actors' names: amongst them are those of Hackett, afterwards bishop of Litchfield and Coventry, and author of *Loiola*; and of Stubbe, author of *Fraus Honesta.*—The scene of *Scyros* is laid in the island of that name in the Aegean Sea, in the valley of Alcander, and the time is twelve hours. It was written by Brookes, a fellow of Trinity, who wrote another pastoral, *Melanthe.*—A third copy of *Scyros* is in Emmanuel College Library, having the 30th instead of the 3d of March 1612, for Prince Charles's visit.

G. C. Moore Smith (*College Plays*, p. 66) reverses the dates of *Scyros* and *Adelphe*.

1612–3. MARCH 10 (WEDNESDAY).

"And one other playe called *the second parte of the Knaues*," before Prince Charles, the Elector Palatine, and the Lady Elizabeth by the Prince's Company. Payment £6. 13*s*. 4*d*., on the same warrant as that for the *First Part*. (Chambers, *Eliz. Stage*, iv, 180. See also Cunningham, in *Shakespeare Society's Papers*, ii, 123–4, in which the date of the play is given as March 5; *Revels*, pp. xlii–xliii.)

1613. APRIL 27 (TUESDAY). CAVERSHAM HOUSE.

A Relation of the late royall Entertainment giuen by the Right Honorable the Lord Knowles, at Cawsome-House neere Redding: to our most Gracious Queene, Queene Anne, in her Progresse toward the Bathe, vpon the seuen and eight and twentie dayes of Aprill. 1613. Whereunto is annexed the Description, Speeches, and Songs of the Lords Maske, presented in the Banquetting-house on the Mariage night of the High and Mightie, Count Palatine, and the Royally descended the Ladie Elizabeth. Written by Thomas Campion. London. 1613.

This entertainment includes a genuine masque, performed before the Queen on the night of the 27th, in the hall of Caversham House. See Reyher, *Masques Anglais*, p. 522. For the *Lords' Masque*, see the entry for 1612–3, February 14.

SUMMER, 1613

1613. JUNE 8 (TUESDAY).

"A playe . . . called *Cardenna*" acted before the Duke of Savoy's Ambassadors by the King's Company (John Hemmynges). Payment £6. 8s. 4d., on warrant dated July 9, 1613. (Chambers, *Eliz. Stage*, iv, 179. See also Cunningham, in *Shakespeare Society's Papers*, ii, 125; *Revels*, p. xliii; Stopes, *Burbage*, p. 255.)

THE SEASON 1613–1614

1613. NOVEMBER 1 (MONDAY).

A play before the King on November 1 by the King's Company (John Hemings). Payment £10, on warrant dated June 21, 1614. (Stopes, *Burbage*, p. 255. See also Cunningham, *Revels*, p. xliii, in which exact dates for the nine plays included in the warrant are not given; Chambers, *Eliz. Stage*, iv, 182.)

1613. NOVEMBER 4 (THURSDAY).

A play before the Prince "on the 4th of Nov^r" by the King's Company (John Hemynges). Payment £6. 13s. 4d., on warrant dated June 21, 1614. (Cunningham, *Revels*, p. xliii. See also Stopes, *Burbage*, p. 255; Chambers, *Eliz. Stage*, iv, 181.)

1613. NOVEMBER 5 (FRIDAY).

A play before the King on November 5 by the King's Company. Payment £10, on the same warrant as that for the play of November 1. (Stopes, *Burbage*, p. 255. See also Cunningham, *Revels*, p. xliii; Chambers, *Eliz. Stage*, iv, 182.)

1613. NOVEMBER 15 (MONDAY).

A play before the King on November 15 by the King's Company. Payment £10, on the same warrant as that for the play of November 1. (Stopes, *Burbage*, p. 255. See also Cunningham, *Revels*, p. xliii; Chambers, *Eliz. Stage*, iv, 182.)

1613. NOVEMBER 16 (TUESDAY).

A play before the Prince on "the 16th of Nov^r" by the King's Company. Payment £6. 13s. 4d., on the same warrant as that for the play of November 4. (Cunningham, *Revels*, p. xliii. See also Stopes, *Burbage*, p. 255; Chambers, *Eliz. Stage*, iv, 181.)

1613. DECEMBER 12 (SUNDAY).

The Dutch Curtezan [John Marston] before the Prince "on the 12th of December last paste" by the Lady Elizabeth's Company (Joseph Taylor). Payment £6. 13s. 4d., on warrant dated June 21, 1614. (Cunningham, *Revels*, p. xliv. See also Chambers, *Eliz. Stage*, iv, 182, in which the warrant is dated at Westminster.)

1613. DECEMBER 26 (SUNDAY). WHITEHALL. THE BANQUETING HOUSE.

The Description of a Maske: Presented in the Banqueting roome at White-hall, on Saint Stephens night last, At the Mariage of the Right Honourable the Earle of Somerset: And the right noble the Lady Frances Howard. Written by Thomas Campion. Whereunto are annexed diuers choyse Ayres composed for this Maske that may be sung with a single voyce to the Lute or Base-Viall. London. 1614.

See Reyher, *Masques Anglais*, p. 523. This is usually entitled *The Squires' Masque*.

1613. DECEMBER 27 (MONDAY). [WHITEHALL.]

A play before the King on December 27 by the King's Company. Payment £10, on the same warrant as that for the play of November 1. (Cunningham, *Revels*, p. xliii; Chambers, *Eliz. Stage*, iv, 182.)

1613. DECEMBER 28 (TUESDAY). [WHITEHALL.]

A play before the King "on the 28th of December" by the Queen's Company (Robte Lee). Payment £10, on warrant dated Whitehall, June 21, 1614. (Cunningham, *Revels*, p. xliii. See also Chambers, *Eliz. Stage*, iv, 182, in which the date is given as December 24, and the warrant dated at Westminster.)

1613. DECEMBER 29 (WEDNESDAY). [WHITEHALL.]

The Irish Masque, by Ben Jonson. (Reyher, *Masques Anglais*, p. 523.)

The title-page, from the 1616 folio, reads: "The Irish Masque at Court." Chamberlain wrote to Carleton, on January 5: "The masquers were so well liked at Court the last week that they were appointed to perform again on Monday; yet their device, which was a mimical imitation of the Irish, was not pleasing to many, who think it no time, as the case stands, to exasperate that nation by making it ridiculous." (*Court and Times of James I*, i, 287.)

1613–4. JANUARY 1 (SATURDAY). [WHITEHALL.]

A play before the King on January 1 by the King's Company. Payment £10, on the same warrant as that for the play of November 1. (Stopes, *Burbage*, p. 255. See also Cunningham, *Revels*, p. xliii; Chambers, *Eliz. Stage*, iv, 182.)

1613–4. JANUARY 3 (MONDAY). [WHITEHALL.]

The Irish Masque, by Ben Jonson, again performed at Court. (Reyher, *Masques Anglais*, p. 523.)

1613–4. JANUARY 4 (TUESDAY). MERCHANT TAILORS' HALL.

"Two severall pleasant Maskes, and a Play," according to Howes, were presented in honor of the marriage of Robert Kerr, Earl of Somerset, to the Lady Frances Howard. One of the masques was the *Masque of Cupid*, by Thomas Middleton. Nichols assumes, upon the evidence of the order made in the Court of Aldermen for payment "for all his disbursements and paynes taken by him and others in the last *Mask of Cupids*, and other Shewes lately made at the aforesaid Hall by the said Mr. Middleton," that he was the author of the other masque and the play. (*Progresses James*, ii, 732.)

The King seems not to have been present on this occasion, although the Lord Mayor had provided the entertainment by royal order, and the bride and bridegroom were accompanied by many members of the Court. See the letter of Chamberlain to Carleton, *Court and Times of James I*, i, 288.

1613–4. JANUARY 4 (TUESDAY). [WHITEHALL.]

A play before the King on January 4 by the King's Company. Payment £10, on the same warrant as that for the play of November 1. (Stopes, *Burbage*, p. 255. See also Cunningham, *Revels*, p. xliii; Chambers, *Eliz. Stage*, iv, 182.)

1613–4. JANUARY 5 (WEDNESDAY). [WHITEHALL.]

A play before the King on "the 5th of January" by the Queen's Company. Payment £10, on the same warrant as that for the play of December 28. (Cunningham, *Revels*, p. xliii. See also Chambers, *Eliz. Stage*, iv, 182.)

1613–4. JANUARY 6 (THURSDAY). WHITEHALL. THE BANQUETING HOUSE.

The Maske of Flowers. Presented By the Gentlemen of Graies-Inne, at the Court of White-hall, in the Banquetting House, vpon Twelfe night, 1613. Being the last of the Solemnities and Magnificences which were performed at the marriage of the right honourable the Earle of Somerset, and the Lady Francis daughter of the Earle of Suffolke, Lord Chamberlaine. London. 1614.

The masque is dedicated to Sir Francis Bacon as the "principall . . . person that did both encourage and warrant the Gentlemen." The dedication is signed "J. G., W. D., T. B." See Reyher, *Masques Anglais*, p. 523.

1613–4. JANUARY 10 (MONDAY).

A play before the Prince on "the 10th of January" by the King's Company. Payment £6. 13s. 4d., on the same warrant as that for the play of November 4. (Cunningham, *Revels*, p. xliii. See also Stopes, *Burbage*, p. 255; Chambers, *Eliz. Stage*, iv, 181.)

1613–4. JANUARY 25 (TUESDAY).

Eastward Howe [Chapman, Jonson, Marston] before the King "on the xxvth of January last past" by the Lady Elizabeth's Company (Joseph Taylor). Payment £10, on warrant dated at Whitehall, June 21, 1614. (Cunningham, *Revels*, p. xliv. See also Chambers, *Eliz. Stage*, iv, 182, in which the warrant is dated at Westminster.)

1613–4. FEBRUARY 2 (WEDNESDAY).

A play before the King on February 2 by the King's Company. Payment £10, on the same warrant as that for the play of November 1. (Stopes, *Burbage*, p. 255. See also Cunningham, *Revels*, p. xliii; Chambers, *Eliz. Stage*, iv, 182.)

1613–4. FEBRUARY 3 (THURSDAY). SOMERSET HOUSE.

Hymens Triumph. A Pastorall Tragicomaedie. Presented at the Queenes Court in the Strand at her Maiesties magnificent intertainement of the Kings most excellent Maiestie, being at the Nuptials of the Lord Roxborough. By Samuel Daniel. London. 1615.

This pastoral, wrote Chamberlain to Carleton on February 3, "shall be represented in a little square paved court." (Nichols, *Progresses James*, ii, 748.) Again on February 10 he wrote:

This day se'ennight the Lord Roxburgh married Mrs. Grace Drummond at Somerset House, or Queen's Court, as it must now be called. The King tarried there till Saturday after dinner. The entertainment was great, and cost the Queen, they say, above £3000. The Pastoral by Samuel Daniel was solemn and dull; but perhaps better to be read than represented. (*Ibid.*, ii, 754.)

Finett (p. 16) gives the date as February 2.

1613–4. FEBRUARY 4 (FRIDAY). SOMERSET HOUSE.

A play at Court before the Lord Mayor and the Aldermen. Possibly this play was acted by the King's Company. See the following entry.

In his letter to Carleton of February 10 (see entry above) in which he describes the festivities connected with Lord Roxborough's marriage, Chamberlain continues:

The Lord Mayor and all the Aldermen were invited for the next day after the Marriage, and had rich gloves. They went thither in pomp, and were graciously used; and besides their great cheer and many healths, had a Play.

1613–4. FEBRUARY 4 (FRIDAY).

A play before the Prince on "the 4th of February" by the King's Company. Payment £6. 13*s*. 4*d*., on the same warrant as that for the play of November 4. (Cunningham, *Revels*, p. xliii. See also Stopes, *Burbage*, p. 255; Chambers, *Eliz. Stage*, iv, 181.)

1613–4. FEBRUARY 8 (TUESDAY).

A play before the Prince on February 8 by the King's Company. Payment £6. 13*s*. 4*d*., on the same warrant as that for the play of November 4. (Cunningham, *Revels*, p. xliii. See also Stopes, *Burbage*, p. 255; Chambers, *Eliz. Stage*, iv, 181.)

1613–4. FEBRUARY 10 (THURSDAY).

A play before the Prince on February 10 by the King's Company. Payment £6. 13*s*. 4*d*., on the same warrant as that for the play of November 4. (Cunningham, *Revels*, p. xliii. See also Stopes, *Burbage*, p. 255; Chambers, *Eliz. Stage*, iv, 181.)

1613–4. FEBRUARY 18 (FRIDAY).

A play before the Prince on "the 18th of the same moneth" by the King's Company. Payment £6. 13*s*. 4*d*., on the same warrant as that for the play of November 4. (Cunningham, *Revels*, p. xliii. See also Stopes, *Burbage*, p. 255; Chambers, *Eliz. Stage*, iv, 181.)

1613–4. MARCH 6 (SHROVE SUNDAY).

A play before the King by the King's Company. Payment £10, on the same warrant as that for the play of November 1. (Chambers, *Eliz. Stage*, iv, 182. See also Cunningham, *Revels*, p. xliii; Stopes, *Burbage*, p. 255, in which the date is given as March 5.)

1613–4. MARCH 8 (TUESDAY).

A play before the King on March 8, by the King's Company. Payment £10, on the same warrant as that for the play of November 1. (Stopes, *Burbage*, p. 255. See also Cunningham, *Revels*, p. xliii; Chambers, *Eliz. Stage*, iv, 182.)

THE SEASON 1614–1615

With regard to the Christmas plays of this season, Chamberlain's much-quoted letter may perhaps be once more quoted. On January 5, [1614–5], he wrote to Sir Dudley Carleton:

I never knew any Christmas to bring forth less variety of occurrences. The world is in motion round about us, and yet we have no news. Here at home we pass on with a slow pace, and nothing fallen out worth the remembrance. They have plays every night, both holidays and working days, wherein they show great ————, being for the most part such poor stuff, that in stead of delight, they send the auditory away with discontent. Indeed, our poets' brains and inventions are grown very dry, insomuch that of five new plays there is not one that pleases, and therefore they are driven to furbish over their old, which stood them in best stead, and bring them most profit. (*Court and Times of James I*, i, 290.)

1614. NOVEMBER 1 (TUESDAY).

Bartholomewe Fayre [Ben Jonson] before the King "on the first of November last past" [by the Lady Elizabeth's Company] (Nathan Fielde). Payment £10, on warrant dated June 11, 1615. (Cunningham, *Revels*, p. xliv. See also Chambers, *Eliz. Stage*, iv, 183.)

1614/1614–5. DATES UNCERTAIN.

Three plays, two before the King and one before Prince Charles, by the Palsgrave's Company (Edward Juby). Payment £26. 13*s.* 4*d.*, on warrant dated April 15, 1615. (Chambers, *Eliz. Stage*, iv, 182. See also *M. L. R.*, iv, 166.)

1614/1614–5. DATES UNCERTAIN.

Three plays before the King by the Queen's Company (Robert Leigh). Payment £10 each, on warrant dated at Westminster, April 25, 1615. (Chambers, *Eliz. Stage*, iv, 182. See also *M. L. R.*, iv, 166.)

1614/1614–5. DATES UNCERTAIN.

Six plays before Prince Charles by Prince Charles's Company (William Rowley). Payment £43. 6*s.* 8*d.*, on warrant dated May 17, 1615. (Chambers, *Eliz. Stage*, iv, 183. See also *M. L. R.*, iv, 165.)

1614/1614–5. DATES UNCERTAIN.

Eight plays before the King by the King's Company (John Hemynges). Payment £10 each, on warrant dated May 19, 1615. (Chambers, *Eliz. Stage*, iv, 182. See also *M. L. R.*, iv, 166. According to Chambers, Cunningham misdates this warrant "1613." See *Revels*, p. xlii. Mrs. Stopes seems to date it "March." See *Burbage*, p. 256.)

1614–5. JANUARY 6 (FRIDAY).

Mercury Vindicated, by Ben Jonson. (Reyher, *Masques Anglais*, p. 523.)

The title-page, from the folio of 1616, reads: "Mercury Vindicated from the Alchemists at Court."

1614–5. JANUARY 8 (SUNDAY).

Mercury Vindicated, by Ben Jonson. (Reyher, *Masques Anglais*, p. 523.)

A few days later Chamberlain again wrote:

The only matter I can advertise, since I wrote the last week, is the success of the Masque on Twelfth-night, which was so well liked and applauded that the King had it represented again the Sunday night after in the very same manner, though neither in device nor show was there anything extraordinary, but only excellent dancing, the choice being made of the best, both English and Scots. (*Court and Times of James I*, i, 356–7.)

CAMBRIDGE, MARCH AND MAY, 1615

King James paid his first visit to the University of Cambridge in March, 1614–5, in response to the invitation of Thomas Howard, Earl of Suffolk, who in 1614 had been elected Chancellor of the University. On March 7 the King and Prince Charles, accompanied by members of the Court, arrived at Cambridge. John Chamberlain, writing from London on March 16 to Sir Dudley Carleton at Turin, thus describes their reception:

My very good Lord; I am newly returned from Cambridge, whither I went some two days after I wrote you my last. The King made his entry there the 7th of this present, with as much solemnity and concourse of gallants and great men as the hard weather and extremely foul ways would permit. The Prince came along with him, but not the Queen, by reason, it is said, that she was not invited; which error is rather imputed to their Chancellor than to the Scholars, that understood not these courses. Another defect was, that there was no Ambassador, which no doubt was upon the same reason. But the absence of women may be better excused for default of language, there being few or none present but of the Howards or that alliance. . . . The King and Prince lay at Trinity College, where the Plays were represented; and the Hall so well ordered for room, that above 2000 persons were conveniently placed. (Nichols, *Progresses James*, iii, 48–9.)

Mullinger (*University of Cambridge*, ii, 578, note) regards the statement of the number of persons who could be accommodated as "a gross exaggeration"; and thinks that, considering the size of the hall, which was 40 by 100 feet, scarcely a thousand persons could have been seated.

1614–5. MARCH 7 (TUESDAY). TRINITY COLLEGE.

Aemilia, a Latin Comedy by T. Cecil of St. John's College, before the King.

Chamberlain, in his letter of March 16 to Carleton, thus continues:

The first night's entertainment was a comedy, made and acted by St. John's men, the chief part consisting of a counterfeit Sir Edward Radcliffe, a foolish doctor of physic, which proved but a lean argument; and though it were larded with pretty shows at the beginning and end, and with somewhat too broad speech for such a presence, yet it was still dry. (Nichols, *Progresses James*, iii, 49.)

1614–5. MARCH 8 (WEDNESDAY). TRINITY COLLEGE.

Ignoramus, a Latin comedy by George Ruggle, before the King.

Chamberlain thus describes the first performance of this famous comedy:

The second night, March 8, was a Comedy of Clare Hall, with the help of two or three good actors from other Houses, wherein David Drummond, in a hobby-horse, and Brakyn, the Recorder of the Town, under the name of Ignoramus, a Common Laywer, bore great parts. The thing was full of mirth and variety, with many excellent actors (among whom the Lord Compton's son, though least, yet was not worst), but more than half marred by extreme length. (Nichols, *Progresses James*, iii, 49–51.)

Francis Brakyn, the Recorder, was very unpopular with the students, and the play was written to ridicule him and the common lawyers, of whom he was a representative. According to Aubrey, "they dressed Sir Ignoramus like Chief Justice Coke," who was the leader of the common-law judges in their struggle against the ecclesiastical courts, "and cutt his beard like him and feigned his voice." (*Brief Lives*, ed. by Clark, i, 180.)

It does not seem likely that James agreed with Chamberlain in finding the play too long. See the entry for May 13.

1614–5. MARCH 9 (THURSDAY). TRINITY COLLEGE.

Albumazar. A Comedy presented before the Kings Maiestie at Cambridge, the ninth of March. 1614. By the Gentlemen of Trinitie Colledge. London. 1615.

On the Stationers' Register the play is entered as having been "acted before his Maiestie at Cambridg[e] 10° Martij 1614." This date seems to be erroneous. Chamberlain, in the letter previously quoted from, wrote that on the third night was "an English comedy called *Albumazar*, of Trinity College's action and invention, but there was no great matter in it, more than one good clown's part." See the article entitled "Comment upon the Old Play of Albumazar" in the *Gentleman's Magazine*, May, 1756.

The author was Thomas Tomkis. In the Bursar's Accounts for 1614-1615 occurs the item: "given Mr Tomkis for his paines in penning and ordering the Englishe Commedie at o^r M^{rs} appoyntment xx^{li}." (Malone Soc. *Collections*, II, 2, p. 172.)

1614–5. MARCH 10 (FRIDAY). TRINITY COLLEGE.

Melanthe, a Latin pastoral by Samuel Brooke, before the King. The pastoral has the following title-page:

Melanthe Fabula pastoralis acta cum Iacobus Magnae Brit. Franc. & Hiberniae Rex, Cantabrigiam suam nuper inviseret, ibidemq́; Musarum, atque eius animi gratiâ dies quinque Commoraretur. Egerunt alumni Coll. San. et Individuae Trinitatis. Cantabrigiae. Excudebat Contrellus Legge. Mart. 27. 1615.

"The last night" wrote Chamberlain, "was a Latin Pastoral of the same House, excellently written and as well acted; which gave great contentment as well to the King as to all the rest." (Nichols, *Progresses James*, iii, 55.)

1614–5. MARCH 13 (MONDAY). KING'S COLLEGE.

Sicelides, a Piscatory, by Phineas Fletcher, was provided for the King's entertainment, but he left before the time for the perform-

ance. It was acted for the benefit of the students, after his departure. (Nichols, *Progresses James*, iii, 55, note.)

1615. MAY 13 (SATURDAY). CAMBRIDGE.

Ignoramus, by George Ruggle, again presented before the King.

James, with his usual royal frankness about what pleased or
bored him, had been delighted by the plays presented at Cambridge during his visit in March. Chamberlain had written:
"But sure the King was exceedingly pleased many times, both at
the plays and disputations; for I had the hap for the most time
to be within hearing, and often at his meals, he would express as
much. He visited all the colleges, save two or three, and com-
mends them beyond Oxford." (*Court and Times of James I*, i, 305.)
His delight in the play of *Ignoramus*, which had been performed
on March 8, led him, after vainly trying to induce the actors to
come to Court, to pay a second visit to Cambridge in May in
order to see the play again. It will be recalled that on his visit to
Oxford in 1605 he found the entertainment offered him dull, and
took no pains to conceal his dislike. Oxford was now smarting
under its eclipse, and the Cantabrigians added to *Ignoramus*, at
its second performance, a derisive "madrigal" by Lake, which
ended thus:

> Then leave it, Scholar, leave it, for yet
> you could not say,
> The King did go from you in March, and
> come again in May.

For this, and other satirical songs on the same subject, see
Nichols, *Progresses*, iii, 66–74. The King was equally pleased with
the second performance. According to James Tabor's brief account, he "laughed exceedingly, and often times, with his
hands, and by words, applauded it." (Mullinger, *The University of
Cambridge*, ii, 545.)

The following extract from Chamberlain's letter of May 20 will
give an idea of the commotion which the satirical play created
among the lawyers:

On Saturday last the King went again to Cambridge, to see the play *Ignoramus*,which has so nettled the lawyers, that they are almost out of all patience; and the lord chief justice, both openly at the King's Bench, and divers other places, hath galled and glanced at scholars with much bitterness; and there be divers Inns of Court have made rhimes and ballads against them, which they have answered sharply enough; and, to say truth, it was a scandal rather taken than given, for what profession is there, wherein some particular persons may not be justly taxed, without imputation to the whole? But it is the old saying, *conscius ipse sibi*, and they are too partial to think themselves *sacro sancti*, that they may not be touched. (*Court and Times of James I*, i, 363. See also Nichols, *Progresses James*, iii, 75–76.)

1615. DATE UNCERTAIN. CAMBRIDGE. TRINITY COLLEGE.

Susenbrotus, or *Fortunia*, a comedy, before the King and Prince Charles?

The title-page of the manuscript runs: "Susenbrotus Comoedia. Acta Cantabrigiae in Collegia Trin. coram Rege Jacobo & Carolo principe Anno 1615." (Morgan, L. B., "The Latin University Drama," in *Jahrbuch*, xlvii, 77.)

There is no record of the performance of more than one play on James's second visit. But two seem at one time to have been contemplated. On March 31 Chamberlain wrote to Carleton:

The King hath a meaning, and speaks much of it, to go again privately to Cambridge to see two of the Plays; and hath appointed the 27th of the next month. But it is not likely he will continue in that mind; for of late he hath made a motion to have the Actors come hither, which will be a difficult thing to persuade some of them. (Nichols, *Progresses James*, iii, 77.)

Possibly the above play was also presented, or at any rate intended. According to Tabor's account (see Mullinger, ii, 544–5) the Prince accompanied his father in May.

THE SEASON 1615–1616

1615–1616. NOVEMBER 1–APRIL 1.

Fourteen plays [before the King] "from the feast of All Saints', 1615, to the 1st of April, 1616," by the King's Company (John

Hemmings). Payment £10 each, on warrant dated April 29, 1616. (Stopes, *Burbage*, p. 256; See also Chambers, *Eliz. Stage*, iv, 183, in which the warrant is dated April 24, 1617.)

1615–1616. NOVEMBER 1–APRIL 1.

Eight plays before the King and the Queen by the King's Company (Heminges). (Chambers, *M. L. R.*, iv, 166. There is possibly an error here. These plays are not given in *Eliz. Stage*.)

1615/1615–6. DATES UNCERTAIN.

Four plays before Prince Charles by Prince Charles's Company (Alexander Foster). Payment £6. 13*s*. 4*d*. each, on warrant dated at Westminster, April 29. (Chambers, *Eliz. Stage*, iv, 183. See also *M. L. R.*, iv, 166.)

1615/1615–6. DATES UNCERTAIN.

Four plays before the King by the Queen's Company (Roberte Lee). Payment £10 each, on warrant dated at Greenwich, May 20, 1616. (Chambers, *Eliz. Stage*, iv, 183. See also *M. L. R.*, iv, 166.)

1615. DECEMBER 17 (SUNDAY). SOMERSET HOUSE.

"One plaie acted before her Matie [at] Queenes Court the xvii^th of December 1615" by the Queen's Company (Ellis Worth). Payment £10, on warrant dated January 7, 1615–6. (Westcott, *New Poems by James I*, p. lxxiii. From Accounts of Anne.)

1615. DECEMBER 21 (THURSDAY). SOMERSET HOUSE.

"One plaie acted before her Matie at Queenes Court on St Thomas daye at night being the xxi^th of December 1615" by the King's Company (John Heminge). Payment £10, on warrant dated January 22, 1615–6. (Westcott, *New Poems by James I*, p. lxxiii. From Accounts of Anne.)

1615–6. JANUARY 1 (MONDAY).

The Golden Age Restored, by Ben Jonson. (Reyher, *Masques Anglais*, p. 523.)

The title-page, from the 1616 folio, reads: "The Golden Age Restor'd. In a Maske at Court, 1615." On account of the squabbles of the ambassadors the masque was repeated on Twelfth Night. Sir John Finett writes:

The King being desirous, that the French, Venetian, and Savoyard Ambassadors should all be invited to a Maske at Court prepared for New-years night, an exception comming from the French, was a cause of deferring their invitation till Twelfe night, when the Maske was to be re-acted. (*Finetti Philoxenis*, p. 31.)

1615–6. JANUARY 6 (SATURDAY).

The Golden Age Restored, by Ben Jonson, again presented at Court. (Reyher, *Masques Anglais*, p. 523.)

1615–6. MARCH. ROYSTON.

A play before the King at Royston, acted by Cambridge students.

On March 27, 1616, John Chamberlain wrote to Sir Dudley Carleton:

As the King came from Newmarket, he had a play at Royston, acted by some of the younger sort of our Cantabrigians. He had heard it commended, and so would needs have it, bearing their charges. (*Court and Times of James I*, i, 393.)

Whether this is "the Comedy to be acted at Court" for which there are two items of expenditure in the Trinity College Bursar's Accounts for 1615–1616 is uncertain. See G. C. Moore Smith, "The Academic Drama at Cambridge," in Malone Soc. *Collections*, II, 2, p. 173.

THE SEASON 1616–1617

1616/1616–7. NOVEMBER 1–FEBRUARY 2.

Thirteen plays before the King "from 1st Nov., 1616, to the 2nd February following" by the King's Company (John Hemmings). Payment £10 each, on warrant dated March 11, 1616–7. (Stopes, *Burbage*, p. 256.)

1616. NOVEMBER 4–6 (MONDAY-WEDNESDAY). WHITE-
HALL.

Plays were acted at Court during the festivities which accompanied the creation of Charles as Prince of Wales.

George Lord Carew, writing to Sir Thomas Roe, concludes his
account of the ceremonies by saying that "the rest of the tryumpe
was barriers, playes, and roninge at the ringe, which lasted two
days." (*Letters*, ed. by Maclean, p. 55.)

1616/1616–7? CHRISTMAS.

The Masque of Christmas, by Ben Jonson.

In the folio of 1640 it is entitled, "Christmas, his Masque; as
it was Presented at Court. 1616."

1616–7. JANUARY 1 (WEDNESDAY). WHITEHALL.

A play at Whitehall on New Year's day.

"After supper," wrote Lady Anne Clifford, "I went to see my
sister Beauchamp and stay'd with her an hour or two for my Lord
was at the play at Whitehall that night." (*Diary*, ed. by Sackville West, p. 46.)

1616–7. JANUARY 5 (SUNDAY). WHITEHALL. THE GREAT
HALL.

The Mad Lover, by Beaumont and Fletcher.

Lady Anne Clifford wrote in her diary:

Upon the 25th [evidently an error for the 5th] I went into the
Court. . . . Supped with my Lord and Lady Arundel and after
supper I saw the play of *the Mad Lover* in the Hall. (*Diary*, ed.
by Sackville-West, p. 47.)

1616–7. JANUARY 6 (MONDAY). WHITEHALL.

The Vision of Delight, by Ben Jonson.

The title-page from the folio of 1640 reads: "The Vision of Delight Presented at Court in Christmas, 1617." The masque was
again performed on January 19. See Reyher, *Masques Anglais*, p.
524.

1616–7. JANUARY 19 (SUNDAY).

The Vision of Delight, by Ben Jonson, again presented at Court. (See Reyher, *Masques Anglais*, p. 524.)

1616–7. FEBRUARY 17 (MONDAY). SOMERSET HOUSE.

A Masque of the Queen's French Musicians. (See Reyher, *Masques Anglais*, p. 524.)

On February 22 Chamberlain wrote to Sir Dudley Carleton:

The Queen's Musicians (whereof she hath more than a good many) made her a kind of Masque or Antick at Somerset House on Monday night last. (Nichols, *Progresses James*, iii, 246.)

1616–7. FEBRUARY 22 (SATURDAY). ESSEX HOUSE.

Louers made Men. A Masque Presented in the House of the Right Honorable The Lord Haye. By diuers of noble qualitie, his friends. For the entertaynment of Monsieur le Baron de Tour, extraordinarie Ambassador for the French King. On Saterday the 22. of February. 1617. London. 1617.

This masque was part of a magnificent entertainment which Lord Hay gave to the Ambassador in payment of a debt of gratitude. The Baron de la Tour, according to Chamberlain, "was the man that first preferred him to the King's service." (See Nichols, *Progresses James*, iii, 244.) Although his presence is not mentioned, it is likely that the King was there. Sir Anthony Weldon, describing the occasion in his *Court and Character of King James* (1650), wrote that "the King, Lords, and all the prime gentlemen then about London" were invited.

1616–7. AFTER MARCH 14.

Three several plays before the King "in his Jorney towardes Scotland" by the Lady Elizabeth's Company (John Townsend and Joseph Moore). Payment £10 each, on warrant dated at Whitehall, July 11, 1617. (Cunningham, *Revels*, p. xliv. A notice of these plays, without the names of the actors, is to be found in the Privy Council Register. See "Dramatic Records from the

Privy Council Register, 1603–1642," ed. by E. K. Chambers and
W. W. Greg, in the Malone Society's *Collections*, VI–V, 376.)
The King set out for Scotland on March 14.

1617. MAY 4 (SUNDAY). DEPTFORD.

"Cupid's Banishment, a Masque presented to her Majesty, by
younge Gentlewomen of the Ladies' Hall, in Deptford at Greenwich, the 4th of May 1617. By Robert White." (Nichols, *Progresses James*, iii, 283.) See also Reyher, *Masques Anglais*, p. 524.

SUMMER, 1617

1617. AUGUST. BROUGHAM CASTLE.

A masque in honor of the King. (Reyher, *Masques Anglais*, p.
524; Nichols, *Progresses James*, iii, 389–92.)
Brougham Castle was the seat of Francis Clifford, fourth Earl
of Cumberland. According to Nichols, the King was there early
in August.

1617. AUGUST 17 (SUNDAY). HOUGHTON TOWER.

A masque before the King, at Houghton Tower.
Nicholas Assheton, who records the performance, attended the
King on his visit. He wrote in his diary:

Aug. 17. Houghton. Wee served the lords with biskett, wyne,
and jellie. The Bushopp of Chester, Dr. Morton, preached before
the King. To dinner. Ab^t 4 o'clock, ther was a rushbearing and
pipeing afore them, affore the King in the middle court; then to
supp. Then, ab^t ten or eleven o'clock, a maske of noblemen,
knights, gentlemen, and courtiers, afore the King, in the middle
round, in the garden. Some speeches: of the rest, dancing the
Huckler, Tour Bedlo, and the Cowp Justice of Peace. (*The Journal
of Nicholas Assheton*, ed by F. R. Raines, pp. 40–45.)

THE SEASON 1617–1618

1617/1617–8. DATES UNCERTAIN.

Fifteen plays before the King by the King's Company (John
Hemmings). Payment £10 each, on warrant dated February 24,
1617–8. (Stopes, *Burbage*, p. 256.)

1617. September 29 (Monday). Hampton Court.

A masque at the marriage of Sir John Villiers to Lady Frances, daughter of Sir Edward Coke, on Michaelmas Day, 1617, at Hampton Court.

This entry is based on a statement by Campbell, in his "Life of Sir Edward Coke" (*Lives of the Chief Justices*, i, 303). I have not been able to find any mention of the masque in the correspondence of the period.

1617–8. January 1 (Thursday).

The Masque of Amazons was prepared by Lady Hay for New Year's night, but the King and Queen refused to allow it to be presented. (See Reyher, *Masques Anglais*, p. 524.)

On January 3 Chamberlain wrote to Carleton:

There was a Masque of nine Ladies in hand at their own cost, whereof the principal was the Lady Hay, as Queen of the Amazons. . . . They had taken great pains in continual practising, and were almost perfect, and all their implements provided; but, whatsoever the cause was, neither the Queen nor King did like or allow of it,—and so all is dashed. (Nichols, *Progresses James*, iii, 454.)

1617–8. January 6 (Tuesday). Whitehall. The Banqueting House.

Pleasure Reconciled to Virtue, by Ben Jonson. (See Reyher, *Masques Anglais*, p. 524.)

The title-page, from the folio of 1640, reads: "Pleasure reconciled to Virtue. A Masque. As it was Presented at Court before King Iames. 1619." The date of the title-page is erroneous, however, as Castelain (*Ben Jonson*, p. 710, *n.* 1) points out. The place of performance is noted in a letter written by Nathaniel Brent:

The Qu: hath caused ye La: maske to be put of wch my Ld Hay should have made at ye robes last night. The other wch ye Prince is to make in the banqueting house on 12th night, and wherein himself is to be an actor, is likely to hould. (*State Papers, Domestic, James I*, xcv, No. 3, quoted by Sullivan, *Court Masques*, p. 106.)

1617–8. JANUARY 9 (FRIDAY). THEOBALDS.

A play of Tom of Bedlam, acted by gentlemen of the Court.

On January 10 Chamberlain wrote to Sir Dudley Carleton:

He [Sir Robert Naunton] is gone this morning after the King, who removes to Royston from Theobalds, where he was to have yesternight a play acted by Sir Thomas Dutton, Sir Thomas Badger, Sir George Goring, Sir Thomas Jerningham, Sir Edward Leech, Sir Robert Yoxely, and the like; of Tom of Bedlam, and other such mad stuff. (*Court and Times of James I,* i, 455.)

On January 17 Chamberlain again wrote that "the play or interlude did not rise to the expectation, but rather fell out the wrong way, especially by reason of a certain song sung by Sir John Finett, wherein the rest bear the burden, of such scurrilous and base stuff, that it put the king out of his good humor, and all the rest that heard it. And I marvel the more that, amongst so many, none had the judgment to see how unfit it was to bring such beastly gear in public places before a prince." (*Ibid.,* ii. 57–58.)

This seems to be the same performance as that called by Reyher the *Masque of the Marriage of a Farmer's Son*. See *Masques Anglais,* p. 524. See also Sullivan, *Court Masques of James I,* pp. 107–8.

1617–8. FEBRUARY 17 (SHROVE TUESDAY). WHITEHALL. THE BANQUETING HOUSE.

Pleasure Reconciled to Virtue, by Ben Jonson, again presented at Court, with the addition of the antimasque *For the Honour of Wales*. (Reyher, *Masques Anglais,* p. 524; Nichols, *Progresses James,* iii, 468, 509.)

On February 21 Chamberlain wrote to Carleton: "On Shrove Tuesday the Prince's Masque for Twelfth-night was represented again with some few alterations and additions, but little bettered."

1617–8. FEBRUARY 19 (THURSDAY). WHITEHALL. THE BANQUETING HOUSE.

The Gray's Inn *Masque of Mountebanks,* by John Marston (?). (Reyher, *Masques Anglais,* p. 525; Nichols, *Progresses James,* iii, 468.)

In the letter previously quoted from Chamberlain thus describes the performance:

On Thursday night the Gentlemen of Gray's Inn came to Court with their show, for I cannot call it a Masque, seeing they were not disguised nor had vizards. For the rest, their fashion and device were well approved, though it were thought to be somewhat out of season to revel in Lent; the cause whereof was they would not be turned into the Hall on Shrove-monday, (as was appointed by reason that the Prince's shows and devices could not be set up and placed in so short a time, if they should possess the Banquetting-room the night before); but seeing no reason or persuasion would serve their turn, they must of necessity be put off till Thursday or some time longer. The Queen was not present at either of them, but keeps close at Denmark House.

The Gray's Inn performance took place on February 2. Concerning the authorship of the masque, see Chambers, *Eliz. Stage*, iii, 435.

1618. APRIL 6 (MONDAY).

"On Easter Monday *Twelfte night* the play soe called" before the King by the King's Company (John Heminges). Payment £10, on warrant dated April 20, 1618. (Cunningham, *Revels*, p. xlv. See also Stopes, *Burbage*, p. 256.)

1618. APRIL 7 (TUESDAY).

"On Easter Tuesday *the Winter's Tale*" before the King by the King's Company. Payment £10, on the same warrant as that for the preceding play. (Cunningham, *Revels*, p. xlv. See also Stopes, *Burbage*, p. 256.)

1618. MAY 3 (SUNDAY).

"The thirde of May the *Merry Divell of Edmonton*" before the King by the King's Company (John Heminges). Payment £10, on warrant dated May 15, 1618. (Cunningham, *Revels*, p. xlv. See also Stopes, *Burbage*, p. 256.)

THE SEASON 1618–1619

On November 15, 1619, Pier Antonio Marioni, Venetian Secretary in England, wrote to the Doge and Senate:

This week his Majesty has been in London, writing, so I hear, night and day in his study, some say it is about these affairs [the coronation of the Prince Palatine as King of Bohemia], some say that he is writing a book. Nevertheless he does not fail to witness almost every evening the comedies which are now being performed at the Court. (*Cal. State Papers, Venetian*, xvi, 47.)

1618/1618–9. NOVEMBER 1; CHRISTMAS.

Eight plays "at Allhollowtide and Christmas, 1618," by the King's Company (John Hemmings). Payment £73. 6s. 8d., on warrant dated April 19, 1619. (Stopes, *Burbage*, p. 256.)

The payment suggests that six of the plays were before the King at £10 each, and two before other members of the royal family, at £6. 13s. 4d. each.

1618–9. JANUARY 6 (WEDNESDAY). WHITEHALL. THE BANQUETING HOUSE.

A masque at Court, performed by Prince Charles, Buckingham, and other lords.

Antonio Donato, Venetian Ambassador, wrote from London on January 17 [O. S. 7]:

Yesterday evening the King had me invited to a masque, which was conducted by the prince in the most charming manner, superbly mounted and proved a great success. (*Cal. State Papers, Venetian*, xv, 432. See also *Cal. State Papers, Domestic*, 1619–1623, p. 2; Reyher, *Masques Anglais*, p. 525.)

According to Finett, the masque was "to be represented in the Hall at White-Hall." (*Finetti Philoxenis*, p. 59.) But, wrote Lady Anne Clifford, "the Prince had the masque at night in the Banqueting House." And she adds, "The King was there but the Queen was so ill she could not remove from Hampton Court all this Xmas, and it was generally thought she would have died." (*Diary*, ed. by Sackville-West, p. 84.)

1618–9. FEBRUARY 2, OR FEBRUARY 7–9 (SHROVETIDE).

A repetition of the Twelfth Night masque was intended for Candlemas or Shrovetide, but, on account of the burning of the Banqueting House, it did not take place. On January 16 Chamberlain wrote to Carleton:

Since my last, we have had here a great mischance by fire at Whitehall, which, beginning in the Banqueting House, hath quite consumed it. . . . There is no doubt that this will hinder the King coming to town this Candlemas, when the masque should have been repeated the second time. (*Court and Times of James I*, ii, 124–5.)

Reverend Thomas Lorkin, writing on January 19, gave the date of the intended repetition as Shrovetide. (*Ibid.*, p. 126.)

1619. MAY 20 (THURSDAY). WHITEHALL. THE GREAT HALL.

Pericles, Prince of Tyre, in honor of the Marquis of Tremouille.

On May 24, 1619, Sir Gerrard Herbert wrote to Sir Dudley Carleton:

The Marquis Trenell [Tremouille], on thursday last tooke leaue of the Kinge: that night was feasted at white hall, by the duke of Lenox in the Queenes greate chamber: where many great Lordes weare to keep them Company but no ladyes. the Sauoy Imbassadour was also there: The english Lordes, was the Marquise Buckingham my lord Pryuy seale, my lord of lenox, my lord of Oxford, my lord Chamberlayne, my l: Hamelton, my lord Arundell, my Lord of Leycester: my lord Cary, my lord Diggby. m^r Treasurer, m^r Secretary Callvart: my lord Beaucham, and my Lord Generall, the rest English gallants, and all mixed wth the french alonge the table. . . . The supper was greate & the banquett curious, serued in 24 greate Chynay worcke platters or voyders, full of glasse scales or bowles of sweete meates: in the middst of each voyder a greene tree of eyther, lemon, orange, Cypers, or other resemblinge. After supper they weare carried to the queenes pryuy chamber, where french singinge was by the Queenes Musitians: after in the Queenes bedd Chamber, they hearde the Irish harpp, a violl, & m^r Lanycr, excellently singinge & playinge on the lute. In the kinges greate Chamber they went to see the play of *Pirrocles, Prince of Tyre*. which lasted till 2 aclocke. after two actes, the players ceased till the french all refreshed them wth sweetmeates brought on Chinay voiders, & wyne & ale in bottells, after the players, begann anewe. The Imbassadour parted next morninge for Fraunce at 8 aclocke. . . . (*State Papers, Domestic, James I*. Vol. cix, No. 46. Quoted from *The Shakespere Allusion-Book*, ed. by J. Munro, 1909, i, 276–7.)

THE SEASON 1619–1620

On January 1, 1619–20, John Chamberlain wrote to Sir Dudley Carleton:

Since I received your letter of the 15th of December, here hath little fallen out worth the writing, but only the king's coming to town the day before Christmas-eve, and little hath passed at court besides plays and revels. (*Court and Times of James I*, ii, 196.)

1619/1619–20. DATES UNCERTAIN.

Ten several plays before the King by the King's Company (John Hemynge). Payment £10 each, on warrant dated March 23, 1619–20. (Stopes, *Burbage*, p. 256.)

1619. CHRISTMAS.

A play before the King by the Prince's Company.

On January 10 [O. S. December 31], 1619–20, Girolamo Lando, Venetian Ambassador in England, wrote to the Doge and Senate:

In connection with the subject of comedies I ought not to conceal the following event from your Secretary, owing to the mystery that it involves. The comedians of the prince, in the presence of the king his father, played a drama the other day in which a king with his two sons has one of them put to death, simply upon suspicion that he wishes to deprive him of his crown, and the other son actually did deprive him of it afterwards. This moved the king in an extraordinary manner, both inwardly and outwardly. In this country, however, the comedians have absolute liberty to say whatever they wish against any one soever, so the only demonstration against them will be the words spoken by the king. (*Cal. State Papers, Venetian*, xvi, 111.)

The play has not been identified.

1619. December 30–31 (Thursday–Friday).

A masque at Court, given by the Prince.

Girolamo Lando, Venetian Ambassador in England, writing on January 2 [O. S. Dec. 23], refers to "the masques which are being prepared by the prince," the first of which is to take place "in seven or eight days." The "other masques" will be given "towards the end of the carnival." (*Cal. State Papers, Venetian*, 1619–1621, pp. 102–3.) We hear, however, of only one other masque given by the Prince. See the entry for January 6.

1619/1619–20. Christmas.

A Pleasant Comedie Called The Two Merry Milkemaids. Or, The best words weare the Garland. As it was Acted before the King, with generall Approbation, by the Companie of the Reuels. By I. C. London. 1620.

Acted at Court, according to Nichols (*Progresses James*, iv, 1105), during Christmas, 1619/1619–20.

1619–20. January 6 (Thursday).

A masque at Court, given by the Prince.

Girolamo Lando, writing on January 14 [O. S. 4], after describing a masque given by Buckingham and others in the houses of the French ambassador (there is no record of the King's presence), says, "On Thursday there will be the Prince's." (*Cal. State Papers, Venetian*, 1619–1621, p. 128.)

Writing again on January 17 [O. S. 7], he says, "Yesterday at the Prince's masque I saw Hay, though hurriedly," etc. (*Ibid.*, p. 135.) Since the masque has not been identified, the Ambassador's description of it may be noted. He writes that the Prince and ten other cavaliers, among whom Buckingham was first, made a brave show; and continues:

His Majesty took part with much gaiety and greatly enjoyed the agility and dancing of his son and of the marquis, who contended against each other for the favour and applause of the King and to give him pleasure. I as representing your Serenity, and the Ambassadors of France and Savoy were honoured and entertained in a seemly manner. We were all placed on a stage to see the dancing and afterwards, following the King, we went to see the supper, in the usual way. At the masque his Majesty sat under his usual large canopy, surrounded by numerous lords. Near him stood the former Archbishop of Spalato, who daily advances in esteem and favour. . . . (*Ibid*, p. 138.) See Reyher, *Masques Anglais*, p. 525.

1619–20. JANUARY 8–21. ESSEX HOUSE.

A masque at Viscount Doncaster's, in honor of the King.

This seems to have been a "running masque." On January 8 Sir Francis Nethersole wrote to Carleton: "Lord Doncaster is entertaining a company, at which the King will be present, and the two Marquises and others will dance a running ballet." (*Cal State Papers, Domestic*, 1619–1623, p. 112.) Compare the letter of Girolamo Lando of January 31 (O. S. 21): "Before the King left London he went with the Prince and the principal gentlemen of the Court to a masque performed in Doncaster's house." (*Cal. State Papers, Venetian*, 1619–1621, p. 155.)

1619–20. JANUARY. FEBRUARY.

The "running masque." For a bibliography, see Reyher, *Masques Anglais*, p. 526. See also the entry for January 6, 1627–8.

Little is known of this kind of performance. Possibly "running" is used in the sense, now obsolete, of "hasty." A "running masque" would therefore be an improvised affair such as that described by Egremont (Fletcher, *Elder Brother*, II, ii): "'Tis not half an hours work, a Cupid, and a Fiddle, and the thing's done." On February 12 Chamberlain wrote to Carleton:

We hear the King will be here within this fortnight, and spend all the Lent hereabout. They pass the time merrily at Newmarket, and the running Masque ranges all over the Country where there be fit subjects to entertain it, as lately they have been at Sir John Croft's near Bury, and in requital those Ladies have invited them to a Masque of their own invention, all those fair sisters being summoned for the purpose, so that on Thursday next the King, Prince, and all the Court go thither a Shroving. (Nichols, *Progresses James*, iii, 587.)

1619–20. FEBRUARY 29 (SHROVE TUESDAY). WHITEHALL.

A repetition of the Prince's masque (apparently the Twelfth-night masque).

On March 6 [O. S. February 25] Girolamo Lando wrote: "They are preparing another representation of the masque given some days ago by the Prince." (*Cal. State Papers, Venetian*, 1619–1621, p. 190.) On March 13 [O. S. 3] he wrote that the performance "took place on the day of carnival according to the calendar here." (*Ibid.*, p. 197.) Compare Chamberlain's letter of March 11, in which he writes that "the Christmas maske" was "repeated on Shrove Tewsday night." (E. P. Stathham, *A Jacobean Letter-Writer*, p. 183.) See Reyher, *Masques Anglais*, p. 526.

1620. APRIL 30 (SUNDAY).

A play before the King on the "30th April, 1620," by the King's Company [John Hemynge]. Payment £10, on warrant dated May 20, 1620. (Stopes, *Burbage*, p. 256.)

SUMMER, 1620

1620. AUGUST. SALISBURY.

A masque at Salisbury. (Reyher, *Masques Anglais*, p. 526.)

The masque was probably presented as a part of the festivities during the King's stay on his progress.

1620. AUGUST 5 (SATURDAY). SALISBURY.

A show or play before the King at Salisbury.

On September 10 [O. S. August 31] the Venetian Ambassador wrote that "the Court at the present moment passes its time in continual amusements, and the leading lords have represented to the king a very familiar comedy in the wilds of the country, wherein the favourite marquis acted as interlocutor." (*Cal. State Papers, Venetian*, xvi, 390.)

A more particular description of the "comedy" is given in a letter of Sir Dudley Carleton's from the Hague:

In England all goeth prosperously and joyfully (thanks to be God) as you will guess by the merry passing of the 5th of August at Salisbury, where there was a show or play of twelve parts, wherein the lord of Buckingham acted an Irish footman with all his habiliments and properties; the Marquis Hamilton a western pirate; the Earl of Montgomery a Welsh advocate of the bawdy court; the Earl of Northampton a cobbler and teacher of Birds to whistle; the Lord of Doncaster a neat barber; the young Lord Compton a tailor; the Lord Cromwell a merryman (also the fool); Sir Henry Rich a curious cook; Sir Edward Zouch a bearwood; Sir John Millecent a carier about of baboons; Sir George Goring a perfumer; and Sir William Fielding a Puritan that marred the play. (*Ibid.*, p. 390, note.)

1620. AFTER AUGUST 28. WOKING.

Masques prepared at Woking in honor of the King and Prince.

On August 28 Sir Edward Zouch, in anticipation of a royal visit, writes from Woking to his brother, Lord Zouch of Odiham Park, that while he cannot equal the good cheer which the Bishop of Winchester will provide for the King's entertainment at Farnham, he will give his Majesty and the Prince more mirth at Woking, and masques each night. He ends by requesting a leash of bucks and a brace of does. (*Cal. State Papers, Domestic*, 1619–1623, p. 175.)

THE SEASON 1620–1621

One of the season's performances was enlivened by satire. In a holiday masque at Hampton Court or Whitehall, it is not clear which, a Puritan was brought in to be "flouted and abused." The incident, as Chamberlain wrote on January 13, was considered by the graver sort to be "unseemly and unseasonable," in view of the state of the French Protestants, and of the fact that a special French embassy was being entertained at Court. (See *Cal. State Papers, Domestic*, 1619–1623, p. 214.) An account at second-hand of the same occurrence is found in Reverend Joseph Mead's letter of February 17 to Sir Martin Stuteville:

I am told there was not long since, (I suppose about new-year's-tide) a play before his Majesty, wherein there was a Puritan brought up, having long asses' ears, who should speak after this manner:—"Is it now a time to give lists and make merry, &c.? This should be a time of fasting and prayer, when the Church of God is in so great affliction in Bohemia and Germany, and other places; and not of masqueing and music, &c."

I will not believe this was entertained with applause; and yet I am told so. (*Court and Times of James I*, ii, 228.)

1620/1620–1. DATES UNCERTAIN.

Nine plays before the King by the King's Company (John Hemmyng). Payment £10 each, on warrant dated March 17, 1620–1. (Stopes, *Burbage*, p. 256.)

1620–1. JANUARY 6 (SATURDAY).

News from the New World Discovered in the Moon, by Ben Jonson. (Reyher, *Masques Anglais*, p. 526.)

The title-page, from the folio of 1640, reads: "Newes from the new World Discover'd in the Moone. A Masque, as it was Presented at Court before King Iames. 1620." The masque was again presented on Shrove Sunday, apparently to appease the Spanish Ambassador, who had not been invited to be present at the first performance. See Sullivan, *Court Masques of James I*, pp. 125–27.

1620–1. JANUARY 8 (MONDAY). ESSEX HOUSE.

A masque at Essex House in honor of the French Ambassador Extraordinary, the Marquis de Cadenet. The King was present. (See Reyher, *Masques Anglais*, p. 526.)

Finett writes:

The Munday after [after Twelfth Night] the Viscount of Doncaster invited the Ambassador and all his company (men of note) to a Supper prepared and set forth with that State and cost as hath been seldome seene. To it were also invited (for honour to the Feast, and Company) the King, the Prince, and most of the great Lords and Ladies in Towne. . . . After Supper, they had the entertainment of a Maske presented by nine young Gentlemen. (*Finetti Philoxenis*, p. 72.)

1620–1. FEBRUARY 11 (SHROVE SUNDAY).

News from the New World Discovered in the Moon, by Ben Jonson. (Reyher, *Masques Anglais*, p. 526.)

1620–1. FEBRUARY 13 (SHROVE TUESDAY). WHITEHALL.
THE GREAT HALL.

A Masque of the Middle Temple. (See Reyher, *Masques Anglais*, p. 526.)

Finett mentions the masque in connection with the visit of six commissioners from the States of the United Provinces. He writes: "For Shrove-Tuesday following I carried them from the King an Invitation to a Maske of the Gentlemen of the Middle-Temple to be represented in the Hall of the Court." (*Finetti Philoxenis*, pp. 73–74.) See also the letter of Girolamo Lando, *Cal. State Papers, Venetian*, 1619-1621, p. 579.

SUMMER, 1621

1621. AUGUST. BURLEIGH.

"Plays" in honor of the King. See the note to the following entry.

1621. AUGUST 3 (FRIDAY). BURLEIGH.

"A Masque of the Metamorphos'd Gypsies. As it was thrice Presented to King Iames. First, at Burleigh on the Hill. Next, at Belvoyr. And lastly, at Windsor. August, 1621." (1640 Folio.) See Reyher, *Masques Anglais*, p. 526.

On August 4 Chamberlain wrote to Carleton:

On yesterday the King was to be entertained by the Lord of Buckingham at Burley in Rutlandshire, a house of the Lord of Harington's that he bought of the Lady of Bedford, where was great provision of Plays, Masques, and all manner of entertainment, and this day the Court removes to Belvoir. (Nichols, *Progresses James*, iv, 709–10.)

1621. AUGUST 5 (SUNDAY). BELVOIR.

The Masque of the Metamorphosed Gipsies, repeated during the entertainment of the King by the Earl of Rutland. Certain lines were added relating to the Gowry Conspiracy, on the anniversary of which it was repeated. (Nichols, *Progresses James*, iv, 710. See also Reyher, *Masques Anglais*, pp. 526-7.)

1621. AUGUST 26 (SUNDAY). WOODSTOCK.

Technogamia: Or The Marriages of the arts. A Comedie. Written by Barten Holyday, Master of Arts, and Student of Christ-Church in Oxford, and acted by the Students of the same House before the Vniuersitie, at Shrouetide. London. 1618.

The following passage from Anthony à Wood's account of Holyday's life explains the circumstances of the court performance of the play:

Technogamia . . . acted publicly in Ch. Ch. hall with no great applause, 13 Febr. 1617. But the wits of those times being minded to shew themselves before the king, were resolved, with leave, to act the said comedy at Woodstock; whereupon the author making some foolish alterations in it, it was accordingly acted on a Sunday night, 26 Aug. 1621. But it being too grave for the King, and too scholastic for the auditory (or as some have said, that the actors had taken too much wine before they began) his majesty (James I) after two acts, offer'd several times to withdraw. At length being persuaded by some of those that were near to him, to have patience till it was ended, least the young men should be discouraged, sate down, tho' much against his will. Whereupon these verses were made by a certain scholar:

> At Christ Church Marriage, done before the king,
> Least that those mates should want an offering,
> The king himself did offer; what, I pray?
> He offer'd twice or thrice to go away.

Several witty copies of verses were made on the said comedy, among which was that of Pet. Heylin of Magd. coll. called Whoop Holyday. Which giving occasion for the making other copies pro and con. Corbet dean of Ch. Ch. who had that day preached (as it seems) before the King with his band starch'd clean, did put in for one; for which he was reproved by the graver sort, but those that knew him well, took no notice of it, for they have several times said, that he loved to the last boys-play very well. (*Athenæ Oxonienses*, ed. Bliss, iii, 522.)

For satirical verses inspired by the King's reception of the performance, see Nichols, *Progresses James*, iv, 1109–1111.

1621. SEPTEMBER 9 (SUNDAY)? WINDSOR.

The Masque of the Metamorphosed Gipsies, again performed, with additions, before the King. (Nichols, *Progresses James*, iv, 716. See also Reyher, *Masques Anglais*, pp. 526–7.)

THE SEASON 1621–1622

1621. NOVEMBER 5 (MONDAY).

"*The womas Plott* [Philip Massinger] plaid before his Matie 5° Novembris last" by the King's Company (John Hemmings). Payment £10, on warrant dated March 27, 1622. (MS. 515, No. 7, Inner Temple Library, quoted by Murray, *English Dramatic Companies*, ii, 193. See also Stopes, *Burbage*, p. 256, in which a warrant dated March 27, probably for this play and the five following plays by the King's Company, is given, without titles or dates.)

1621. NOVEMBER 26 (MONDAY).

"*The Woman is to Hard for him* 26° of the same Monethe" before the King by the King's Company. Payment £10, on the same warrant as that for the preceding play. (MS. 515. Murray, *Eng. Dr. Com.*, ii, 193. See also Stopes, *Burbage*, p. 256.)

1621. DECEMBER. SAXHAM.

A masque at Sir John Croft's, in honor of the King. (Reyher, *Masques Anglais*, p. 527; *Cal. State Papers, Domestic*, 1619–1623, p. 324.)

1621. DECEMBER 26 (WEDNESDAY).

"*The Island Princes* [Beaumont and Fletcher] vppon St Stephens day" before the King by the King's Company. Payment £10, on the same warrant as that for the play of November 5. (MS. 515. Murray, *Eng. Dr. Com.*, ii, 193. See also Stopes, *Burbage*, p. 256; Adams, *Dramatic Records*, p. 49.)

1621. December 27 (Thursday).

"27° Decembris 1621 . . . *the man in the moone drinks Clarett*" [before the King] by the Prince's Company. Payment £10, on warrant dated March 6, [1621–2]. (MS. 515. Murray, *Eng. Dr. Com.*, ii, 193.)

1621. December 29 (Saturday).

"The 29 of the same Moneth . . . *the Witch of Edmonton*" [W. Rowley, Dekker, Ford] by the Prince's Company [before the King]. Payment £10, on the same warrant as that for the preceding play. (MS. 515. Murray, *Eng. Dr. Com.*, ii. 193.)

The title-page of the edition of 1658 records that this play was acted "once at Court, with singular Applause."

1621. December 30 (Sunday).

"The play called *gramarcie witt* on of 30th of December 1621" [before the King] "by Ellisworth and his fellowes late servaunts to Queene Anne and now the Companie of the Revells." Payment £10, on warrant dated March 2, [1621–2]. (MS. 515. Murray, *Eng. Dr. Com.*, ii, 192–3.)

1621–2. January 1 (Tuesday).

"*The Pilgrim* on new yeares day" before the King by the King's Company. Payment £10, on the same warrant as that for the play of November 5. (MS. 515. Murray, *Eng. Dr. Com.*, ii, 193. See also Stopes, *Burbage*, p. 256; Adams, *Dramatic Records*, p. 49.)

1621–2. January 6 (Sunday). Whitehall. The Banqueting House.

The Masque of Augurs, by Ben Jonson. (Reyher, *Masques Anglais*, pp. 527, 344.)

The title-page, from the folio of 1640, reads: "The Masque of Augures. With the several Antimasques Presented on Twelfe-night, 1622." The masque was repeated on May 5 or 6.

1621–2. JANUARY 24 (THURSDAY).

"*The Wildgoose Chase* [Beaumont and Fletcher] the xxiiii of Januarie" before the King by the King's Company. Payment £10, on the same warrant as that for the play of November 5. (MS. 515. Murray, *Eng. Dr. Com.*, ii, 193. See also Stopes, *Burbage*, p. 256; Adams, *Dramatic Records*, p. 49.)

1621–2. MARCH 3–5 (SHROVETIDE).

A Shrovetide repetition of the *Masque of Augurs* seems to have been contemplated. On March 18 [O. S. 8] Girolamo Lando, Venetian Ambassador in England, wrote to the Doge and Senate:

At Theobalds the King's gout grew worse, and kept him almost completely confined. . . . Accordingly they gave up repeating the masque at the Court, much business being postponed and the audiences of ambassadors put off. (*Cal. State Papers, Venetian*, 1621–1623, p. 265.)

On February 25 was issued "a warrant to the Tower for hangings for the Banqueting house against the maske at Shrouetide to be delivered to Richard Higgins," (MS. 515. Murray, *Eng. Dr. Com.*, ii, 192.)

1621–2. MARCH 5 (SHROVE TUESDAY).

"*The Coxcombe* [Beaumont and Fletcher] the 5 of this instant Marche" before the King by the King's Company. Payment £10, on the same warrant as that for the play of November 5. (MS. 515. Murray, *Eng. Dr. Com.*, ii, 193; See also Stopes, *Burbage*, p. 256.)

1622. MAY 6 (MONDAY). WHITEHALL. THE BANQUETING HOUSE.

The Masque of Augurs repeated. (Reyher, *Masques Anglais*, pp. 344, 527. See also *Finetti Philoxenis*, pp. 105–6.) A Chamberlain letter gives the date of the repetition as May 5.

THE SEASON 1622–1623

1622/1622–3. DATES UNCERTAIN.

Nine plays [before the King] by the King's Company (John Hemynges). Payment £10 each, on warrant dated March 14, 1622–3. (Stopes, *Burbage*, p. 256.)

It is possible that the five plays the names of which are given in the following entries were paid for on this warrant.

1622. DECEMBER 26 (THURSDAY). WHITEHALL.

"Upon St. Steevens daye at night *The Spanish Curate* [John Fletcher] was acted by the kings players." (Adams, *Dramatic Records*, p. 49.)

The "Revels and Playes" of the holidays were "acted at Christmas in the court at Whitehall." (*Ibid.*, p. 49.)

1622. DECEMBER 27 (FRIDAY). WHITEHALL.

"Upon St. Johns daye at night was acted *The Beggars Bush* [Beaumont and Fletcher] by the Kings players." (Adams, *Dramatic Records*, p. 49.)

1622. DECEMBER 28 (SATURDAY).

"Upon Childermas daye no playe." (Adams, *Dramatic Records*, p. 49.)

1622. DECEMBER 29 (SUNDAY). WHITEHALL.

"Upon the Sonday following *The Pilgrim* [John Fletcher] was acted by the kings players." (Adams, *Dramatic Records*, p. 49.)

1622–3. JANUARY 1 (WEDNESDAY). WHITEHALL.

"Upon New-years day at night *The Alchemist* [Ben Jonson] was acted by the kings players." (Adams, *Dramatic Records*, p. 49.)

1622–3. JANUARY 6 (MONDAY).

Time Vindicated, by Ben Jonson, prepared for Twelfth Day, was postponed. See the following entry.

1622–3. JANUARY 6 (MONDAY). WHITEHALL.

"Upon Twelfe night, the Masque being put off, the play called *A Vowe and a Good One* was acted by the prince's servants." (Adams, *Dramatic Records*, p. 50.)

This play is identified by Fleay (*Drama*, i, 200) as Fletcher's *The Chances*; again as Middleton's *A Fair Quarrel* (ii, 98.)

1622–3. JANUARY 12 (SUNDAY).

Time Vindicated was again intended, and again postponed. On January 20 [O. S. 10] Alvise Valaresso, Venetian Ambassador in England, wrote: "Sunday next has now been appointed for the Prince's masque." (*Cal. State Papers, Venetian*, 1621–1623, p. 549.)

1622–3. JANUARY 19 (SUNDAY). WHITEHALL. THE BANQUETING HOUSE.

Time Vindicated, by Ben Jonson. (Reyher, *Masques Anglais*, p. 527.)

The title-page, from the folio of 1640, reads: "Time Vindicated to himselfe, and to his Honors. In the presentation at Court on Twelfth night. 1623." The date here given is incorrect. The performance was more than once postponed. Sir John Astley, Master of the Revels, recorded in his Office Book:

Upon Sonday, being the 19th of January, the *Princes Masque* appointed for Twelfe daye, was performed. The speeches and songs composed by Mr. Ben Johnson, and the scene made by Mr. Inigo Jones. . . . (Adams, *Dramatic Records*, p. 50.)

On January 25 Chamberlain wrote that "the departure of the French Ambassador's lady, with her niece, Mademoiselle St. Luc, who bore a principal part in all those meetings, was the cause that the masque could not well be put off longer than Sunday last." (*Court and Times of James I*, ii, 356.)

1622–3. FEBRUARY 2 (SUNDAY). WHITEHALL.

"At Candlemas *Malvolio* [Shakespeare's *Twelfth Night*] was acted at court, by the kings servants." (Adams, *Dramatic Records*, p. 50.)

It appears from Archbishop Laud's *Diary* that the Court was still in London on February 5.

1622–3. FEBRUARY 23–25 (SHROVETIDE).

"At Shrovetide, the king being at Newmarket, and the prince out of England, there was neyther masque nor play, nor any other kind of Revells held at court." (Adams, *Dramatic Records*, p. 50.)

The King intended to visit Cambridge at Shrovetide in order to see "certain plays," but altered his plans. On February 22 Chamberlain wrote to Carleton:

Boschet, the ambassador from the Archduchess, arrived here on Wednesday, and lodgeth with the Spanish Ambassador, refusing to be defrayed, as was intended; and that he should have had his audience at Cambridge, where the King meant to have been this Shrovetide, to see certain plays, about which there hath been much ado 'twixt the masters and seniors of Trinity College on the one side, and the younger fellows on the other, who would have them by all means; so that, the matter being referred to the Vice-Chancellor, he, loth to displease either party, sent it to the Lord Keeper, who, acquainting the King with it, certain of both parties were sent for, about Christmas, to show their reasons, which, being not admitted on the seniors' side, but willed to bring better or more pregnant, the ancientest of them said, that these times required rather prayers and fasting than plays and feasting; which was ill taken, and order given for the plays to go on. But, as matters are fallen out, I think he has altered his intention, and will not be there. (*Court and Times of James I*, ii, 365.)

The King's change of plan seems to have been caused by the disturbance which arose when it was discovered that Prince Charles and Buckingham had set out incognito for Spain. But it may have been in part occasioned by the nature of one of the plays, deemed by the University unsuitable for presentation before the ambassadors, whom the King proposed to bring. On February 22 Reverend Joseph Mead wrote from Christ College to Sir Martin Stuteville:

I will tell you a pretty Cambridge accident, as I am informed. On Ash Wednesday there is a comedy at Trinity College: whereupon the Spanish Ambassador and the Ambassador of Brussels being at Court, his Majesty sent word that they meant to come both to see the comedy. The name of the comedy is *Ignatius Loyola*, and, as I guess, the argument according. Hereupon, the seniors of Trinity have been much puzzled, and have moved the doctors to write to his Majesty how the case stands; and that either the ambassadors must not come, or the comedy must not be acted. (*Ibid.*, p. 368.)

The King went to Cambridge on March 12, accompanied by the ambassadors, who, however, did not attend the play. As Chamberlain wrote, "being made acquainted beforehand, for fear of offence, that the argument of it consisted chiefly of a Jesuit and a Puritan, they would not adventure, but wished they had not had notice; for they seemed to like all their entertainment so well, that they desired to have all the orations, and other exercises and disputations, that they might be printed." (*Ibid.*, p. 373.)

1622–3. MARCH 12 (WEDNESDAY). CAMBRIDGE. TRINITY COLLEGE.

Loyola, a comedy by John Hacket, before the King.

On March 21, 1622–3, John Chamberlain wrote to Sir Dudley Carleton:

After two or three disappointments, the 12th of this month, the king went to Cambridge, was there by ten o'clock, had dined before eleven, then went to the Hall, which being darkened, the play began presently, they having had order to abbreviate it or contract it, from six to seven hours to four or five, which he sat out with good satisfaction, and went back to Newmarket that night. (*Court and Times of James I*, ii, 375–76.)

The date of March 12 is confirmed by a letter of Mr. Mead's to Sir Martin Stuteville, on March 15:

The King heard our Comedie on Wednesday, but expressed no remarkable mirth thereat. He laughed once or twice toward the end. (Ellis, *Original Letters*, iii, 132.)

The performance is dated March 19 by Nichols (*Progresses James*, iv, 835), and Fleay (*Drama* i, 268). This is evidently an error.

1622–3. MARCH? NEWMARKET?

Fucus Histriomastix, a Cambridge Latin comedy probably by Robert Ward, acted at Queen's College in Lent 1623, was later acted before the King, as the court prologue and epilogue testify. According to Professor G. C. Moore Smith, the editor of the play (Cambridge, 1909), this court performance probably took place in March, at Newmarket. See also his *College Plays Performed in the University of Cambridge* (1923), p. 9.

1622–3. DATE UNCERTAIN.

Labyrinthus, a Cambridge play by W. Hawkesworth, acted before the King. (G. C. Moore Smith, *College Plays*, p. 92.)

Fleay (*Drama*, i, 275), probably on the authority of the article in the *Retrospective Review* (xii, 35), assigns the play to Shrovetide, 1621–2, and states that it was acted at Trinity College. At that time, however, the King was ill with gout at Theobalds, and would scarcely have undertaken a journey to the University. Smith dates the court performance 1622–3, and suggests that it may have taken place away from Cambridge.

THE SEASON 1623–1624

1623/1623–4. DATES UNCERTAIN.

Ten plays before the King by the King's Company (John Hemmings). Payment £10 each, on warrant dated February 17, 1623–4. (Stopes, *Burbage*, p. 257.)

Possibly the seven plays by the King's Company, the names of which follow, were paid for on this warrant.

1623. SEPTEMBER 29 (MONDAY). HAMPTON COURT.

"Upon Michelmas night att Hampton Court, *The Mayd of the Mill* [Beaumont and Fletcher] by the K. company." (Adams, *Dramatic Records*, p. 51.)

1623. NOVEMBER 1 (SATURDAY). ST. JAMES'S.

"Upon Allhollows night at St. James, the prince being there only, *The Mayd of the Mill* againe, with reformations." (Adams, *Dramatic Records*, p. 51.)

1623. NOVEMBER 5 (WEDNESDAY). WHITEHALL.

"Upon the fifth of November att Whitehall, the prince being there only, *The Gipsye* [Middleton and Rowley], by the Cockpitt company." (Adams, *Dramatic Records*, p. 51.)

1623. NOVEMBER 18 (TUESDAY). YORK HOUSE.

A masque by John Maynard, given by the Duke of Buckingham in honor of Don Diego de Mendoza and Don Carlos de Colonna, Spanish ambassadors.

Sir John Finett writes: "After Supper there was a Maske with a faire appearance of Ladies at it, and after the Maske, a most sumptuous Banquet." (*Finetti Philoxenis*, p. 132.) The King was present "as a guest inviting himselfe," he adds.

Finett leaves the date a little obscure. According to an entry in Archbishop Laud's *Diary*, and other contemporary accounts, the feast took place on November 18. In the Venetian State Papers (xviii, 157–8) the date is given as Wednesday, November 19.

Chamberlain describing the occasion in a letter written on November 21, says:

There was a Masque of young Maynard's invention, whereof I hear little or no commendation, but rather that the Spainards took offence at it. The main argument of it was a congratulation of the Prince's return. (Nichols, *Progresses James*, iv, 941.)

Upon sending a copy to Sir Dudley Carleton, he wrote, on December 6, that "the masque, at York House, were not worth the sending but that it is so free from flattery."

1623. DECEMBER 26 (FRIDAY). WHITEHALL.

"Upon St. Stevens daye, the king and prince being there, *The Mayd of the Mill*, by the K. company. Att Whitehall." (Adams, *Dramatic Records*, p. 51.)

The third performance. See the entries for September 29 and November 1.

1623. DECEMBER 27 (SATURDAY). WHITEHALL.

"Upon St. John's night, the prince only being there, *The Bondman* [Philip Massinger], by the queene [of Bohemia's] company. Att Whitehall." (Adams, *Dramatic Records*, p. 51.)

1623. DECEMBER 28 (SUNDAY). WHITEHALL.

"Upon Innocents night, falling out upon a Sonday, *The Buck is a Thief*, the king and prince being there. By the king's company. At Whitehall." (Adams, *Dramatic Records*, p. 51.)

1623–4. JANUARY 1 (THURSDAY). WHITEHALL.

"Upon New-years night, by the K. company, *The Wandering Lovers* [John Fletcher], the prince only being there. Att Whitehall." (Adams, *Dramatic Records*, p. 51.)

1623–4. JANUARY 4 (SUNDAY). WHITEHALL.

"Upon the Sonday after, being the 4 of January 1623, by the Queene of Bohemias company, *The Changelinge* [Middleton, W. Rowley], the prince only being there. Att Whitehall." (Adams, *Dramatic Records*, p. 51.)

1623–4. JANUARY 6 (TUESDAY).

Neptune's Triumph, by Ben Jonson, prepared for representation in the Banqueting House, but not performed, on account of rivalry between the French and Spanish ambassadors. (See Reyher, *Masques Anglais*, p. 527.)

The title-page, from the folio of 1640, reads: "Neptunes Triumph for the Returne of Albion. Celebrated in a Masque At the Court on the Twelfth night. 1624."

1623–4. JANUARY 6 (TUESDAY). WHITEHALL.

"Upon Twelfe Night, the maske being put off, *More Dissemblers besides Women* [Thomas Middleton], by the king's company, the prince only being there. Att Whitehall." (Adams, *Dramatic Records*, p. 51.)

According to Malone, Herbert wrote in the margin of his Office Book, "The worst play that ere I saw." (*Ibid.. n.* 8.)

1623–4. JANUARY 18 (SUNDAY). WHITEHALL.

"To the Duchess of Richmond, in the kings absence, was given *The Winter's Tale*, by the K. company, the 18 Janu. 1623. Att Whitehall." (Adams, *Dramatic Records*, p. 51.)

1623–4. FEBRUARY 8–10 (SHROVETIDE).

A Shrovetide masque seems to have been contemplated. On February 16 [O. S. 6] Alvise Valaresso, Venetian Ambassador in England, wrote: "The usual masque will not be performed, or will be performed without ambassadors, in order not to offend any." (*Cal. State Papers, Venetian*, xviii, 217.) Possibly the reference is to *Neptune's Triumph*, which had been postponed from Twelfth Day.

SUMMER, 1624

1624. AUGUST 5 (THURSDAY)? BURLEIGH.

A masque by John Maynard. (Reyher, *Masques Anglais*, p. 528; *Court and Times of James I*, ii, 472.)

On August 21 Chamberlain wrote to Carleton that "we have nothing from the court, but of a masque at Burleigh, made by young Maynard, with no great approbation."

This may have been the "sylvan masque" performed at Burleigh, the Duke of Buckingham's residence, on August 5. On August 23 [O. S. 13] Alvise Valaresso, Venetian Ambassador in England, wrote from London:

The Ambassador Fiat has left the King, but has not yet arrived here. He has the Earl of Warwick always with him. Buckingham gave him a state banquet; he ate with the King and Prince on the anniversary of the Gowrie conspiracy, when they also performed a sylvan masque. (*Cal. State Papers, Venetian*, xviii, 420.)

1624. AUGUST 19 (THURSDAY). KENILWORTH.

The Masque of Owls, by Ben Jonson, presented before Prince Charles. (Reyher, *Masques Anglais*, p. 528.)

The title-page, from the folio of 1640, reads: "The Masque of Owles at Kenelworth . . . 1626." The date is incorrect, as

Reyher points out. Chamberlain continues, in the letter quoted above: "Another was lately presented before the Prince at Killingworth, by Ben Jonson, whilst the King was at Warwick, but with what success we do not yet hear, because it was but two days since." (*Court and Times of James I*, ii, 472.)

1624? DATE UNCERTAIN.

Pan's Anniversary, or *The Shepherd's Holiday*, by Ben Jonson.

In the folio of 1640 it has the following title-page: "Pans Anniversarie; or, the Shepherds Holy-day . . . As it was presented at Court before King James. 1625."

On account of the fact that James died early in 1625, that other masques are misdated in the folio, and that *Pan's Anniversary* seems to be intended for a summer presentation, scholars have questioned the date given on the title-page. The original conjecture of Nichols (*Progresses James* iv, 986) that the order in the folio is presumably correct, and that the masque therefore should be assigned to the year 1624 is favored by Greg (*Pastoral Poetry and Pastoral Drama*, p. 263, *n.* 1) and Castelain (*Ben Jonson*, p. 736, *n.*).

THE SEASON 1624–1625

1624/1624–5. DATES UNCERTAIN.

Five plays by the King's Company. Payment £10 each, on warrant dated March 22, 1624-5. (Stopes, *Burbage*, p. 257.)

Possibly the four plays by the King's Company, the titles of which follow, were paid for on this warrant. The payment, however, indicates the King's presence.

1624. NOVEMBER 1 (MONDAY).

"Upon All-hollows night, 1624, the king beinge at Roiston, no play." (Adams, *Dramatic Records*, p. 52.)

1624. NOVEMBER 2 (TUESDAY).

"The night after, my Lord Chamberlain had *Rule a Wife and Have a Wife* [John Fletcher] for the ladys, by the kings company." (Adams, *Dramatic Records*, p. 52.)

1624. December 10 (Friday). Cambridge.

A comedy was prepared for the King's last visit to Cambridge, but was not performed. On December 18 Chamberlain wrote to Carleton: "There should have been a comedy, but the shortness of the time, the king's indisposition, and their hasting away, cut it off." (*Court and Times of James I*, ii, 485.)

1624. December 26 (Sunday). Whitehall.

"Upon St. Steevens night, the prince only being there, [was acted] *Rule a Wife and Have a Wife*, by the kings company. Att Whitehall." (Adams, *Dramatic Records*, p. 52.)

The presence of the King is not recorded at any of the entertainments of the season. On January 8 John Chamberlain wrote: "The king kept his chamber all this Christmas, not coming once to the chapel nor to any of the plays." (*Court and Times of James I*, ii, 488.) He died, it will be recalled, on March 27, 1625.

1624. December 27 (Monday). Whitehall.

"Upon St. John's night, [the prince] and the duke of Brunswick being there, *The Fox* [Ben Jonson], by the ————. At Whitehall." (Adams, *Dramatic Records*, p. 52.)

The Fox was owned by the King's Company. (*Ibid.*, *n.* 3.)

1624. December 28 (Tuesday). Whitehall.

"Upon Innocents night, the [prince] and the duke of Brunswyck being there, *Cupid's Revenge*, by the Queen of Bohemia's Servants. Att Whitehall, 1624." (Adams, *Dramatic Records*, p. 52.)

1624–5. January 1 (Saturday). Whitehall.

"Upon New-years night, the prince only being there, *The First Part of Sir John Falstaff* [Shakespeare's *Henry IV*, Part I], by the kings company. Att Whitehall, 1624." (Adams, *Dramatic Records*, p. 52.)

1624–5. January 6 (Thursday). Whitehall.

The Fortunate Isles, by Ben Jonson, prepared for Twelfth Night, but postponed. See the entry for January 9.

1624–5. JANUARY 6 (THURSDAY). WHITEHALL.

"Upon Twelve night, the Masque being putt of, and the prince only there, *Tu Quoque*, by the Queene of Bohemias servants. Att Whitehall, 1624." (Adams, *Dramatic Records*, p. 52.)

1624–5. JANUARY 9 (SUNDAY).

"The Fortunate Isles, and their Vnion. Celebrated in a Masque Design'd for the Court, on the Twelfth night. 1626." [Error for "1624". 1640 Folio.] (See Reyher, *Masques Anglais*, p. 528.)

By Ben Jonson. Although the masque was intended for Twelfth Night, it was presented three days later. Finett writes:

The fourth of January I received Order for the invitation of the French ambassador (the Marquess de Fiat) the Venetian Seignior Pesaro . . . and two Agents Monsieur Brumeau for the King of Spaine, and Monsieur Van Mal for the Archdutches to a Maske of the Prince, with certaine Lords and Gentlemen on Twelfnight . . . but being the next morning, assured by the Prince himself, that the Maske was to be put off till Sunday the ninth of January. I was upon his Highness intimation sent to disinvite them all which I performed with the French personally and with the rest by Letter. But on Saturday reinvited them for the next day. (*Finetti Philoxenis*, pp. 143–44.)

1624–5. JANUARY 12 (WEDNESDAY).

A play by the King's Company on January 12. Payment £10, on warrant dated February 20, 1624–5. (Stopes, *Burbage*, p. 257.)

1624–5. FEBRUARY 2 (WEDNESDAY).

"On Candlemas night the 2 February, no play, the king being att Newmarket." (Adams, *Dramatic Records*, p. 52.)

MISCELLANEOUS COURT PERFORMANCES OF UNCERTAIN DATE

The Phoenix, As It hath beene sundry times Acted by the Children of Paules. And presented before his Maiestie. London. 1607.

By Thomas Middleton. Entered S. R. May 9, 1607.

[*Mucedorus.*] *Amplified with new additions, as it was acted before the Kings Maiestie at White-hall on Shroue-sunday night. By his Highnes Seruants vsually playing at the Globe. Very delectable, and full of conceited Mirth.* London. 1610.

This edition of the play has not been found in the Stationers' Register. It is therefore difficult to date the Shrove Sunday referred to.

The Masque of the Four Seasons.

Collier, who prints this masque for the first time in *Inigo Jones . . . and Five Court Masques* (1848), assigns it, on internal evidence, to a date previous to 1612. (p. xx.)

The Masque of the Twelve Months.

Collier, who prints the masque in *Inigo Jones . . . and Five Court Masques*, says:

The fourth piece, *The Masque of the Twelve Months*, is anonymous, and is printed from a manuscript of the time, belonging to the editor of this portion of the work. It is quite evident that it was a court performance; and although nothing is said to fix the place of representation, we may be pretty certain that it was at Whitehall, and before James I.

Brotanek (*Englische Maskenspiele*, pp. 345–6) assigns it on internal evidence to January 1, 1611–12(?). See also Reyher, *Masques Anglais*, p. 522; Chambers, *Eliz. Stage*, iv, 58–9.

A Faire Quarrell. As it was Acted before the King and diuers times publikely by the Prince his Highnes Seruants. Written by Thomas Midleton and William Rowley Gentl. London. 1617.

According to Professor M. W. Sampson (*Thomas Middleton*, pp. 26, 202) the play was written in 1617, after March 13. It must therefore have been acted at Court in the year 1617. No payment to the Prince's company is recorded for that year.

A Courtly Masque: The Deuice Called The World tost at Tennis. As it hath beene diuers times Presented to the Contentment of many Noble and Worthy Spectators, By the Prince his Seruants. Inuented, and set downe, By Tho: Middleton & William Rowley Gent. London. 1620.

The Induction is preceded by this statement: "An Introduction to the Masque prepared for his Majesty's Entertainment at Denmark-House."

With regard to the date, Fleay says: "There is small doubt that this was the 'play' presented at Denmark House to the peers 1619, Mar. 4, when the Prince was practising at the ring against the King's Day." (*Drama*, ii, 100.) This date seems improbable when it is recalled that the Queen died on March 2, and that her body was taken to Denmark House four days later. See *Court and Times of James I*, ii, 144.

THE REIGN OF CHARLES I
1625-1642

THE REIGN OF CHARLES I

THE SEASON 1625–1626

ON DECEMBER 18, 1625, Sir Benjamin Rudyerd wrote to Sir Francis Nethersole that Christmas was to be spent at Hampton in plays, the common players having leave to come to Court since the plague had been reduced to six. (*Cal. State Papers, Domestic*, 1625–1626, p. 179.) On New year's eve he wrote that the Court would remove on "Tuesday next" [January 3], and that the end of Christmas would be kept at Whitehall. (*Ibid.*, p. 193.)

On December 30 the King gave his company of players ("who are to attend us daily at our Court this Christmas") the sum of one hundred marks "for the better furnishing them with apparel."

1625–1626. DATES UNCERTAIN.

Ten plays by the King's Company (John Hemmings). Payment £10 each, on warrant dated May 30, 1626. (Stopes, *Burbage*, p. 257.)

1625–6. FEBRUARY 21 (SHROVE TUESDAY). SOMERSET HOUSE.

A pastoral of the Queen's. (See Reyher, *Masques Anglais*, p. 528.)

In the Venetian State Papers this pastoral is said to have been performed on Shrove Tuesday, which fell on February 21. On March 6 [O. S. February 24] the Venetian Ambassador wrote:

On Shrove Tuesday the Queen and her maidens represented a pastoral, followed by a masque, with rich scenery and dresses, and remarkable acting on her part. The King and Court enjoyed it, those present being picked and selected, but it did not give complete satisfaction, because the English objected to the first part (attione) being declaimed by the Queen. (*Cal. State Papers, Venetian*, xix, 345–6.)

1625–6. February 21 (Shrove Tuesday). Somerset House.

A masque followed the performance of the Queen's pastoral. See the note to the preceding entry.

In a letter of Henry Manners to Sir George Manners, the date of the masque is given as Shrove Monday. (*MSS. of the Duke of Rutland, Hist. MSS. Com., Twelfth Report*, Part 4, p. 476.)

THE SEASON 1626–1627

1626. November 5 (Sunday). York House.

A masque given by the Duke of Buckingham, in honor of the King, Queen, and the French Ambassador, M. Bassompierre.

Sir John Finett writes:

On Sunday the 15th of November, the Duke of Buckingham having prepared a sumptuous entertainment of a Supper and a Maske at York-house for the French Ambassador Monsieur Bassompierre, had his feast honored with the presence of both their Majesties. (*Finetti Philoxenis*, p. 191.)

This date seems to be an error for November 5. November 15 fell not on Sunday, but Wednesday. Moreover, Bassompierre, in his *Journal de ma Vie* (iii, 274) describes the occasion under the date of "le dimanche 15me." This is, of course, according to the Gregorian calendar, and would correspond in the Old Style to November 5. Reyher (*Masques Anglais*, p. 528) dates the masque November 15, but he seems here, as in the case of the masque of November 16, not to have converted the ambassador's date into the Old Style, which then prevailed in England.

The date is confirmed by a correspondent of Reverend Joseph Mead, who writes, on November 10:

Last Sunday, at night, the Duke's grace entertained their Majesties and the French Ambassador at York House, with great feasting and show, where all things came down in clouds; amongst which, one rare device was a representation of the French King and the two Queens, with their chiefest attendants, and so to the life that the Queen's Majesty could name them. It was four o'clock in the morning before they parted. . . . (*Court and Times of Charles I*, 1, 166.)

1626. NOVEMBER 6 (MONDAY). YORK HOUSE.

A comedy before the King, Queen, and the French Ambassador.
Bassompierre writes:

Le lundy 16me [O. S. 6] le roy quy avoit couché a Iorchaus m'envoya querir pour ouir la musique de la reine sa femme; puis en suitte il fit tenir le bal, apres lequel il y eut comedie, et se retira a Houaithall avec la reine sa femme. (*Journal de ma Vie*, iii, 274.)

1626. NOVEMBER 16 (THURSDAY). SOMERSET HOUSE.

A masque of the Queen's, in honor of the French Ambassador. (*Finetti Philoxenis*, p. 192.)

Reyher, (*Masques Anglais*, p. 528) says: "Finett, *Observations*, p. 190 [192] speaks of a ballet given by the Queen the 16th of November. Is this not an error for the 26th? I find no mention of this masque in Bassompierre." The ambassador, however, writes in the *Journal de ma Vie:*

Le jeudy 26me [O. S. 16] les comtes de Brischwater et de Salisberi me vindrent voir. Le soir je fus trouver la reine a Sommerset, quy fit en ma consideration ce jour là une tres belle assemblée, puis un ballet, et de là une collation de confitures. (iii, 276-7.)

See also the letter of Alvise Contarini, Venetian Ambassador, who wrote on November 27 [O. S. 17], "Last evening her Majesty gave him a masque, which proved very elegant." (*Cal. State Papers, Venetian*, 1626-1628, p. 32.)

1626. NOVEMBER 19 (SUNDAY). WHITEHALL. THE GREAT HALL.

A comedy before the King, Queen, and the French Ambassador. (*Finetti Philoxenis*, p. 193.)

Bassompierre writes in the *Journal de ma Vie:*

Lucnar [Sir Lewis Lewknor] me vint apporter de la part du roy un tres riche present de quattre diamans mis en une losenge et une grosse perle au bout; et le mesme soir le roy m'envoya encor querir pour me faire ouir une excellente comedie angloise. (iii, 277-8.)

1626–7. CHRISTMAS.

A play before the King.

On February 3, 1626–7, the Reverend Joseph Mead wrote to Sir Martin Stuteville: "I doubt not but you have heard of the play in Christmas, which was begun again at the Duke's entering, the King having heard one full act." (*Court and Times of Charles I,* i, 191.) The reference is, of course, to the King's favorite, the Duke of Buckingham.

1626–7. JANUARY 14 OR 15 (SUNDAY OR MONDAY). WHITEHALL.

A masque of the Queen's.

This masque was intended for Twelfth Night. Finett writes: "There being a Maske in practice of the Queen in person, with other great Ladies for the end of Christmas, I three or foure dayes before Twelftide, asked my Lord Chamberlain what course would be taken with the Ambassadors here resident, Contareni for Venice, and Joachimi for the States?" The Venetian, however, "desired time for the consideration" of the proposal made to him, and the masque took place "the Moneday seavennight after following after Twelfday," with the Venetian Ambassador sitting on the right hand and the States Ambassador on the left of the King.

In the Venetian State Papers (1626–1628, p. 107) the date is given as Sunday, January 14. On January 29 [O. S. 19] Contarini wrote: "On Sunday last the Queen performed her masque, which was very pretty." Likewise, a correspondent writing on January 19 to Reverend Joseph Mead, says that the Queen's masque was held "last Sunday," and adds that it was said to have been "preparing and performing from three in the afternoon till four next morning." (*Court and Times of Charles I,* i, 185.) See Reyher, *Masques Anglais,* p. 529.

1627. MAY 15 (TUESDAY). YORK HOUSE.

A masque given by the Duke of Buckingham in honor of the King and Queen. (Reyher, *Masques Anglais,* p. 529.)

The title and author of the masque are unknown. The following letters, however, indicate its nature. On May 16 a correspondent wrote to Reverend Joseph Mead:

On Tuesday night last, the duke gave his farewell supper at York House, and a masque unto their majesties, wherein first comes forth the duke, after him Envy, with divers open-mouthed dogs' heads, representing the people's barking; next came Fame, then Truth, &c. (*Court and Times of Charles I*, i, 226.)

The Venetian Ambassador wrote that it represented "the putting to sea of the fleet, to inflame the King's ardour" against the French. (*Cal. State Papers, Venetian*, 1626–1628, p. 239.)

THE SEASON 1627–1628

1627/1627-8. SEPTEMBER 29–JANUARY 31.

Ten plays "acted before the King at several times between Michaelmas last 1627 and the last of January following" by the King's Company (John Hemings, John Lowen, Joseph Taylor). Payment £10 each, on warrant dated April 10, 1628. (Stopes, in *Jahrbuch*, xlvi, 94. See also her *Burbage*, p. 257–8.)

A schedule containing the names of the plays has been lost.

1627. NOVEMBER 1 (THURSDAY). WHITEHALL.

A play at Court.

Finett mentions this play as the occasion of an exhibition of coolness between two ambassadors:

While these Puntillio's were in agitation, a Play on all Saints day (being appointed at Court to begin Christmas with) I was told the day before by the Venetian (when he visited me at my House) that he was invited to the sight of it, and to a Supper by the Countess of Denbigh as was the Savoy Ambassador at the same time by the Earle of Carliel, understanding thus much, I did (to prevent all inconveniences that might happen by any suddain incounter) let fall a word or two in hearing of the Savoy Ambassador for his knowledge of it; who answerably took his course in such sort, as that after the Venetian was (before the Kings comming into the Hall) entered there, leading the Countesse of Denbigh, and seating himselfe uppermost at the end of the Lords seat towards the Kings right hand, next above the Lady mentioned the Ambassador of Savoy entered with the King passing promiscously amongst the Lords, and (as I had before prepared the Dutches of Buckingham, were seated next above her, the other great Ladies) the Lord of Carliel sitting next above the Ambassador, but sidewayes upon another seate on the Kings left hand, neither of these Ambassadors so much as looking one towards another, much lesse saluting, either entering, or parting, that of Savoy going out, as he entered after the King, leaving the Dutchess, and the other of Venice after those were gone following with the Countesse. (*Finetti Philoxenis*, pp. 235–6.)

1627–8. January 6 (Sunday).

A masque at Court was planned, but not presented. (See Reyher, *Masques Anglais*, p. 529.)

This was to have been a "running masque." On January 2 Rowland Woodward wrote to Francis Windebank: "A thin Court and a dead Christmas, only there will be a running masque on Sunday, which is not of above six days' conception." (*Cal. State Papers, Domestic*, 1627–1628, p. 502.) Possibly the masque was postponed until Shrovetide, and the plans for it elaborated. See the following entry.

1627–8. February 24–26 (Shrovetide).

Two masques were planned for Shrovetide, one by the "gentlemen of the Temple" and one by the King.

On January 12 Reverend Joseph Mead wrote to Sir Martin Stuteville:

The gentlemen of the Temple being this Shrovetide to present a masque to their Majesties, over and besides the King's own great masque, to be performed in the Banqueting House by an hundred actors. (*Court and Times of Charles I*, i, 312.)

On February 11 a warrant was issued to pay Edmund Taverner £600 "towards the expense of a masque to be presented shortly before the King at Whitehall." (*Cal. State Papers, Domestic*, 1627–1628, p. 556.) There is no record, however, that either of the masques took place. The King was not in London during Shrovetide. On February 20 Mr. Beaulieu wrote to Sir Thomas

Puckering that "his Majesty is going this day towards New-market, to remain in the journey till the 15th of March." (*Court and Times of Charles I*, i, 322.)

1627–8. FEBRUARY 24–26 (SHROVETIDE).

It was rumored that the King would visit Cambridge, to see the Shrovetide plays there. Mead wrote, on February 22:

We have two or three Comedies at Trinity this Shrovetide, and the stage there built to that purpose. But of the King's coming, it was not talked of, when I wrote last, and if it be, it is but private and accidental. Some say, he will be here on the Monday; and my Lord of Durham, that was, is now in the town, as is thought, for some direction to that purpose. Yet others doubt whether he will come or not. (*Court and Times of Charles I*, i, 325.)

The King did not go to Cambridge until March 3. He returned to London, or at least to Theobalds, on March 8. See the letter of Mr. Beaulieu, *op. cit.*, p. 326.

1627–8. MARCH 3 (MONDAY). CAMBRIDGE. TRINITY COLLEGE.

Paria, a Latin play by Thomas Vincent, of Trinity College, before the King. (G. C. Moore Smith, *College Plays*, pp. 9, 69. Cf. Fleay, *Drama*, ii, 265.)

1628. APRIL 15 (EASTER TUESDAY).

A play on "Easter Tuesday at night" by the King's Company [John Hemmings]. Payment £10, on warrant dated April 20, 1628. (Stopes, *Burbage*, p. 257.)

THE SEASON 1628–1629

1628/1628–9. CHRISTMAS—CANDLEMAS.

Sixteen plays before the King "between Christmas and Candlemas 1628" by the King's Company (John Hemings). Payment on warrant of February 27, 1628–9. (Stopes, in *Jahrbuch*, xlvi, 94. See also *Burbage*, p. 528.)

1629. April 6 (Easter Monday).

"*Ye Love Sicke Maid* [Richard Brome] before the King on Easter Monday by the King's Company (John Hemings). Payment £10, on warrant dated May 6, 1629. (Stopes, in *Jahrbuch*, xlvi, 94. See also *Burbage*, p. 258.)

THE SEASON 1629-1630

1629-30. Date Uncertain.

A masque at Court? (Reyher, *Masques Anglais*, p. 529.)

1629/1629-30. October-February.

Ten plays "between October and February 1629-30" by the Queen's Company. Payment £10 each, on warrant dated July 5, 1630. (Stopes, in *Jahrbuch*, xlvi, 95.)

1629/1629-30. Christmas.

Twelve plays before the King "at Christmas 1629" by the King's Company (John Hemings). Payment £10 each, on warrant dated April 3, 1630. (Stopes, in *Jahrbuch*, xlvi, 95. See also *Burbage*, p. 258.)

On December 30 Mr. Beaulieu wrote Sir Thomas Puckering that there had "wanted no plays for the solemnizing of the Christmas holidays."

THE SEASON 1630-1631

1630/1630-1. Dates Uncertain. Hampton Court.

Four plays at Hampton Court, by the King's Company (John Lowen). Payment £20 each, "in respect of the travaile and expenses of the whole company in Dyet and Lodging during the time of their attendance there," on warrant dated March 17, 1630-1. (Stopes, in *Jahrbuch*, xlvi, 95. See also *Burbage*, p. 258.)

1630/1630-1. Date Uncertain. Whitehall.

"And the like sum of £20 for one play" by the King's Company "which was acted at Whitehall in the daytime, whereby the players lost the benefitt of their house for that day." Paid on the same warrant as that for the preceding plays. (Stopes, in *Jahrbuch*, xlvi, 95. See also *Burbage*, p. 258.)

1630/1630–1. SEPTEMBER 30–FEBRUARY 21. WHITEHALL.

Sixteen other plays before the King at Whitehall "between the 30th September and 21st Feb. last past" by the King's Company. Payment £10 each, on the same warrant as that for the preceding plays. An annexed schedule containing the titles has been lost. (Stopes, in *Jahrbuch*, xlvi, 95. See also *Burbage*, p. 258.)

1630–1. JANUARY 9 (SUNDAY).

Loues Triumph through Callipolis. Performed in a Masque at Court 1630. By his Maiestie with the Lords, and Gentlemen assisting. The Inuentors. Ben Ionson. Jnigo Iones. London. 1630. (See Reyher, *Masques Anglais*, p. 529.)

1630–1. FEBRUARY 22 (SHROVE TUESDAY).

Chloridia. Rites to Chloris and her Nymphs. Personated in a Masque, at Court. By the Queenes Maiesty And her ladies. At Shroue-tide. 1630. London. [n. d.] By Ben Jonson. (See Reyher, *Masques Anglais*, p. 529.)

THE SEASON 1631–1632

1631/1631–2. DATES UNCERTAIN. WHITEHALL.

Three plays "at Whitehall in 1631" by the Children of the Revels (William Blagrave). Payment £10 each, on warrant dated January 24, 1634–5. (Chalmers, *Apology*, p. 508. See also *Jahrbuch*, xlvi, 97.)

W. J. Lawrence (*Times Literary Supplement*, Nov. 25, 1923) is of the opinion that one of these plays was Thomas Randolph's *Amyntas*. He shows that this play was licensed by Herbert on November 26, 1630, and acted by the Children of the Revels. It was first published in 1638 as having been "acted before the King and Queene at White-Hall."

1631/1631–2. DATES UNCERTAIN.

Three plays "in 1631" by the Children of the Revels (William Blagrave). Payment £10 each, on warrant dated January 30, 1634–5. (Chalmers, *Apology*, p. 508.)

1631/1631–2. OCTOBER 10–FEBRUARY 20.

Sixteen plays "between 10th of October 1631 and 20th Feb. 1631–2" by the Queen's Company (Christopher Beeston). "£170 for 16 Playes . . . and £10 extra for three plays each performed at Hampton Court." (Stopes, in *Jahrbuch*, xlvi, 96.)

1631/1631–2. CHRISTMAS.

Eleven plays before the King "at Christmas 1631" by the King's Company (John Lowing, Joseph Taylor, and Eilliard Swanston). Payment £10 each for ten, and £20 for one at Hampton Court, on warrant dated February 22, 1631–2. (Stopes, in *Jahrbuch*, xlvi, 96. See also *Burbage*, p. 259.)

1631–2. JANUARY 8 (SUNDAY). WHITEHALL. THE BANQUETING HOUSE.

Albions Triumph. Personated in a Maske at Court. By the Kings Maiestie and his Lords. The Sunday after Twelfe Night. 1631. London. 1631. (See Reyher, *Masques Anglais*, p. 530.)

On January 12 Mr. Pory wrote to Sir Thomas Puckering:

The last Sunday night the King's masque was acted in the Banqueting House, the Queen's being suspended till another time by reason of a soreness which fell into her delicate eyes. The inventor or poet of this masque was Mr. Aurelian Townshend, sometimes towards the Lord Treasurer Salisbury, Ben Jonson being for this time discarded, by reason of the predominant power of his protagonist, Inigo Jones, who this time twelvemonth was angry with him for putting his own name before his in the title-page, which Ben Jonson made the subject of a bitter satire or two against Inigo. (*Court and Times of Charles I*, ii, 158–59.)

1631–2. February 14 (Shrove Tuesday). Whitehall. The Great Hall.

Tempe Restord. A Masque Presented by the Queene, and foureteene Ladies, to the Kings Maiestie at Whitehall on Shrove-Tuesday. 1631. London 1631.

By Aurelian Townsend. See Reyher, *Masques Anglais*, p. 530. The masque was performed, according to a letter of the Venetian Ambassador's, "in the great hall of the royal palace." (*Cal. State Papers, Venetian*, xxii, 592.)

1631–2. March 19 (Monday). Cambridge.

The Rivall Friends. A Comoedie, As it was Acted before the King and Queens Maiesties, when out of their princely favour they were pleased to visite their Vniversitie of Cambridge, upon the 19. day of March. 1631. Cryed downe by Boyes, Faction, Envie, and confident Ignorance, approv'd by the judicious, and now exposed to the publique censure, by The Authour, Pet. Hausted Mr. in Artes of Queenes Colledge. London. 1632.

On February 23 Mr. Pory wrote to Sir Thomas Puckering: "But on Tuesday [February 21] his Majesty carried the Queen a pleasanter voyage, namely, from hence to Theobalds, thence to Royston, so on to Cambridge, where three comedies are provided for their entertainment." (*Court and Times of Charles I*, ii, 170.)

We have a record of only two comedies. For a detailed account of the *Rival Friends*, see the article by Professor J. Q. Adams in the *Journal of English and Germanic Philology* for July, 1912.

1631–2. March 22 (Thursday). Cambridge.

The Jealous Lovers. A Comedie presented to their gracious Majesties at Cambridge, by the Students of Trinity-Colledge. Written by Thomas Randolph, Master of Arts, and Fellow of the House. Cambridge. 1632.

See the note to the preceding entry. General accounts of the royal visit, and the reception of the play, more favorable than that of the *Rival Friends*, are to be found in Masson, *Life of Milton*, i, 251–54, and Mullinger, *The University of Cambridge*, iii, 107–109. For the date of the performance, see G. C. Moore Smith, *College Plays*, p. 69.

THE SEASON 1632–1633

1632/1632–3. May 3–March 3. Whitehall and Denmark House.

Twenty-one plays before the King "at Whitehall and Denmark House, acted between 3rd May 1632, and 3rd of March following" by the King's Company (John Lowen, Joseph Taylor, Eilliard Swanston). Payment £10 each, on warrant dated March 16, 1632–3. (Stopes, in *Jahrbuch*, xlvi, 96–7. See also *Burbage*, p. 259.)

1632/1632–3. Date Uncertain. Whitehall. The Cockpit.

The "rehearsal" of a play at the Cockpit by the King's Company, "by which means they lost their afternoon at the House." Payment £20, on the same warrant as that for the twenty-one plays. (Stopes, in *Jahrbuch*, xlvi, 96–7. See also *Burbage*, p. 259.)

1632/1632–3. Dates Uncertain. Hampton Court.

Two plays before the King at Hampton Court, by the King's Company. Payment £20 each, on the same warrant as that for the twenty-one plays. (Stopes, in *Jahrbuch*, xlvi, 96–7. See also *Burbage*, p. 259.)

1632–1633. Dates Uncertain.

Fourteen plays by the Queen's Company. Payment £10 each, on warrant dated October 27, 1633. (Stopes, in *Jahrbuch*, xlvi, 97. Mrs. Stopes gives £240 as the sum paid for the fourteen plays. Evidently this is an error.)

1632. October–November.

Nine plays by the Queen's Company (Christopher Beeston). Payment £10 each for eight, and "£20 for one acted at Hampton Court in October," on warrant dated December 5, 1632. (Stopes, in *Jahrbuch*, xlvi, 96.)

1632. November 19 (Tuesday)?

A performance of Walter Montague's *Shepherd's Paradise* was contemplated in November, probably for the King's birthday.

There is no evidence, however, that the performance took place. See the entry for 1632–3, January 9.

Preparation for the play was begun early in the autumn. On September 20 Mr. Pory wrote to Sir Thomas Puckering:

That which the Queen's Majesty, some of her ladies, and all her maids of honour are now practicing upon, is a pastoral penned by Mr. Walter Montagu, wherein her Majesty is pleased to act a part, as well for her recreation as for the exercise of her English. (*Court and Times of Charles I*, ii, 176.)

On November 12 [O. S. 2] Vicenzo Gussoni, the Venetian Ambassador, wrote:

The Court is preparing for the dancing and festivities which are to take place within a few days upon the occasion of a comedy in which, for the gratification and pleasure of the King, the Queen herself will perform publicly. (*Cal. State Papers, Venetian*, xxiii, 28.)

1632–3. JANUARY 9 (WEDNESDAY). SOMERSET HOUSE.

The Shepheard's Paradise. A Comedy. Privately Acted before the Late King Charls by the Queen's Majesty, and Ladies of Honour. Written by W. Mountague Esq. London. 1629 [misprint for 1659].

The performance probably occurred on January 9, although one correspondent gives the date as January 10. On January 3 Mr. Pory wrote to Sir Thomas Puckering that the Queen's pastoral was to be acted "on Wednesday next" in the lower court of Denmark House. (*Court and Times of Charles I*, ii, 214.) Mr. Beaulieu, however, wrote on January 10: "This night our Queen hath acted her costly pastoral in Somerset House, which hath lasted seven or eight hours." (*Ibid.*, p. 216.) Perhaps he dated his letter on the next morning. A correspondent writing on January 13 to Sir Robert Philips refers to the play as having been acted on Wednesday. (*Northumberland MSS., Hist. MSS. Com., Ap. to Third Report*, p. 282.) See Reyher, *Masques Anglais*, p. 530.

1632–3. FEBRUARY 2 (SATURDAY).

A repetition of the *Shepherd's Paradise* was planned for Candle- mas.

On January 13 a correspondent wrote to Sir Robert Philips that the Queen's pastoral was "again to be performed on Candlemas next." (*Northumberland MSS.*, *op. cit.*, p. 282.) See Reyher, *Masques Anglais*, p. 530.

1632–3. MARCH 5 (SHROVE TUESDAY). WHITEHALL.

A "masque" given by the Queen. Possibly this was the second performance of the *Shepherd's Paradise*.

On March 18 [O. S. 8] Vicenzo Gussoni, Venetian Ambassador in England, wrote from London to the Doge and Senate:

On the night of Tuesday last, the end of the carnival according to their reckoning here, the queen produced her masque in the public hall, when the king gladly took part in the dancing until near daybreak. (*Cal. State Papers, Venetian*, xxiii. 86.)

THE SEASON 1633–1634

1633–1634. DATES UNCERTAIN.

Twenty-two plays by the King's Company (John Lowen, Joseph Taylor, and Elliard Swanston) "by them acted before his Majesty within a whole year." Payment £10 each; on warrant dated April 27, 1634. (Chalmers, *Apology*, p. 507. See also Stopes, in *Jahrbuch*, xlvi, 97; *Burbage*, p. 259.)

It is probable that this warrant covers the plays by the King's Company, the titles of which follow.

1633. DATES UNCERTAIN.

[Seven] plays "in 1633" by the Queen's Company (Christopher Beeston). Payment £10 each, on warrant dated December 31, 1634. (Chalmers, *Apology*, p. 507.)

1633. NOVEMBER 16 (SATURDAY). ST. JAMES's.

"On Saterday, the 17th of Novemb. being the Queens birthday, *Richard the Thirde* was acted by the K. players at St. James, wher the king and queene were present, it being the first play the queene sawe since her M.^tys delivery of the Duke of York, 1633." (Adams, *Dramatic Records*, p. 53.)

The writer was apparently trusting to memory. Saturday fell on November 16. Moreover, the Queen's birthday, November 26, according to the New Style, was celebrated in England on the corresponding Old Style date, November 16.

1633. NOVEMBER 19 (TUESDAY). ST. JAMES'S.

"On tusday, the 19th of November, being the king's birth-day, *The Yong Admirall* [James Shirley] was acted at St. James by the queen's players, and likt by the K. and Queen." (Adams, *Dramatic Records*, p. 53.)

1633. NOVEMBER 26 (TUESDAY). ST. JAMES'S.

"On tusday night at St. James, the 26th of Novemb. 1633, was acted before the King and Queene, *The Taminge of the Shrew.* Likt." (Adams, *Dramatic Records*, p. 53.)

1633. NOVEMBER 28 (THURSDAY). ST. JAMES'S.

"On thursday night at St. James, the 28 of Novemb. 1633, was acted before the King and Queene, *The Tamer Tamd*, made by Fletcher. Very well likt." (Adams, *Dramatic Records*, p. 53.)

1633. DECEMBER 10 (TUESDAY). WHITEHALL.

"On tusday night at Whitehall the 10 Decemb. 1633, was acted before the King and Queen, *The Loyal Subject*, made by Fletcher, and very well likt by the king." (Adams, *Dramatic Records*, p. 53.)

1633. DECEMBER 16 (MONDAY). WHITEHALL.

"On Monday night the 16 of December, 1633, at Whitehall was acted before the King and Queen, *Hymens Holliday* or *Cupids Fegarys*, an ould play of Rowley's. Likte." (Adams, *Dramatic Records*, p. 53.)

1633–4. JANUARY 1 (WEDNESDAY). WHITEHALL.

"On Wensday night the first of January, 1633, *Cymbeline* [William Shakespeare] was acted at Court by the Kings players. Well likte by the kinge." (Adams, *Dramatic Records*, p. 53.)

1633–4. JANUARY 6 (MONDAY). DENMARK HOUSE.

"On Monday night, the sixth of January and the Twelfe Night, was presented at Denmark-house, before the King and Queene, Fletchers pastorall called *The Faithfull Shepheardesse*, in the clothes the Queene had given Taylor the year before of her owne pastorall.

"The scenes were fitted to the pastorall, and made, by Mr. Inigo Jones, in the great chamber, 1633." (Adams, *Dramatic Records*, p. 53. See also *Cal. State Papers, Venetian*, xxiii, 184.)

The reference is to Montague's *The Queen's Pastoral*, which had been performed at Denmark House on January 10, 1632–3.

On January 9 Mr. Garrard wrote to the Lord Deputy:

I never knew a duller Christmas than we had at Court this year, but one Play all the Time at Whitehall, and no dancing at all. The Queen had some little infirmity . . . which made her keep in, only on Twelfthnight she feasted the King at Somerset-house, and presented him with a Play, newly studied, long since printed, *The Faithful Shepherdess*, which the King's Players acted in the Robes she and her Ladies acted their Pastoral in the last year. (*Strafford Letters*, i, 177.)

1633–4. JANUARY 12 (SUNDAY).

"*The Guardian*, a play of Mr. Messengers, was acted at court on Sunday the 12 January, 1633, by the King's players, and well likte." (Adams, *Dramatic Records*, p. 54.)

1633–4. JANUARY 14 (TUESDAY).

"*The Tale of the Tub* [Ben Jonson] was acted on tusday night at Court, the 14 Janua. 1633, by the Queenes players, and not likte." (Adams, *Dramatic Records*, p. 54.)

1633–4. JANUARY 16 (THURSDAY).

"*The Winters Tale* was acted on thursday night at Court, the 16 Janua. 1633, by the K. players, and likt." (Adams, *Dramatic Records*, p. 64.)

1633–4. JANUARY 28 (TUESDAY).

"*The Witts* [William Davenant] was acted on tusday night the 28 January, 1633, at Court, before the Kinge and Queene. Well likt. It had a various fate on the stage, and at court, though the kinge commended the language, but dislikt the plott and characters." (Adams, *Dramatic Records*, p. 54.)

1633–4. JANUARY 30 (THURSDAY).

"*The Night-Walkers* was acted on thursday night the 30 Janua. 1633, at Court, before the King and Queen. Likt as a merry play. Made by Fletcher." (Adams, *Dramatic Records*, p. 54.)

1633–4. FEBRUARY 3 (MONDAY). WHITEHALL. THE BANQUETING HOUSE.

"*The Triumph of Peace. A Masque, presented by the Foure Honourable Houses, or Jnnes of Court. Before the King and Queenes Majesties, in the Banquetting-house at White Hall, February the third, 1633. Invented and Written, By James Shirley, of Grayes Inne, Gent.* London. 1633."

The masque was requested by the King. "There came a desire for the King about a fortnight ago to the Inns of Court by my Lord Keeper," wrote Thomas Coke on October 17, "that the gentlemen of the several Inns would show themselves at Court by the presentation of a mask, which desire was suddenly accepted and speedily concluded upon." (*MSS. of Earl Cowper, Hist. MSS. Com., Ap. to Twelfth Report*, Part 2, p. 34. See also Reyher, *Masques Anglais*, p. 530; Adams, *Dramatic Records*, p. 54.)

1633–4. FEBRUARY 6 (THURSDAY).

"On thursday night the 6 of Febru. 1633, *The Gamester* was acted at Court, made by Sherley, out of a plot of the king's, given him by mee; and well likte. The King sayd it was the best play he had seen for seven years." (Adams, *Dramatic Records*, p. 54.)

1633–4. FEBRUARY 11 OR 13 (TUESDAY OR THURSDAY). MERCHANT TAILORS' HALL.

The Triumph of Peace, by James Shirley, again performed before the King and Queen. (Reyher, *Masques Anglais*, p. 530.)

1633–4. FEBRUARY 18 (SHROVE TUESDAY). WHITEHALL. THE BANQUETING HOUSE.

Coelum Britanicum. A Masque at White-Hall in the Banquetting-house, on Shrove-Tuesday-night, the 18. of February, 1633. London. 1634.

By Thomas Carew. See Reyher, *Masques Anglais*, p. 530; Adams, *Dramatic Records*, p. 55.

1634. APRIL 7 (EASTER MONDAY). WHITEHALL. THE COCKPIT.

"Bussy d'Amboise [George Chapman] was played by the king's players on Easter-monday night, at the Cockpitt in court." (Adams, *Dramatic Records*, p. 55.)

1634. APRIL 8 (TUESDAY). WHITEHALL. THE COCKPIT.

"The Pastorall was playd by the king's players on Easter-tusday night, at the Cockpitt in court." (Adams, *Dramatic Records*, p. 55.)

Probably "Fletcher's pastoral, called *The Faithful Shepherdess*" which had been presented at Court on January 6, 1633–4. (*Ibid., n.* 3.)

1634. MAY 13 (TUESDAY). BLACKFRIARS.

"The 13 May, 1634, the Queene was at Blackfriars to see Messengers playe." (Adams, *Dramatic Records*, p. 65.)

According to Malone, the play was the *Tragedy of Cleander*, which had been acted on May 7. (*Ibid., n.* 2.) It was not unusual for the Queen to see a play at Blackfriars. See the entries for 1635–6, Date Uncertain; 1636, May 5; 1638, April 23. The Queen probably engaged the playhouse for an evening performance. The public, of course, would be excluded, and only the invited guests admitted. See Adams, *Shakespearean Playhouses*, p. 232.

SUMMER, 1634

On August 25, 1634, a warrant for £100 was issued "for ye Prince's Players for their attendance abroad." On July 20 "a tent for the Prince's players during progress" had been furnished. (See Stopes, in *Jahrbuch*, xlvi, 97.)

THE SEASON 1634–1635

1634–1635. MAY 13–MARCH 30.

Twenty plays "acted between 13 May 1634, and 30th March 1635" by the King's Company (John Lowen). Payment £10 each for fifteen, and £20 each for five at Hampton Court, on a warrant dated May 24, 1635. (Stopes, *Jahrbuch*, xlvi, 98. See also *Burbage*, p. 259.) Cf. Chalmers, *Apology*, p. 508, in which the dates of acting are given as between "13th May 1624, and the 30th of March 1626." These dates are probably erroneous. Payment would scarcely have been so long deferred.

1634. DATES UNCERTAIN.

Eight plays "acted by the Queen's players at court, in 1634, whereof one at Hampton-court" (Christopher Beeston). Payment £10 each for seven, and £20 for the one at Hampton Court, on a warrant dated March 24, 1635–6. (Chalmers, *Apology*, p. 509. See also Stopes, in *Jahrbuch*, xlvi, 98.)

1634. SEPTEMBER 3 (WEDNESDAY).

Comedies in honor of the Marquis of San Germano.

On September 15 [O. S. 5] Francesco Zonca, Venetian Secretary in England, wrote to the Doge and Senate:

In the mean time the Queen herself has had various amusements arranged for him, and the day before yesterday, in particular, he dined here in London with her Majesty, entertained by Lord Gorin, her Master of the Horse, when they represented comedies, dancing, music and other agreeable pastimes. (*Cal. State Papers, Venetian*, xxiii, 275.)

1634. September, October. Hampton Court.

Three plays at Hampton Court "in September and October 1634" by the Prince's Company (Joseph Moore, Andrew Kayne, Ellis Worth). Payment £20 each, on warrant dated December 10, 1635. (Chalmers, *Apology*, pp. 508–9. See also *Jahrbuch*, xlvi, 98.)

1634. October.

A masque given by the Queen in honor of the birth of a son to her sister, the Duchess of Savoy.

On October 15 [O. S. 5] Vicenzo Gussoni, Venetian Ambassador in England, wrote from London to the Doge and Senate:

The Queen here desired to have special rejoicings over the birth of the little prince of Savoy. She herself danced in a masque, which was arranged and studied by her Majesty for this purpose in a country village, a pleasure resort not far from this city. She invited to it Buonporto, the gentleman sent on purpose to this Court with the news by the Duchess to her sister. (*Cal. State Papers, Venetian*, xxiii, 15–16.)

The little prince referred to was Francis Hacinth, afterwards duke of Savoy, born on September 4. The arrival of the messenger, the Sieur de Bonport, is announced by Gussoni in a letter dated October 8 [N. S.]. I have not identified the "country village" where the masque was performed.

1634–5. Christmas.

The Conspiracy A Tragedy, As it was intended for the Nuptialls, of the Lord Charles Herbert, and the Lady Villers. Written by Mr. Henry Killigraew. London. 1638.

On January 11, 1634–5, Garrard wrote to Strafford:

At the end of Christmas was married by the Archbishop of Canterbury my Lord Chamberlain's eldest Son to the Lady Mary Villiers, Daughter to the Duke of Buckingham, in the Closet at Whitehall. It was done privately, and few invited, and sooner than was intended, by reason the young lady began to affect the younger Brother Philip Herbert, and of herself had moved the Chamberlain, that she might marry him, saying he did apply himself to her more than my Lord Herbert did: But the Dutchess chid her out of that Humour, and now she is married that affection will vanish. (*Letters and Dispatches of the Earl of Strafford*, i, 359.)

According to Archbishop Laud's *Diary*, this marriage was celebrated on January 8, 1634–5. From the title-page we may infer that Killigrew's play, though "intended for the Nuptialls," may not have been acted. The authorized edition was issued in 1653 with the title *Pallantus and Eudora*.

Anzolo Correr, Venetian Ambassador in England, bears witness to the absorption of the Court in amusements. On January 19 [O. S. 9] he wrote to the Doge and Senate:

I find it hard to inform your Excellencies of the impression made by this [the proposed peace between the Emperor and the Duke of Saxony] upon the Court here, because the ministers here persist in the notion I have so often reported, and at present they are devoting most of their time to the jollities of the carnival, not a day passing without dancing and comedies at Court. (*Cal. State Papers, Venetian*, xxiii, 323.)

1634–1635. January, February, May. Whitehall and The Cockpit.

Four plays "at Whitehall, and the Cockpit, in January, February, and May following" by the Prince's Company. Payment £10 each, on warrant dated December 10, 1635. (Chalmers, *Apology*, pp. 508–9. See also Stopes, in *Jahrbuch*, xlvi, 98.)

1634–5. February–May 10. Whitehall. The Cockpit.

Three plays at the Cockpit by the French players (Josias Floridor). Payment £10 each, on warrant dated May 10, 1635. (Chalmers, *Apology*, p. 508.)

The French players arrived in London in February, 1635.

1634–5. February 10 (Shrove Tuesday). Whitehall. The Banqueting House.

The Temple of Love. A Masque. Presented by the Queenes Majesty, and her Ladies, at White-hall on Shrove-Tuesday, 1634. By Inigo Iones,

Surveyour of his Majesties Workes; and William Davenant, her Majesties Servant. London. 1634. (See Reyher, *Masques Anglais*, pp. 344, 531.)

On February 23 [O. S. 13] the Venetian Ambassador wrote:

During these last days of carnival there has been little room for business amid the dances, comedies, and other pleasant diversions. The Court has been fully occupied with these and in particular with the representation of a masque, which the Queen has repeated three times, set out with the most stately scenery, machines, and dresses. (*Ibid.*, 334.)

The other performances doubtless took place on Shrove Sunday and Monday.

1634–5. February 15 (Sunday). Denmark House.

A play before the Queen, at Denmark House, by the French players. (Adams, *Dramatic Records*, p. 60.)

See the following entry.

1634–5. February 17 (Tuesday). Whitehall. The Cockpit.

"On tuesday night the 17 of February, 1634, a Frenche company of players, being approved by the queene at her house too nights before, and commended by her majesty to the kinge, were admitted to the Cockpitt in Whitehall, and there presented the King and queene with a Frenche comedy called *Melise* [Du Rocher] with good approbation: for which play the king gives them ten pounds." (Adams, *Dramatic Records*, p. 60.)

SUMMER, 1635

Private theatricals seem to have constituted a part of the Queen's summer amusement. On August 31 [O. S. 21] Anzolo Correr, Venetian Ambassador in England, wrote to the Doge and Senate:

They expect his Majesty at Windsor, back from his progress, within a fortnight. He proposes to stay there some weeks. The Queen has spent her time so far at Oatlands, where she has passed it in getting her maids to perform pastorals and comedies and other pleasant diversions. (*Cal. State Papers, Venetian*, xxiii, 445.)

THE SEASON 1635–1636

The young Prince Palatine, eldest son of the Queen of Bohemia, was a visitor at the English Court during the season, having arrived in England on November 21. On December 21 [O. S. 11] the Venetian Ambassador wrote:

It seems that his Majesty wishes the second Prince Palatine also to come to this realm, and they were thinking of sending a man of war to fetch him, but this is not settled yet. Comedies, festivities, and balls are the order of the day here, and are indulged in every day at Court for the prince's sake. (*Cal. State Papers, Venetian*, xxiii, 491.)

1635. DATE UNCERTAIN.

A play before the King by the Spanish players (John Navarro). Payment £10, on warrant dated December 23, 1635. (Chalmers, *Apology*, p. 509. See also Stopes, in *Jahrbuch*, xlvi, 98.)

1635/1635–6. DATES UNCERTAIN.

[Eighteen?] plays "acted in 1635" by the King's Company. Payment £180, on warrant dated May 10, 1636. (Chalmers, *Apology*, p. 509. Mrs. Stopes, in *Jahrbuch*, xlvi, 98, and *Burbage*, p. 259, gives the amount as £80.)

1635/1635–6. DATES UNCERTAIN. HAMPTON COURT.

Four plays at Hampton Court in 1635 by the Queen's Company (Christopher Beeston). Payment £20 each, on warrant dated May 10, 1637. (Chalmers, *Apology*, p. 510. See also Stopes, in *Jahrbuch*, xlvi, 99.)

1635/1635–6. DATES UNCERTAIN. WHITEHALL.

Five plays at Whitehall in 1635 by the Queen's Company. Payment £10 each, on the same warrant as that for the plays of the preceding entry. (Chalmers, *Apology*, p. 510. See also Stopes, in *Jahrbuch*, xlvi, 99.)

1635–1636. DATE UNCERTAIN. BLACKFRIARS.

The Second Part of *Arviragus and Philicia* [Lodowick Carlell] before the Queen at Blackfriars.

In an undated letter Charles, the Prince Palatine, wrote to his mother, the Queen of Bohemia:

The King sat yesternight at Van Dyke's for the Prince of Orange, but y^r Mat^y hath forgate to send me the measure of the picture; his house is close by Blake Friers, where the Queen saw Lodwick Carlile's second part of *Arviragus and Felicia* acted, wch is hughly liked of every one, he will not fail to send it to your Mat^y. (*MSS. of the Duke of Northumberland, Ap. to Third Report*, p. 118.)

The young Prince Elector was in England from November, 1635, to June, 1637. The letter quoted above is tentatively assigned by C. H. Gray (*Lodowick Carliell*, p. 36) to 1636.

1635. OCTOBER. HAMPTON COURT.

Two plays before the King at Hampton Court in October, 1635, by the Salisbury Court Players (Richard Heton). Payment £20 each, on warrant dated February 8, 1636–7. (Chalmers, *Apology*, p. 509. Mrs. Stopes, *Jahrbuch*, xlvi, 99, gives the date of the warrant as February 18.)

1635. DECEMBER.

A tragedy before the King "in December last" by the French Players (Josias Floridor). Payment £10, on warrant dated December 23, 1635. (Chalmers, *Apology*, p. 509. See also Stopes, *Jahrbuch*, xlvi, 98, in which the date of the warrant is given as January 8, 1635–6.)

1635. DECEMBER 21 (MONDAY). WHITEHALL. THE GREAT HALL.

"Le pastorale de *Florimene* fust representé devant le roy et la royne, le prince Charles, et le prince Palatin, le 21 Decem. jour de St. Thomas, par les filles Françoise de la royne, et firent tres bien,

dans le grande sale de Whitehall, aux depens de la royne.''
(Adams, *Dramatic Records*, p. 55. See also Simpson and Bell,
Designs by Inigo Jones, p. 98.)

On January 4 [O. S. December 25] the Venetian Ambassador
wrote to the Doge and Senate:

On Monday evening the Queen presented a most beautiful
pastoral to her maids in French. She has now withdrawn to
Somerset House for the devotions of Christmas. (*Cal. State
Papers, Venetian*, xxiii, 499.)

1635–6. FEBRUARY. CAMBRIDGE.

Comedies at Cambridge, in honor of the Prince Elector.

On January 25 George Garrard wrote to the Earl of Strafford:

The Prince Elector . . . goes this Monday the 25th after his
Majesty to Newmarket. He is to be entertained with Feasting
and Comedies at Cambridge.'' (*Strafford Letters*, i, 510.)

1635–6. FEBRUARY 16 (TUESDAY).

"The Second part of *Arviragus and Philicia* [Lodowick Carlell]
playd at court the 16 Febru. 1635, with great approbation of K.
and Queene." (Adams, *Dramatic Records*, p. 55.)

1635–6. FEBRUARY 18 (THURSDAY). ST. JAMES'S.

"*The Silent Woman* [Ben Jonson] playd at Court of St. James on
thursday yᵉ 18 Febr. 1635." (Adams, *Dramatic Records*, p. 55.)

1635–6. FEBRUARY 22 (MONDAY). ST. JAMES'S.

"*The Dukes Mistres* played at St. James the 22 of Feb. 1635.
Made by Sherley." (Adams, *Dramatic Records*, p. 56.)

"Since Herbert is giving a continuous account of Court performances in chronological order, and since this entry follows the
entry of February 24, and precedes the entry of February 28
I believe that the correct date is February 25. The numerals 2
and 5 may have been confused by the transcriber or the printer."
(*Ibid.*, note 1.)

1635–6. FEBRUARY 23 OR 24 (TUESDAY OR WEDNESDAY). THE MIDDLE TEMPLE.

The Triumphs of the Prince d'Amour. A Masque presented by His Highnesse at His Pallace in the Middle Temple, the 24ᵗʰ of Februarie 1635. London, 1635.

By William Davenant. The Queen was present at the performance. The following account is taken from the Herbert records:

On Wednesday the 23 of Febru. [the 23rd fell on Tuesday] 1635, the Prince d'Amours gave a masque to the Prince Elector and his brother, in the Middle Temple, wher the Queen was pleasd to grace the entertaynment by putting of majesty to putt on a citizens habitt, and to sett upon the scaffold on the right hande amongst her subjects.

The queene was attended in the like habitts by the Marques Hamilton, the Countess of Denbighe, the Countess of Holland, and the Lady Elizabeth Feildinge. Mrs. Basse, the law-woman, leade in this royal citizen and her company.

The Earle of Holland, the Lord Goringe, Mr. Percy, and Mr. Jermyn, were the men that attended.

The Prince Elector satt in the midst, his brother Robert on the right hand of him, and the Prince d'Amours on the left.

The Masque was very well performed in the dances, scenes, cloathinge, and musique, and the Queene was pleasd to tell mee at her going away, that she liked it very well.

Henry Lause
William Lause } made the musique.

Mr. Corseilles made the scenes. (Adams, *Dramatic Records*, p. 56.)

1635–6. FEBRUARY 24 (WEDNESDAY). ST. JAMES'S.

"*Loves Aftergame*, played at St. James by the Salisbury Court players, the 24 of Feb. 1635." (Adams, *Dramatic Records*, p. 56.)

£10 was paid, on a warrant dated February 8, 1636–7, for a play before the King at St. James by the Salisbury Court players in "February 1635." (Chalmers, *Apology*, p. 509. See also Stopes, in *Jahrbuch*, xlvi, 99.)

1635–6. FEBRUARY 25 (THURSDAY).

See entry for February 22, note.

1635–6. FEBRUARY 27 (SATURDAY). COLLEGE OF THE MUSEUM MINERVAE.

Corona Minervae. Or a Masque Presented before Prince Charles his Highnesse, The Duke of Yorke his Brother, and the Lady Mary his Sister, the 27ᵗʰ of February, at the Colledge of the Museum Minervae. London. 1635.

The College of the Museum Minervae in Covent Garden was founded in 1634 by Sir Francis Kinaston. On December 12, 1635, it was endowed by the King. An extract from the grant will explain the nature of the institution:

Whereas our trustie and wel-beloved Sir ffrancis Kynaston, hath lately provided and furnished a faire house in Comon Garden, commonly called Museum Minervae, being for the furtherance of the studies and exercises of the youth of this Kingdome, wee having ever shewed our self a fauourer and nourisher of all such good deseignes, especially such as serue for the better educacon and breeding Are graciously pleased as of our princely bountie, to give vnto our said servant one hundred pounds to be by him imployed for the benefit of that house.

Sir Francis Kinaston himself, says E. F. Rimbault, was the author of the masque. For the full text of the grant, see *Notes and Queries*, Third Series, vi, 265. Other interesting particulars of the institution are given by Rimbault, *ibid.*, First Series, iii, 317.

1635–6. FEBRUARY 28 (SUNDAY). ST. JAMES'S.

"The 28 Feb. *The Knight of the Burning Pestle* [Beaumont and Fletcher], playd by the Q. men at St. James." (Adams, *Dramatic Records*, p. 56.)

1635–6. MARCH 1 (SHROVE TUESDAY).

A masque was given by Lady Hatton, in honor of the King, the Queen, the Palsgrave and his brother, on Shrove Tuesday night. (*Gawdy MSS., Hist. MSS. Com., Tenth Report*, Part 2, p. 157.)

1636. APRIL 4 (MONDAY). WHITEHALL. THE COCKPIT.

"The 4th of Aprill at the Cockpitt *the Silent woman.*" (Adams, *Dramatic Records*, p. 75.)

1636. APRIL 18, 19 (EASTER MONDAY AND TUESDAY). WHITEHALL. THE COCKPIT.

"The first and second part of *Arviragus and Philicia* [Lodowick Carlell] were acted at the Cockpitt before the Kinge and Queene, the Prince, and Prince Elector, the 18 and 19 Aprill, 1636, being monday and tusday in Easter weeke." (Adams, *Dramatic Records*, p. 56.)

In the bill presented by the actors the entries read, "Easter munday at the Cockpitt the firste parte of *Arviragus,*" and "Easter tuesday at the Cockpitt the second parte of *Arviragus.*" (*Ibid.*, p. 75.)

On March 12, 1636–7, upon the presentation of an itemized bill by the King's Company, for "Playes acted before the Kinge and Queene this present yeare of the Lord 1636," the Lord Chamberlain authorized the Treasurer of the Chamber "to pay or cause to bee payd unto John Lowen and Joseph Taylor or either of them for themselves and the rest of the Company of his Ma^{ts} Players the summe of Two hundred and tenne pounds (beeing after usuall and accustomed rate of Tenne pounds for each play) for One and Twenty Playes by them acted before his Ma^{ty} at Hampton Court and elsewhere within the space of a yeere ended in February last: And that you likewise pay unto them the summe of Thirtye pounds more for their paynes in studying and acting the new Play sent from Oxford called *The Royall Slaue* which in all amounteth to the summe of Two Hundred and Forty Pounds." (Cunningham, *Revels*, p. xxiv. See also Stopes, *Burbage*, p. 260.)

This warrant provides for the payment of plays by the King's Company from Easter, 1636, to February 21, 1636–7.

The bill presented by the actors is printed by Cunningham, *Revels*, pp. xxiv–xxv, and by Adams, *Dramatic Records of Sir Henry Herbert*, pp. 75–76.

1636. MAY 5 (THURSDAY). BLACKFRIARS.

"The 5th of May at the Blackfryers for the Queene and the prince Elector—*Alfonso*" [Greene? Peele?]. (Adams, *Dramatic Records*, p. 75.)

OXFORD, AUGUST, 1636

Players passes were issued on May 17 to the King's Company, the members of which were "commanded to attend his Majesty and be nigh about the Court this somer progresse in readiness when they shall be called on to act before his Majesty." (See Stopes, in *Jahrbuch*, xlvi, 98; *Burbage*, p. 259.) No record of a performance by the company during the progress has survived.

On August 29, the King, Queen, Prince Charles, the Elector Palatine and his brother, Prince Rupert, together with many members of the Court, arrived at Oxford. Three plays were presented before them, and Wood states that a fourth, Jasper Mayne's *City Match*, was intended.

1636. AUGUST 29 (MONDAY). OXFORD. CHRIST CHURCH HALL.

The Floating Island: A Tragi-Comedy, Acted before his Majesty at Oxford, Aug. 29. 1636. By the Students of Christ-Church. Written by William Strode, late Orator of the University of Oxford, The Aires and Songs set by Mr. Henry Lawes, servant to his late Majesty in his publick and private Musick. London, 1655.

The principal account of the performance is given by Anthony à Wood in his *History and Antiquities of the University of Oxford:*

That night, after the King, Queen, and two Princes had supped, they saw a comedy acted in Christ Church Hall, but such an one it was, that had more of the Moralist than Poet in it. And though it was well penned, yet it did not take with the Courtiers so well, as it did with the togated crew. It was intituled *Passions Calmed*, or *The Setling of the floating Island*, made by Strode the Orator, and performed by the Scholars beyond expectation. It was acted on a goodly stage, reaching from the upper end of the Hall almost to the hearth place, and had on it three or four openings on each side thereof, and partitions between them much resembling the desks or studies in a Library, out of which the Actors issued forth. The said partitions they could draw in and out at their pleasure upon a sudden, and thrust out new in their places according to the nature of the Screen, whereon were represented Churches, Dwelling-houses, Palaces, &c. which for its variety bred very great admiration. Over all was delicate painting resembling the Sky, Clouds, &c. At the upper end a great fair shut of two leaves that opened and shut without any visible help. Within which was set forth the emblem of the whole Play in a mysterious manner. Therein was the perfect resemblance of the billows of the Sea rolling, and an artificial Island, with Churches and Houses waving up and down and floating, as also rocks, trees and hills. Many other fine pieces of work and Landscapes did also appear at sundry openings thereof, and a Chair also seen to come gliding on the Stage without any visible help. All these representations, being the first (as I have been informed) that were used on the English stage, and therefore giving great content, I have been therefore the more punctual in describing them, to the end that posterity might know that what is now seen in the Play-houses at London belonging to his Majesty, and the Duke of York, is originally due to the invention of Oxford Scholars. (ii, 408–9.)

The royal visitors found the play dull. On September 26 George Evelyn, then a student at Oxford, wrote to his father that "it was generally misliked of the Court, because it was so grave; but especially because they understood it not." (*Diary and Correspondence*, ed. Bray, i, 421.) Likewise George Garrard wrote to Viscount Conway that "there was a play at Christ-church 'fitter for scholars than a court'," and reported Lord Carnavon's remark that "it was the worst that ever he saw but one that he saw at Cambridge." (*Cal. State Papers, Domestic*, 1636–1637, p. 114.)

1636. AUGUST 30 (TUESDAY). OXFORD. CHRIST CHURCH HALL.

Love's Hospital, by George Wilde, acted before the King and Queen by the students of St. John's College.

The play was performed in the afternoon. The best account of the occasion is from the pen of Wood:

> When dinner was ended he [the Chancellor] attended the King and Queen, together with the Nobles, into several withdrawing Chambers, where they entertained themselves for the space of an hour. In the mean time he caused the windows of the Common Hall or Refectory to be shut, candles lighted, and all things to be made ready for the Play, which was then to begin, called *the Hospitall of Lovers*, made for the most part (as 'tis said) by Mr. George Wild, Fellow of St. John's College. When these things were fitted, he gave notice to the King and Queen, and attended them into the Hall, whither he had the happiness to bring them by a way prepared from the presence Lodgings to the Hall without any the least disturbance. He had the Hall kept so fresh and cool that there was not any one person when the King and Queen came into it. The Princes, Nobles and Ladies entered the same way with the King, and then presently another door was opened below, to fill the Hall with the better sort of company. All being settled the Play began and was acted. The plot good and the action. It was merry and without offence, and so gave a great deal of content, which I doubt cannot be said of any play acted in the Play-houses belonging to the King and Duke, since 1660. In the middle of the Play, the Chancellor ordered a short banquet for the King and Queen, Lords and Ladies. And the College was at that time so well furnisht, as that they did not borrow any one Actor from any College in the University. (*History and Antiquities*, ii, 411.)

The play is extant in manuscript, with the title, "Love's Hospitall, as it was acted before the Kinge and Queenes Majestyes and by the students of St. Jo. Baptists Coll. in Oxon. August 29° 1636 authore Georgio Wilde." (See Louise B. Morgan, "The Latin University Drama," *Jahrbuch*, xlvii, 87.) The date given in the title, however, is incorrect. *The Floating Island* was acted on August 29, and there were two plays on the next day.

1636. AUGUST 30 (TUESDAY). OXFORD. CHRIST CHURCH HALL.

The Royall Slave. A Tragi-Comedy. Presented to the King and Queene by the Students of Christ-Church in Oxford. August 30, 1636. Presented

since to both their Majesties at Hampton-Court by the Kings Servants.
London. 1639.

Again the principal account is furnished by Wood:

The play [*Love's Hospital*] ended, the King and the Queen went to Christ Church, retired and supped privately, and about 8 of the clock went into the Common Hall there to see another Comedy called *The Royal Slave*, made by Mr. Will Cartwright of that House. It contained much more variety than that of *Passions calmed.* Within the shuts were seen a curious Temple, and the Sun shining over it, delightful forests also, and other prospects. Within the great shuts mentioned before, were seen villages, and men visibly appearing in them, going up and down, here and there about their business. The Interludes were represented with as much variety of scenes and motions as the great wit of Inigo Jones (well skilled in setting out a Court Masque to the best advantage) could extend unto. It was very well pen'd and acted, and the strangeness of the Persian habits gave great content. (*History and Antiquities*, ii, 413.)

The royal visitors were pleased with the performance. George Evelyn recorded the fact that the play "much delighted his Majesty and all the nobles, commending it for the best that ever was acted" (*Diary*, ed. Bray, i, 421), and Garrard wrote that it was "generally liked, and the Lord Chamberlain so transported with it, that he swore mainly he never saw such a play before." (*Cal. State Papers, Domestic*, 1636–1637, p. 114.) This unbounded success led to a second performance at Hampton Court. See the entry for 1636–7, January 12.

THE SEASON 1636–1637

The London theatres were closed on account of the plague, and the members of the Court had taken refuge at Hampton. The King had commanded his players "to assemble their companie and keepe themselves togither neere our Court for our service." An allowance of £20 per week, which began on November 1 and was to continue during his Majesty's pleasure, was paid to John Lowen and Joseph Taylor, on behalf of the Company.

According to Wood, Jasper Mayne's *City Match* was acted at Hampton Court during the season:

Mr. Jasper Maine's Play called the *City Match*, though not acted at Christ Church before the King and Queen as was intended, yet it was sent for to Hampton Court, and he went there about Christmas following to see the setting forth of his Play. It took so well, that it was afterwards acted before the King and Queen at Whitehall, and several times by his Majesty's Servants at the Black Fryers in London, and at length published an. 1639, fol. (*History and Antiquities*, ii, 413.)

1636. September 12 (Monday). Richmond.

The King and Queenes Entertainement at Richmond. After their departure from Oxford: In a Masque, presented by the most Illustrious Prince, Prince Charles, Sept. 12. 1636. Oxford. 1636.

The author is unknown. See Reyher, *Masques Anglais*, p. 531.

1636. November 17 (Thursday). Hampton Court.

"The 17th of November at Hampton Courte. *the Coxcombe*" [Beaumont and Fletcher]. (Adams, *Dramatic Records*, p. 75.)

1636. November 19 (Saturday). Hampton Court.

"The 19th of November at Hampton Court. *beggers bush.*" (Adams, *Dramatic Records*, p. 75.)

1636. November 29 (Tuesday). Hampton Court.

"The 29th of November at Hampton Court. *the maides tragedie*" [Beaumont and Fletcher]. (Adams, *Dramatic Records*, p. 75.)

1636. December 6 (Tuesday). Hampton Court.

"The 6th of December at Hampton Court. *the loyall subiect.*" (Adams, *Dramatic Records*, p. 76.)

1636. December 8 (Thursday). Hampton Court.

"The 8th of December at Hampton Court. *the moore of Venice.*" (Adams, *Dramatic Records*, p. 76.)

1636. DECEMBER 16 (FRIDAY). HAMPTON COURT.

"The 16th of December at Hampton Court. *Loues pilgrimage*" [Beaumont and Fletcher]. (Adams, *Dramatic Records*, p. 76.)

1636. DECEMBER 26 (MONDAY AFTERNOON). HAMPTON COURT.

"The first part of *Arviragus*, Monday Afternoon, 26 Decemb." (Adams, *Dramatic Records*, p. 57.)

In the bill presented by the actors the entry reads, "St Stephens day at Hampton Court. the first pte of *Arviragus*." (*Ibid*., p. 76.)

1636. DECEMBER 27 (TUESDAY). HAMPTON COURT.

"The second part of *Arviragus*, tusday 27 Decemb." (Adams, *Dramatic Records*, p. 57.)

In the bill presented by the actors the entry reads, "St Johns Day at Hampton Court. the second parte of *Arviragus*." (*Ibid*., p. 76.)

1636–7. JANUARY 1 (SUNDAY). HAMPTON COURT.

"*Love and Honour* [William Davenant], on New-years night, sonday." (Adams, *Dramatic Records*, p. 57.)

In the bill presented by the actors the entry reads, "The first day of January at Hampton Court. *loue and honor*." (*Ibid*., p. 76.)

1636–7. JANUARY 5 (THURSDAY). HAMPTON COURT.

"*The Elder Brother* [John Fletcher], on thursday the 5 Janua." (Adams, *Dramatic Records*, p. 57.)

In the bill presented by the King's Company the entry reads, "The 5th of January at Hampton Court. *the Elder brother*." (*Ibid*., p. 76.)

1636–7. JANUARY 10 (TUESDAY). HAMPTON COURT.

"*The King and no Kinge*, on tusday ye 10 Janua." (Adams, *Dramatic Records*, p. 57.)

In the bill presented by the actors the entry reads, "The 10th of January at Hampton Court. *the Kinge and noe Kinge*." (*Ibid*., p. 76.)

1636–7. JANUARY 12 (THURSDAY). HAMPTON COURT.

"*The Royal Slave*, on thursday the 12 of Janu.—Oxford play, written by Cartwright. The king gave him forty pounds." (Adams, *Dramatic Records*, p. 51.)

In the bill presented by the actors the entry reads, "The 12th of January the new play from Oxford. *the Royall slave*." (*Ibid.*, p. 76.)

£20 was paid to the King's Company for acting the play, on a warrant dated March 16, 1636–7. (Cunningham, *Revels*, p. xxiv. See also Stopes, in *Jahrbuch*, xlvi, 99.)

The play had previously been acted before the Court at Oxford, on August 30. Concerning the second performance Anthony à Wood wrote:

In November following, the Queen sent to the Chancellor that he would procure of Christ Church the Persian attire of the *Royall Slave* and other apparell wherein it was acted, to the end that she might see her own Players act it over again, and whether they could do it as well as 'twas done by the University. Whereupon the Chancellor caused the Cloaths and Perspectives of the Stage to be sent to Hampton Court in a Waggon, for which the University received from her a letter of thanks. So that all of it being fitted for use (the author thereof being then present) 'twas acted soon after, but by all mens confession, the Players came short of the University Actors. At the same time the Chancellor desired of the King and Queen that neither the Play, or Cloaths, nor Stage, might come into the hands and use of the common Players abroad, which was graciously granted. (*History and Antiquities*, ii, 413.)

Concerning the reluctance of the University, see also the letter of Mr. E. R. to Sir Thomas Puckering (*Court and Times of Charles I*, ii, 266). This letter, dated January 11, states that the performance took place on Twelfth Night. There is, of course, a possibility that there were two performances at Hampton Court. It seems more likley, however, that E. R. is guilty of an error arising from a confusion of dates.

The production was an expensive one. Besides the payments to the author and actors, £154 was paid, on April 4, 1637, for "ye alterations, reparations, and additions which were made unto ye scene, apparell, and propertyes." It was expended as follows: "to Peter le Huc, propertymaker, 50*l.*; to George Portmans, painter, 50*l.*; and to Estienne, Nan, and Sebastian le Pierre for themselves and 12 dancers, 54*l.*" (*Cal. State Papers, Domestic*, 1636–1637, p. 563.)

1636–7. JANUARY 17 (TUESDAY). HAMPTON COURT.

"The 17th of January at Hampton Court—*Rollo.*" (Adams, *Dramatic Records*, p. 76.)

See the following entry.

1636–7. JANUARY 24 (TUESDAY). HAMPTON COURT.

"The 24th of January at Hampton Court—*hamlett.*" (Adams, *Dramatic Records*, p. 76.)

In the Office Book of Sir Henry Herbert, however, the performance of *Rollo* (see the preceding entry) is dated January 24, and no performance of *Hamlet* is mentioned. See Adams, *op. cit.*, p. 57.

1636–7. JANUARY 31 (TUESDAY). ST. JAMES'S.

"*Julius Caesar*, at St. James, the 31 Janu. 1636." (Adams, *Dramatic Records*, p. 57.)

In the bill presented by the actors the entry reads, "The 31th of January at S[t] James. the *tragedie of Cesar.*" (*Ibid.*, p. 76.)

1636–7. FEBRUARY 7 (TUESDAY). ST. JAMES'S.

"*Cupides Revenge*, at St. James, by Beeston's boyes, the 7 Febru." (Adams, *Dramatic Records*, p. 57.)

It is probable that this play, and *Wit without Money*, on February 14, were the "two plays acted by the New Company" for which Beeston was paid £10 each on May 10, 1637. (Chalmers, *Apology*, p. 510. See also Stopes, in *Jahrbuch*, xlvi, 99.)

1636–7. FEBRUARY 9 (THURSDAY). ST. JAMES'S.

"*A Wife for a Monthe* [Beaumont and Fletcher], by the K. players, at St. James, the 9 Febru." (Adams, *Dramatic Records*, p. 58.)

In the bill presented by the actors the entry reads, "The 9th of ffebruary at S[t] James. *the wife for a moneth.*" (*Ibid.*, p. 76.)

1636–7. FEBRUARY 14 (TUESDAY). ST. JAMES'S.

"*Wit without Money* [Beaumont and Fletcher] by the B. boyes at St. James, the 14 Feb." (Adams, *Dramatic Records*, p. 58.)

For payment, see the entry for February 7.

1636–7. FEBRUARY 17 (FRIDAY). ST. JAMES'S.

"*The Governor* [Sir Cornelius Formido] by the K. players, at St. James, the 17 Febru. 1636." (Adams, *Dramatic Records*, p. 58.)

This play was dated by the actors February 16: "The 16th of ffebruary at S[t] James. *The Governour.*" (*Ibid.*, p. 76.)

1636–7. FEBRUARY 21 (SHROVE TUESDAY). ST. JAMES'S.

"*Philaster*, by the K. players, at St. James, shrovetusday, the 21 Febru. 1636." (Adams, *Dramatic Records*, p. 58.)

In the bill presented by the actors the entry reads, "The 21th of ffebruary at S[t] James. *Philaster.*" (*Ibid.*, p. 76.)

THE SEASON 1637–1638

1637/1637–8. DATE UNCERTAIN.

The Cid, A Tragi comedy, out of French made English: And acted before their Majesties at Court, and on the Cock-pit Stage in Drury-lane by the servants to both their Majesties. London. 1637.

Translated from Corneille by Joseph Rutter. The play was entered on the Stationers' Register January 29, 1637–8. The court performance must have taken place between the date of the formation of the King and Queen's Company, early in 1637, and that of the entry of the play in 1637–8.

1637/1637–8. SEPTEMBER 30–FEBRUARY 3.

Fourteen plays before the King "between the 30th of September and the 3d of February following, 1637" by the King's Company (John Lowen, Joseph Taylor and Elliardt Swanston). Payment £10 each for thirteen, and £20 for one at Hampton Court, on warrant dated March 15, 1637–8. (Chalmers, *Apology*, p. 510. See also Stopes, in *Jahrbuch*, xlvi, 100; *Burbage*, p. 261.)

1637. NOVEMBER, DECEMBER.

Three plays before the King "in November, and December last" by the Prince's Company (Joseph Moore). Payment £10 each for two, and £20 for one at Hampton Court, "in consideration of their travel, and remove of goods," on warrant dated March 21, 1637–8. (Chalmers, *Apology*, p. 510. See also Stopes, in *Jahrbuch*, xlvi, 101.)

1637/1637–8. CHRISTMAS.

Aglaura, a tragedy by Sir John Suckling.

The only officially recorded court performance of *Aglaura* is that of April 3, 1638. It is evident from the following letter, however, that a play by Suckling was acted earlier in the year. On February 7, 1637–8, George Garrard wrote to the Earl of Strafford:

Two of the King's Servants, Privy-Chamber Men both, have writ each of them a Play, Sir John Sutlin and Will Barclay, which have been acted in Court, and at the Black Friars, with much Applause. Sutlin's play cost three or four hundred Pounds setting out, eight or ten Suits of new Cloaths he gave the Players; an unheard of Prodigality. (*Strafford Letters*, ii, 150.)

Undoubtedly this was *Aglaura*. The *Aglaura* presented on April 3 was in a revised form. The author had turned it from a tragedy into a comedy by writing an alternative fifth act, which has a separate title-page: "Aglaura Represented At the Court, by his Majesties Servants. Written by Sir John Suckling, 1646." There is also a new "Prologue to the Court," which refers to a Christmas performance of the play as it was originally written, with a tragic close. The prologue begins thus:

> 'Tis strange, perchance you'll think, that she, that died
> At Christmas, should at Easter be a bride:
> But 'tis a privilege the poets have
> To take the long-since dead out of the grave.

and closes,

> Aglaura's but repriev'd this night; and, though
> She now appears upon a poet's call,
> She's not to live, unless you say she shall.

Aubrey refers to the splendor of the performance:

When his *Aglaura* was acted, he bought all the cloathes him-selfe, which were very rich; no tinsill, all the lace pure gold and silver, which cost him . . . I have forgott. He had some scaenes to it, which in those days were only used at masques. (*Brief Lives*, ed. Clark, ii, 245.)

1637–8. JANUARY 7 (SUNDAY). WHITEHALL. THE MASQUING HOUSE.

Britannia Triumphans: a Masque, Presented at White Hall, by the Kings Majestie and his Lords, on the Sunday after Twelfth-night, 1637. By Inigo Iones Surveyor of his Majesties workes, and William Davenant her Majesties servant. London. 1637.

A letter from George Garrard to the Earl of Strafford on November 9, 1637, affords some particulars of the structure in which this masque and *Luminalia* (on February 6) were presented:

Here are to be two Masks this Winter, one at Christmas, which the King with the young noblesse do make; the other at Shrove-tide, which the Queen and her Ladies do present to the King. A great Room is now in building only for this use betwixt the Guard-Chamber and the Banquetting-house, of Fir, only weather-boarded and slightly covered. At the Marriage of the Queen of Bohemia I saw one set up there, but not of the Vastness that this is, which will cost too much Money to be pulled down, and yet down it must when the Masks are over. (*Strafford Letters*, ii, 130.)

1637–8. FEBRUARY 6 (TUESDAY). WHITEHALL. THE MASQUING HOUSE.

Luminalia, or The Festival of Light. Personated in a Masque at Court, By the Queenes Majestie, and her Ladies. On Shrovetuesday Night, 1637. London. 1637.

See Reyher, *Masques Anglais*, p. 531; and cf. the preceding entry.

1638. MARCH 26 (MONDAY). WHITEHALL. THE COCKPIT.

"At the Cocpit the 26th of march *The lost ladie*" [Sir William Berkeley]. (Adams, *Dramatic Records*, p. 76.)

See the letter of George Garrard quoted under the entry for 1637–8, Christmas. Possibly an earlier performance of this play is referred to.

The name of this play, with the names of the twenty-three which follow (entries for 1638, March 27, to 1638–9, January 7, inclusive) is taken from a bill presented by the actors of the King's Company. The bill was discovered by George R. Wright, F. S. A., and was reproduced in facsimile in *The Journal of the British Archaeological Association* for 1860. It is printed in *Shakespearean Playhouses*, p. 404, and *The Dramatic Records of Sir Henry Herbert*, pp. 76–77, by Professor J. Q. Adams. Because the reference to the "Cocpit" was misunderstood, however, by the discoverer and other scholars, it remained for Professor Adams to point out the fact that the little "theatre royal" at Whitehall, not the public playhouse in Drury Lane, was the scene of these plays, and to establish the genuineness of the document.

On the original bill the Lord Chamberlain made checks at the left of the entries of the plays performed at Somerset House, Hampton Court, and Richmond, to show how many times the actors lost their day at their house. For these plays they received £20 instead of the usual £10. The actors received payment on the following warrant:

12th March 1638–9—Forasmuch as his Majesty's servants, the company at the Blackfriars, have by special command, at divers times within the space of this present year 1638; acted 24 plays before his Majesty; six whereof have been performed at Hampton Court, and Richmond by means whereof, they were not only at the loss of their day at home, but at extraordinary charges, by travelling, and carriage of their goods; in consideration whereof they are to have £20 a piece, for those plays; and £10 a piece, for the other 18 acted at Whitehall, which in the whole amounteth to the sum of £300, etc. (Chalmers, *Apology*, pp. 510–11. Cf. Stopes, in *Jahrbuch*, xlvi, 101; *Burbage*, p. 261.)

1638. MARCH 27 (TUESDAY). WHITEHALL. THE COCKPIT.

"At the Cocpit the 27ᵗʰ of march *Damboyes*" [Bussy D'Ambois, by George Chapman]. (Adams, *Dramatic Records*, p. 76.)

1638. APRIL 3 (TUESDAY). WHITEHALL. THE COCKPIT.

"At the Cocpit the 3ᵈ of Aprill *Aglaura*" [Sir John Suckling]. (Adams, *Dramatic Records*, p. 76.)

See the note to the entry for 1637–8, Christmas.

1638. APRIL 23 (MONDAY). BLACKFRIARS.

"At the blackfryers the 23 of Aprill for the queene *the vnfortunate lou[ers]*" [Sir William Davenant]. (Adams, *Dramatic Records*, p. 76.)

1638. APRIL 29 (SUNDAY). WHITEHALL. THE COCKPIT.

"At the Cocpit the 29ᵗʰ of may the princes berthnight *ould Castel*" [Shakespeare's *Henry IV*]. (Adams, *Dramatic Records*, p. 76.)

1638. MAY 29 (TUESDAY).

"A Presentation Intended for the Prince his Highnesse on his Birth-day, the 29 of May, 1638. annually celebrated." (In Thomas Nabbes, *The Spring's Glorie*, 1638.) See Reyher, *Masques Anglais*, p. 532.

The wording of the title-page leads one to suspect that the masque was not performed on the occasion for which it was written. Compare the entry for 1634–5, Christmas.

1638. MAY 31 (THURSDAY). WHITEHALL. THE COCKPIT.

"At the Cocpit the last of may agayne *the vnfortunate louers*." (Adams, *Dramatic Records*, p. 76.)

SUMMER, 1638

1638. JULY 10 (TUESDAY). SOMERSET HOUSE.

"At Somerset-house the 10ᵗʰ of July & our day lost at our house mʳ Carlels play the first part of *the passionate louers*" [Lodowick Carlell]. (Adams, *Dramatic Records*, p. 76.)

THE SEASON 1638–1639

1638–1639. DATES UNCERTAIN.

Seven plays "acted at court in 1638, & 1639" by the Queen's Company (Henry Turner). Payment £10 each for six, and £20 for one at Richmond, on warrant dated March 6, 1639–40. (Chalmers, *Apology*, p. 510. See also Stopes, in *Jahrbuch*, xlvi, 106.)

1638. SEPTEMBER 30 (SUNDAY). HAMPTON COURT.

"At Hampton Court the 30th of September *The vnfortunate louers*." (Adams, *Dramatic Records*, p. 77.)

1638. NOVEMBER 6 (TUESDAY). RICHMOND.

"At Richmount the 6th of november for the ladie maries berth-night & the day lost at our house *The mery divell of Edmonto[n]*." (Adams, *Dramatic Records*, p. 77.)

1638. NOVEMBER 8 (THURSDAY). WHITEHALL. THE COCKPIT.

"At the Cocpit the 8th of november *The fox*." (Adams, *Dramatic Records*, p. 77.)

1638. NOVEMBER 13 (TUESDAY). WHITEHALL. THE COCKPIT.

"At the Cocpit the 13th of november *Ceaser*" [Shakespeare's *Julius Caesar*?]. (Adams, *Dramatic Records*, p. 77.)

1638. NOVEMBER 15 (THURSDAY). WHITEHALL. THE COCKPIT.

"At the Cocpit the 15th of november *The mery wifes of winser*." (Adams, *Dramatic Records*, p. 77.)

1638. NOVEMBER 20 (TUESDAY). WHITEHALL. THE COCKPIT.

"At the Cocpit the 20th of november *The fayre favorett*" [Sir William Davenant]. (Adams, *Dramatic Records*, p. 77.)

1638. NOVEMBER 22 (THURSDAY). WHITEHALL. THE COCKPIT.

"At the Cocpit the 22th of november *Chances*" [Beaumont and Fletcher]. (Adams, *Dramatic Records*, p. 77.)

1638. NOVEMBER 27 (TUESDAY). WHITEHALL. THE COCKPIT.

"At the Cockpit the 27th of november *The Costome of the C[oun-try]*" [Beaumont, Fletcher, Massinger]. (Adams, *Dramatic Records*, p. 77.)

1638. NOVEMBER 29 (THURSDAY). WHITEHALL. THE COCKPIT.

"At the Cocpit the 29th of november *The northern las*" [Richard Brome]. (Adams, *Dramatic Records*, p. 77)

1638. DECEMBER 6 (THURSDAY). WHITEHALL. THE COCKPIT.

"At the Cocpit the 6th of desember *The spanish Curatt*" [Beaumont and Fletcher]. (Adams, *Dramatic Records*, p. 77.)

1638. DECEMBER 11 (TUESDAY). WHITEHALL. THE COCKPIT.

"At the Cocpit the 11th of desember agayne *The fayre favorett.*" (Adams, *Dramatic Records*, p. 77.)

1638. DECEMBER 18 (TUESDAY). WHITEHALL. THE COCKPIT.

"At the Cocpit the 18th of desember m Carlels play agayne the first part of *The passionate louers.*" (Adams, *Dramatic Records*, p. 77.)

1638. DECEMBER 20 (THURSDAY). WHITEHALL. THE COCKPIT.

"At the Cocpit the 20th of desember the 2d part of *The pasionate louers.*" (Adams, *Dramatic Records*, p. 77.)

For a description of sketches for a scene, and for the costume of a Druid in Part II of this play, see Simpson and Bell, *Designs by Inigo Jones*, p. 118.

1638. DECEMBER 27 (THURSDAY). WHITEHALL. THE COCKPIT.

"At the Cocpit the 27 of desember the 2^d part agayne of *the pasionate louers*." (Adams, *Dramatic Records*, p. 77.)

1638. DECEMBER 28 (FRIDAY). RICHMOND.

"At Richmount the 28 of desember the ladie Elsabeths berthnight & our day lost at our house *The northern las*." (Adams, *Dramatic Records*, p. 77.)

1638–9. JANUARY 1 (TUESDAY). RICHMOND.

"At Richmount on newyeares day and our day lost at our house *beggers bush*." (Adams, *Dramatic Records*, p. 77.)

1638–9. JANUARY 7 (MONDAY). RICHMOND.

"At Richmount the 7th of Janeuarye and our day lost at our house *The spanish Cura[tt]*." (Adams, *Dramatic Records*, p. 77.)

THE SEASON 1639–1640

1639/1639–40. AUGUST 6–FEBRUARY 11.

Twenty-one plays before the King and Queen "acted between the 6th of August 1639, and the 11th of Febry following" by the King's Company (John Lowen, Joseph Taylor, and Elliardt Swanston). Payment £10 each for nineteen, and £20 each for two at Richmond, on warrant dated April 4, 1640. (Chalmers, *Apology*, p. 511. See also Stopes, in *Jahrbuch*, xlvi, 102; *Burbage*, p. 262.)

Fleay (*Chronicle*, ii, 85) states, without giving his authority, that Jasper Mayne's *City Match*, printed in 1639 as it was "Presented to the King and Queene at White-Hall," by the King's Company, was acted by royal command in 1639.

1639. NOVEMBER. RICHMOND.

Three plays at Richmond "in the month of November" by the Prince's Company (Joseph Moore and Andrew Kayne). Payment £20 each, "in consideration of their travelling expences, and loss of the days at home," on warrant dated May 4, 1640. (Chalmers, *Apology*, p. 511. See also Stopes, in *Jahrbuch*, xlvi, 102.)

1639–40. JANUARY 21 (TUESDAY). WHITEHALL. THE MASQUING HOUSE.

Salmacida Spolia. A Masque. Presented by the King and Queenes Majesties, at White-hall, On Tuesday the 21. day of January 1639. London. 1639.

By Sir William Davenant. See Reyher, *Masques Anglais*, pp. 345, 532, and Simpson and Bell, *Designs by Inigo Jones*, p. 119.

1639–40. FEBRUARY 16–18 (SHROVETIDE).

A repetition of *Salmacida Spolia?*

On February 14 Secretary Vane wrote from Whitehall to Sir Thomas Roe that their Majesties, with their royal children, were in perfect health, and for their recreation intended to dance again their masque this Shrovetide. (*Cal. State Papers, Domestic*, 1639–40, p. 459.)

It is worth noting, also, that among the designs for this masque one sketch is inscribed "febyary 5 1640," indicating, apparently, that some alteration was contemplated for a subsequent performance. See Simpson and Bell, *Designs by Inigo Jones*, p. 128.

1640. APRIL 9 (THURSDAY). WHITEHALL. THE GREAT HALL.

"On thursday the 9 of Aprill, 1640, my Lord Chamberlen bestow'd a play on the Kinge and Queene, call'd *Cleodora, Queene of Arragon*, made by my cozen Abington [William Habington]. It was performed by my lords servants out of his own family, and his charge in the cloathes and sceanes, which were very riche and curious. In the hall at Whitehall.

"The king and queen commended the generall entertaynment, as very well acted, and well set out.

"It was acted the second tyme in the same place before the king and queene." (Adams, *Dramatic Records*, p. 58.)

Scenery for this play is described by Simpson and Bell, *Designs by Inigo Jones*, pp. 131–2.

1640. AFTER APRIL 9. WHITEHALL. THE GREAT HALL.

Cleodora, Queen of Aragon, by William Habington, before the King and Queen.

See the preceding entry.

THE SEASON 1640–1641

1640/1640–1. NOVEMBER 10–FEBRUARY 22.

[Sixteen?] plays "acted before his Majesty, the Queen, and Prince, between the 10th of November 1640, and the 22d of February 1640–1" by the King's Company (John Lowen, Joseph Taylor, and Ellardt Swanston). Payment £160, on warrant dated March 20, 1640–1. (Chalmers, *Apology*, pp. 511–12. See also Stopes, in *Jahrbuch*, xlvi, 104; *Burbage*, p. 262.)

THE SEASON 1641–1642

1641–2. JANUARY 6 (THURSDAY). WHITEHALL. THE COCKPIT.

"On Twelfe Night, 1641, the prince had a play called *The Scornful Lady* [Beaumont and Fletcher], at the Cockpitt, but the kinge and queene were not there; and it was the only play acted at courte in the whole Christmas." (Adams, *Dramatic Records*, p. 58.)

1641–2. MARCH 12 (SATURDAY). CAMBRIDGE. TRINITY COLLEGE.

[*Cutter of Coleman Street.*] *The Guardian. A Comedie Acted before Prince Charles his Highness, at Trinity Colledge in Cambridge, upon the twelfth of March, 1641. Written by Abraham Cowley.* London. 1650.

Joseph Beaumont, in a letter to his father, says of this performance: "From yᵉ Regent house his Highnes went to Trinity College, where after dinner he saw a Comedy in English, & gave all sighnes of great acceptance wʰ he could, & more than yᵉ Univʳsity dared expect." (*Archaeologia*, xviii, 30.)

Beaumont mentions only one play. The writer in the *Retrospective Review* (xii, 40) states that Vincent's *Paria* was also performed. But G. C. Moore Smith (*College Plays*, p. 97) says that this statement "appears to be groundless."

MISCELLANEOUS COURT PERFORMANCES OF UNCERTAIN DATE

The Deseruing Fauorite. As it was lately Acted, first before the Kings Maiestie, and since publikely at the Black-Friers. By his Maiesties Seruants. Written by Lodowicke Carlell, Esquire, Gentle-man of the Bowes, and Groome of the King and Queenes Priuie Chamber. London. 629.

The title-page of the edition of 1659 reads, "As it was presented before the King and Queenes Majesties at White-Hall."

The Fair Maid Of The West. Or, A Girle worth gold. The first part. As it was lately acted before the King and Queen, with approved liking, By the Queens Majesties Comedians. Written by T. H. [Thomas Heywood.] London. 1631.

Entered S. R. June 16, 1631. The prologue was "spoken to their two Majesties at Hampton Court."

The Staple of Newes. A Comedie Acted in the yeare, 1625. By His Maiesties Seruants. The Author Ben: Ionson. London. 1631. Fol.

There is a court prologue. The play was entered S. R. April 14, 1626, but no edition earlier than the Folio is known. Concerning the date of the court performance Fleay (*Drama*, i, 384) makes this statement: "The mention of Shrovetide (which began Feb. 19 in

1626) in the Induction, coupled with 'now at the Coronation,' 1626, Feb. 2, fixes the public performance to Candlemas, the Court to Shrovetide."

The Emperour of the East. A Tragae-Comoedie. The Scaene Constantinople. As it hath bene diuers times acted, at the Black-friers, and Globe Play-houses, by the Kings Maiesties Seruants. Written by Philip Massinger. London. 1632.

There is a court prologue. The play was licensed by Herbert on March 11, 1630–1, and entered on the Stationers' Register November 19, 1631. It must therefore have been acted at Court between these dates.

The Famous Tragedy of the Rich Iew of Malta. As it was played before the King and Queene, in his Majesties Theatre at White-Hall, by her Majesties Servants at the Cock-pit. Written by Christopher Marlo. London. 1633.

The play was probably acted at Court in 1632. Thomas Heywood prefixes a court prologue, and the entry on the Stationers' Register is November 20, 1632. Moreover, "his Majesties Theatre at White-Hall," the Cockpit-in-Court, was new at Christmas, 1632–3. See Adams, *Shakespearean Playhouses*, pp. 394–95.

A Fine Companion. Acted before the King and Queene at White-Hall, And sundrie times with great applause at the private House in Salisbury Court, By the Prince his Servants. Written by Shakerley Marmyon. London. 1633.

Entered S. R. June 15, 1633.

The Shepheards Holy-Day. A Pastorall Tragi-Comaedie. Acted Before Both Their Maiesties at White-Hall, by the Queenes Servants. With an Elegie on the death of the most noble Lady, the Lady Venetia Digby. Written by J. R. [Joseph Rutter.] London. 1635.

According to Fleay, Lady Venetia Digby died in 1633.

Loves Maistresse: Or, The Queens Masque. As it was three times presented before their two Excellent Maiesties, within the space of eight dayes; In the presence of sundry Forraigne Ambassadors. Publikely Acted by the Queens Comoedians, At the Phoenix in Drury-lane. London. 1636.

By Thomas Heywood. Two court prologues are prefixed to the play. The first is preceded by this statement: "Her Majestie Inviting the King to Denmarke House, in the Strand, upon His Birth-day, being November 19. This Play (bearing from that time) the Title of *the Queenes Masque*, was againe presented before Him: Cupid speaking the Prologue." Upon this occasion, Heywood states in the address *To the Reader*, the play "came the second time to the Royall viewe." The second prologue is entitled, "The Prologue To the King and Queene, at the second time of the Authors Play called *Cupids Mistresse or Cupid and Psiche*, presented before them the same weeke: Spoken by Cupid." This apparently means, as Fleay notes, that the third performance was the second "of the same Weeke." The natural inference is that the first presentation of the play was given the preceding week, perhaps on the Queen's birthday, November 16. The play was entered on the Stationers' Register September 30, 1635. Fleay's conjecture is that the performances were given the preceding year. See Nos. 10 and 11 of Heywood's Court Prologues and Epilogues, in *Pleasant Dialogues and Dramma's*.

Argalus and Parthenia. As it hath been Acted at the Court before their Maiesties: And At the Private-House in Drury-Lane, By their Maiesties Servants. By Hen. Glapthorne. London. 1639.

Entered S. R. January 11, 1638–9. The young company of the King and Queen was formed early in 1637.

The Hollander. A Comedy written 1635. The Author Henry Glapthorne. And now Printed as it was then Acted at the Cock-pit in Drury lane, by their Majesties Servants, with good allowance. And at the Court before both their Majesties. London. 1640.

Entered S. R. May 22, 1640. As Fleay points out, the play could not have been acted by "their Majesties Servants" in 1635, for that company had not then been formed. The play was licensed by Herbert on March 12, 1635–6, for the Queen's Company. See

W. J. Lawrence, "New Facts from Sir Henry Herbert's Office Book," *The Times Literary Supplement*, November 29, 1923.

The Ladies Priviledge. As it was Acted with good allowance at the Cock-pit in Drury-lane, And before their Majesties at White-hall twice. By their Maiesties Servants. The Author Henry Glapthorne. London. 1640.
Entered S. R. April 4, 1640.

King Iohn and Matilda, A Tragedy. As it was Acted with great Applause by Her Majesties Servants at the Cock-pit in Drury Lane. Written by Robert Davenport Gent. London. 1655.

Prefixed to the list of *dramatis personae* is this statement: "The Names of the Persons in the Play, And of the Actors that first Acted it on the Stage, and often before their Majesties." The play is assigned by Fleay to a date between 1625 and 1636. Murray (*Dramatic Companies*, vol. i, table op. p. 266, *n.* 3) says: "The appearance of Young in the cast indicates that the play was acted before 1629, when he probably joined the King's Revels Company."

The Careles Shepherdess. A Tragi-Comedy Acted before the King & Queen, And at Salisbury-Court, with great Applause. Written by T. G. [Thomas Goffe] *Mr. of Arts. With an Alphebeticall Catologue of all such Plays that ever were Printed.* London. 1656.

Homer Smith, in his "Pastoral Influence in the English Drama," assigns the court performance of the play to a date between 1625 and 1629, noting that it took place before the death of the author, since he wrote the prologue addressed "to their Majesties at White hall." (*Pub. Mod. Lang. Asso. Amer.*, 1902.)

The Excellent Comedy, called The Old Law; Or A new way to please you. By Phil. Massenger. Tho. Middleton. William Rowley. Acted before the King and Queene at Salisbury House, and at severall other places, with great Applause. Together with an exact and perfect Catalogue of all the Playes, with the Authors Names, and what are Comedies, Tragedies, Histories, Pastoralls, Masks, Interludes, more exactly Printed then ever before. London. 1656.

E. C. Morris, in *The Date and Composition of The Old Law*, conjectures that the play may have been revised by Massinger for presentation before the King and Queen as a part of the coronation ceremonies in 1625. (*Pub. Mod. Lang. Asso. Amer.*, 1902.)

The Sun's-Darling: A Moral Masque: As it hath been often presented at Whitehall, by their Majesties Servants; and after at the Cock-pit in Drury Lane, with great Applause. Written by John Foard and Tho. Decker Gent. London. 1656.

The masque was acted by the company of the King and Queen, which was formed early in 1637.

HEYWOOD'S COURT PROLOGUES AND EPILOGUES

(In *Pleasant Dialogues and Dramma's, 1637*.)

Most of Heywood's prologues and epilogues addressed to the Court and published in his *Pleasant Dialogues and Dramma's*, 1637, cannot be associated with his known plays, but some of them may be approximately dated.

1. "The Queene feasting the King at Somerset House, upon his Birth-day, hers falling in the same weeke, this was there spoken unto them."

Spoken after the birth of Prince Charles, which occurred on May 29, 1630. The King's birthday was November 19, the Queen's November 16.

2. "A speech spoken to their two excellent Majesties, at the first Play play'd by the Queenes Servants, in the new Theatre at White Hall."

According to Adams, *Shakespearean Playhouses*, pp. 394–95, the Cockpit-in-Court was "new" at Christmas, 1632–3. This prologue apparently belongs to the year 1632, since it must precede Heywood's court prologue to *The Jew of Malta*, published in 1633 as having been acted in "his Maiesties Theatre at White-Hall" and entered on the Stationers' Register November 20, 1632.

3. "To the King and Queene upon a New-yeares day at night: the Two-fac't Ianus with a great golden Key in his hand, the Presenter."

There is some difficulty here. The "one thousand six hundred thirty one" of the prologue is sufficiently definite; but Heywood mentions an "Heire" who is "as yet alone," and at New Year's, 1631–2, there were two children, Princess Mary having been born on November 4, 1631.

4. "A Prologue spoke before the King, when her Majesty was great with child."

Spoken in 1631, at the beginning of the seventh year of the marriage of the King and Queen.

5. "Another spoken at White Hall before their sacred Majesties."

This prologue is assigned by Fleay, without explanation, to the year 1634.

6. "A Prologue spoken to their sacred Majesties at Hampton Court."

In the "factious peevish male-content" Fleay sees an allusion to Prynne.

7. "Spoken to their Majesties at Hampton Court."

This prologue belongs to *The Fair Maid of the West*, published in 1631 as having been "lately acted before the King and Queen."

8. "Spoken to their two Majesties at White Hall."

The date of this prologue is uncertain.

9. "Spoken to their excellent Majesties upon the like occasion."

Again the date is uncertain.

10. "Spoken to the King and Queene, at the second time of the Authors Play cald *Cupids Mistresse or Cupid and Psiche*, presented before them."

This prologue belongs to *Love's Mistress, or the Queen's Masque*, published in 1636 as having been "three times presented before their two excellent Majesties, within the space of eight dayes."

11. "The speech spoken to their two Majesties, eight dayes before, being the King's birth-day: presented at Somerset house, by the Queenes appointment, she then feasting the King."

This prologue belongs to *Love's Mistress* (see above). There seems to be some confusion here. In the address *To the Reader* prefixed to the play, Heywood states that upon this occasion it "came the second time to the Royall viewe." (See the note to the play, under "Miscellaneous Court Performances.") If this statement is correct, the second performance could not have taken place "eight dayes before" the third, when all three were given within eight days.

12. "Spoken to his Majesty upon a New-yeares day at night." The date is uncertain.

13. "Another spoken at the Court to the like purpose." The date is uncertain.

[Prologues 14, 15, 16, 17, and 18 were not addressed to the Court.]

19. Vpon his Majesties last birth-night, he being then thirty five yeares of age, and the Queene great with child."

This prologue was spoken on November 19, 1635, Charles having been born in 1600.

20. "Spoken to the Palsgrave at his first comming over, in the presence of his Majesty, etc."

The prologue is dated by Fleay November 22, 1635. The Palsgrave arrived on November 21.

A LIST OF THE PRINCIPAL
WORKS CITED AND INDEX

A LIST OF THE PRINCIPAL
WORKS CITED

ADAMS, J. Q. *The Dramatic Records of Sir Henry Herbert, Master of the Revels, 1623–1673.* New Haven, 1917.

A Life of William Shakespeare. New York, 1923.

Peter Hausted's *The Rivall Friends.* (*Journal of English and Germanic Philology,* July, 1912.)

Shakespeare, Heywood, and the Classics. (*Modern Language Notes,* June, 1919.)

Shakespearean Playhouses. New York, 1917.

ARBER, E. *A Transcript of the Stationers' Registers, 1554–1640.* 5 vols. London, 1875–1894.

AUBREY, JOHN. *Brief Lives,* ed. by A. Clark. 2 vols. Oxford, 1898.

BANG, W. Heywood's *Pleasant Dialogues and Dramma's.* (*Materialen,* vol. iii, 1903.)

BASSOMPIERRE (Maréchal de). *Journal de ma Vie.* 4 vols. Paris, 1870–1877.

BEAUMONT, JOSEPH. Account of the Reception of King Charles the Second, when Prince of Wales, at Cambridge, in 1641. (*Archaeologia,* xviii, 30.)

BIRCH, THOMAS. *The Life of Henry, Prince of Wales.* London, 1760.

BIRCH, T., and R. F. WILLIAMS. *The Court and Times of James I.* 2 vols. London, 1849.

The Court and Times of Charles I. 2 vols. London, 1848.

BOAS, F. S. *University Drama in the Tudor Age.* Oxford, 1914.

BOAS, F. S., and W. W. GREG. James I at Oxford in 1605. Property Lists from the University Archives. (The Malone Society's *Collections,* i, 3.)

BLISS, P. *Athenæ Oxonienses.* 4 vols. London, 1813–1820.

DE BRANTÔME, PIERRE DE BOURDEILLES. *Oeuvres Complètes,* ed. by Merimée and Lacour. 13 vols. Paris, 1875. Vol. iv.

BRAY, W. *Diary and Correspondence of John Evelyn.* 4 vols. London, 1857.

BROTANEK, R. *Die Englische Maskenspiele.* Wien, 1902.

BRUCE, J. *Diary of John Manningham,* 1602–3. Camden Society, 1868.

CALENDAR OF STATE PAPERS, DOMESTIC SERIES. 1547–1660. London, 1856–.

CALENDAR OF STATE PAPERS, SPANISH. London, 1892–.

CALENDAR OF STATE PAPERS, VENETIAN. London, 1884–.

CAMPBELL, J. The Life of Edward Coke (*Lives of the Chief Justices of England.* 2 vols. London, 1849.)

CHALMERS, GEORGE. *An Apology for the Believers in the Shakespeare-Papers.* London, 1797.

CHAMBERS, E. K. Court Performances under James I. (*Modern Language Review,* iv, 153ff.)

Court Performances before Queen Elizabeth. (*Modern Language Review,* ii, 1ff.)

The Elizabethan Stage. 4 vols. Oxford, 1923.

Four Letters on Theatrical Affairs. (The Malone Society's *Collections,* ii, 2.)

CHAMBERS, E. K., and W. W. GREG. Dramatic Records from the Landsdowne MSS. (Malone Society's *Collections,* ii.)

Dramatic Records from the Privy Council Register, 1603–1642. (Malone Society's *Collections,* iv, v.)

COLLIER, J. P. *Five Court Masques.* (Printed with Cunningham's *Inigo Jones,* for the Shakespeare Society. London, 1848.)

History of English Dramatic Poetry. 3 vols. London, 1879.

COLLINS, ARTHUR. *Letters and Memorials of State.* 2 vols. London, 1746.

CUNNINGHAM, P. *Extracts from the Accounts of the Revels at the Court in the Reigns of Queen Elizabeth and King James I.* Printed for the Shakespeare Society, 1848.

Plays at Court, Anno 1613. (*The Shakespeare Society's Papers,* ii, 123.)

LIST OF THE PRINCIPAL WORKS CITED

DASENT, J. R. *Acts of the Privy Council of England.* New Series. London, 1890–.

DELACOURT, R. Christmas in 1603. (*Notes and Queries*, 2nd Series, x, 461.)

DURAND, W. Y. *Palaemon and Arcyte, Progne, Marcus Geminus,* and the Theatre in which they were acted, as described by John Bereblock (1566). (*Publications of the Modern Language Association of America.* 1905.)

ELLIS, H. *Original Letters.* 3 vols. London, 1825.

FEUILLERAT, A. *Documents Relating to the Office of the Revels in the Time of Queen Elizabeth.* Louvain, 1908.

FINETT, SIR JOHN. *Finetti Philoxenis.* London, 1656.

FLEAY, F. G. *A Biographical Chronicle of the English Drama, 1559–1642.* 2 vols. London, 1891.

A Chronicle History of the London Stage, 1559–1642. London, 1890.

GEMSEGE, P. Comment upon the Old Play of Albumazar. (*The Gentleman's Magazine*, May, 1756.)

GOFFIN, R. C. *The Life and Poems of William Cartwright.* Cambridge, 1918.

GRAY, C. H. *Lodowick Carliell.* Chicago, 1905.

GREG, W. W. *A List of English Plays Written before 1643 and Printed before 1700.* London, 1900.

A List of Masques, Pageants, &c. London, 1902.

Henslowe's Diary. 2 vols. London, 1904.

HALLIWELL-PHILLIPPS, J. O. *Illustrations of the Life of Shakespeare.* London, 1874.

JEAYES, I. H. *Letters of Philip Gawdy, 1579–1616.* London, 1906.

KNOWLES, W. *The Earl of Strafford's Letters and Dispatches.* 2 vols. Dublin, 1740.

Latin Plays Acted before the University of Cambridge. (*The Retrospective Review*, xii, 31.)

LAW, E. *The History of Hampton Court Palace.* 2 vols. London, 1898.

LAWRENCE, W. J. New Facts from Sir Henry Herbert's Office Book. (*The Times Literary Supplement*, Nov. 29, 1923.)

MACLEAN, JOHN. *Letters from George Lord Carew to Sir Thomas Roe, 1615–1617.* Camden Society, 1860.

MANNING, J. A. *Memoirs of Sir Benjamin Rudyerd.* London, [n. d.].

MARTIN, C. T. *Journal of Sir Francis Walsingham, 1570–1583.* Camden Society, 1870.

MASSON, DAVID. *The Life of Milton in Connexion with the History of His Time.* 6 vols. London, 1881.

MORGAN, L. B. The Latin University Drama. (The Shakespeare *Jahrbuch*, xlvii, 69.)

MORRIS, E. C. The Date and Composition of the Old Law. (*Publications of the Modern Language Association of America.* 1902.)

MULLINGER, J. B. *The University of Cambridge.* 3 vols. Cambridge, 1873–1911.

MURRAY, J. T. *English Dramatic Companies.* 2 vols. London, 1910.

NICHOLS, J. G. *The Progresses and Public Processions of Queen Elizabeth.* 3 vols. London, 1788–1805.

The Progresses, Processions, and Magnificent Festivities of King James the First. 4 vols. London, 1828.

The Diary of Henry Machyn, 1550–1563. Camden Society, 1848.

PARK, THOMAS. *Nugae Antiquae.* 2 vols. London, 1804.

RAINES, F. R. *The Journal of Nicholas Assheton.* Chetham Society, 1848.

REYHER, P. *Les Masques Anglais.* Paris, 1909.

RIMBAULT, E. F. The Academies of Sir Francis Kynaston and Sir Balthazar Gerbier. (*Notes and Queries*, 1st Series, iii, 317.)

ROYAL COMMISSION ON HISTORICAL MANUSCRIPTS. MSS. of the Duke of Northumberland, Appendix to Third Report, 1872; MSS. of the Earl de la Warr, Appendix to Fourth Report, 1874; Gawdy MSS., Appendix to Tenth Report, Part II, 1885; MSS. of Earl Cowper, Appendix to Twelfth Report, Part II, 1888; MSS. of the Duke of Rutland, Appendix to Twelfth Report, Part IV, 1888.

LIST OF THE PRINCIPAL WORKS CITED

SACKVILLE-WEST, VICTORIA. *The Diary of Lady Anne Clifford*. London, 1923.

SCHELLING, F. E. *Elizabethan Drama, 1558–1642*. 2 vols. New York, 1908.

SCOTT, E. J. L. Westminster Play Accounts of 1564 and 1606. (*Athenæum* i, 220.)

SIMPSON, PERCY, and C. F. BELL. *Designs by Inigo Jones for Masques and Plays at Court*. London, 1924.

SMITH, G. C. MOORE. *College Plays Performed in the University of Cambridge*. Cambridge, 1923.

The Academic Drama at Cambridge: Extracts from College Records. (The Malone Society's *Collections*, ii, 2.)

SMITH, H. Pastoral Influence in the English Drama. (*Publications of the Modern Language Association of America*. 1897.)

STATHAM, E. P. *A Jacobean Letter-Writer. The Life and Times of John Chamberlain*. London, [n. d.]

STOPES, C. C. Shakespeare's Fellows and Followers. (The Shakespeare *Jahrbuch*, xlvi, 12.)

William Hunnis and the Revels of the Chapel Royal. Louvain, 1910.

Burbage and Shakespeare's Stage. London, 1913.

The Earliest Official Record of Shakespeare's Name. (Shakespeare *Jahrbuch*, xxxii, 182.)

SULLIVAN, M. *Court Masques of James I*. New York, 1913.

WALLACE, C. W. *Evolution of the English Drama*. Berlin, 1912.

WELDON, ANTHONY. *The Court and Character of King James*. London, 1817.

WESTCOTT, ALLAN F. *New Poems by James I of England*. New York, 1911.

WILLIAMS, SARAH. *Letters Written by John Chamberlain during the Reign of Queen Elizabeth*. Camden Society, 1861.

WINWOOD, R. *Memorials of Affairs of State*. 3 vols. London, 1725.

WOOD, ANTHONY à. *The History and Antiquities of the University of Oxford*, ed. by John Gutch. 2 vols. Oxford, 1792–6.

YORKE, P. *Miscellaneous State Papers, 1501–1762*. 2 vols. London, 1778.

INDEX OF AUTHORS

293

INDEX OF TITLES